Latin American Studies

Social Sciences and Law

Edited by
David Mares
University of California, San Diego

A Routledge Series

Latin American Studies

David Mares, *General Editor*

Observing our Hermanos de Armas
U.S. Military Attachés in Guatemala, Cuba, and Bolivia, 1950-1964
Robert O. Kirkland

Land Privatization in Mexico
Urbanization, Formation of Regions, and Globalization in Ejidos
María Teresa Vázquez-Castillo

The Politics of the Internet in Third World Development
Challenges in Contrasting Regimes, with Case Studies of Costa Rica and Cuba
Bert Hoffmann

Contesting the Iron Fist
Advocacy Networks and Police Violence in Democratic Argentina and Chile
Claudio A. Fuentes

Contesting the Iron Fist

Advocacy Networks and Police Violence in Democratic Argentina and Chile

Claudio A. Fuentes

LONDON AND NEW YORK

Published in 2005 by Routledge
2 Park Square Milton Park, Abingdon Oxon OX14 4RN
52 Vanderbilt Avenue, New York, NY 10017

Routledge is an imprint of the Taylor & Francis Group, an informa business

First published in paperback 2012

Library of Congress Cataloging-in-Publication Data

Fuentes, Claudio.
Contesting the iron fist : advocacy networks and police violence in democratic Argentina and Chile / Claudio A. Fuentes.
p. cm. -- (Latin American studies. Social sciences and law)
Includes bibliographical references and index.
ISBN 0-415-97169-1 (hardback : alk. paper)
1. Human rights advocacy--Chile. 2. Police brutality--Chile. 3. Human rights advocacy--Argentina. 4. Police brutality--Argentina. I.I Title. II. Latin American studies (Routledge (Firm)). Social sciences and law.

JC599.C5F84 2005
363.2'32--dc22 2005012933

ISBN 13: 978-0-415-64697-0 (pbk)

To those anonymous activists
who dream of and work for a better world.

Contents

List of Tables, Graphs, and Figures

Tables

Graphs

Figures

Glossary of Abbreviations

AI	Amnesty International
AMIA	Buenos Aires Jewish Cultural Center
BAPP	Buenos Aires Provincial Police
CAJ	Corporation of Legal Assistance
ChCHR	Chilean Commission of Human Rights
CEDEJU	Commission for the Rights of Young People
CEJIL	Center for Justice and International Law
CELS	Center for Legal and Social Studies
CEP	Center for Public Studies
CERC	Center for the Study of Contemporary Reality
CEUNM	Center of Studies for the New Majority
CODEPU	Commission for the Rights of the People
CPU	Center for the Promotion of University Studies
FASIC	Social Help Foundation of the Christian Churches
FLACSO	Latin American Faculty of Social Sciences
FREPASO	Popular and Social Front Party (*Frente Popular y Social*)
INJ	National Institute for the Youth
NGOs	Non-governmental organizations
PDC	Christian Democratic Party (*Partido Demócrata Cristiano*)
PPD	Party for Democracy (*Partido por la Democracia*)
POS	Political Opportunity Structure
PS	Socialist Party (*Partido Socialista*)
RN	National Renovation Party (*Partido Renovación Nacional*)
UCR	Civic Radical Union Party (*Unión Cívica Radical)*
UDI	Independent Democrat Union Party (*Unión demócrata Independiente*)
U.N.	United Nations
U.S.	United States
USAID	U.S. Agency for International Development

Acknowledgments

This book is the result of a long process that began in 1997, when I decided to complete my doctoral degree at the University of North Carolina at Chapel Hill. Since then, I have received the support of many friends and colleagues who have provided me with valuable advice, support, and friendship.

I owe a particular debt of thanks to professors Jonathan Hartlyn and Lars Schoultz at the department of political science at the UNC-Chapel Hill for their constant guidance and instructive critiques. They provided me with useful comments and personal support to make this project possible. Other professors in the same department who deserve special thanks are Evelyne Huber and Thomas Oatley. I specially thank professor Augusto Varas for his intellectual advice since I met him in Chile, back in 1991. His advice and support were crucial when I decided to study in the United States, and his work has inspired me to continue in academia, observing problems from a broad comparative perspective. Moreover, I benefited greatly from discussions with and advice from Merike Blofield. She offered encouragement and support at every stage of this project. Many arguments of this book emerged from fascinating conversations with Merike, and I am sure she is the origin of several of them.

My academic work would not have been possible without the support of several institutions. The Ford Foundation, the Institute for the Study of World Politics, and the Duke-UNC Consortium of Latin American Studies all gave me crucial financial support during my time in the United States and my field research in Argentina and Chile. I specially thank Ford Foundation (Santiago) for the grant that allowed me to finish this project between August 2002 and February 2003.

There are many people and organizations in Argentina, Chile, and the United States who helped me obtain key information for this book. The Center of Legal and Social Studies (CELS-Argentina) and the Latin American Faculty of Social Science (FLACSO-Chile), where I maintained an institutional affiliation during trips to Argentina and Chile, were both particularly helpful. I thank the following people for their help and support: Nelson Caucoto and his team (Chile), Gustavo Palmieri (Argentina), Francisco Rojas (Chile), Marcelo Saín (Argentina), and María del Carmen Verdú (Argentina).

Writing a book is not only an academic journey but a personal one. My deepest thanks are due to my family and friends who, in different ways, have tolerated my long moments of silence and have encouraged me to open my eyes to what really matters in life. Thanks Erin Redfern, Simon Barth, Bennett Hazlip, Liz Markovit, Alan Mcpherson, Aruna Radakhrisna, Tiffany Tung, Amy Mortensen, Paul Dionne, Elisa Canal-Beeby, Juan Pablo Luna, Leticia Ruiz-Rodríguez, Mireya Dávila, Oscar Chamosa, Sharon Mújica, Claudia Heiss, (my dad in heaven) and my mom.

Claudio A. Fuentes
New York

Introduction

Most citizens in the Western world consider that controlling crime and delinquency are main priorities governments should focus on. The problem is deciding on the costs a society should pay for public safety. In some cases, like in the province of Buenos Aires, a governor suggested that "we need to shoot delinquents. I am not saying kill them, but shoot them in their arms or legs."[1] In other less extreme cases, delivering public safety means providing the police with more legal tools to arrest individuals. In most cases, politicians frame the problem as a trade-off between protecting citizens' rights and providing public safety.

While all democratic societies have accepted the inviolability of citizens' physical integrity as a core principle of social life, there is a constant tension between the protection of such right and the actual use of force by security forces to prevent crime, delinquency, and even terrorism. This trade-off is particularly acute in the developing world where governments faces simultaneous pressures to solve socioeconomic problems, reinforce the rule of law, generate a more efficient state apparatus, and overcome institutional and political legacies of past authoritarian regimes. Social protests are likely to rise in a context in which structural economic reforms have increased social inequality and reduced the capacity of the state to deliver services. As an expected outcome, governments are tempted to use force to deal with internal conflicts. Moreover, higher levels of unemployment and poverty have been generally associated with higher levels of crime which, in turn, affect policies regarding the use of force to control crime. Additionally, public opinion generally supports "tough" policies against delinquency. Thus, it is not surprising to observe governments implementing "iron fist" policies to cope with crime and delinquency.

In theory, democracies prevent the violation of citizens' rights by establishing rules regulating the relationship between law enforcement officers and citizens and sanctions against those who violate citizen rights.

Moreover, societies have set up specific institutional tools such as ombudsmen and cost-free counseling to advance citizens' interests. The central idea behind these regulations is to create a balance between the protection of citizens' rights and the need to maintain public safety in a given country.

The question becomes how societies define rules enhancing citizens' rights as well as protecting public security in a context in which "iron fist" policies are demanded. I began to explore this question when I realized that many Latin American countries did not have basic rules protecting citizens' rights from police abuse. For instance, until the early 1990s, in many parts of the region security forces were not mandated to read detainees their rights and detainees were not able to contact their relatives or a legal counselor at the moment of arrest.

Reforms of the judiciary and the police after transitions to democracy in Latin America brought new hopes for citizens regarding the protection of their rights. Indeed, during the 1990s several countries in Latin America enacted reforms such as stricter regulations on police powers to detain individuals and an equivalent to the U.S. *Miranda* rights for detainees.[2] For the first time in the history of these countries, individuals had been granted certain basic rights such as the right to remain silent and the right to contact an attorney. These seemingly basic reforms should have a profound impact on the relationship between citizens and the police. However, many of these changes have been difficult to implement, several of them have been contested by the police, and—by the mid-1990s—security forces were being reissued with some of the powers they had lost.[3] Moreover, the actual record of police violence in the region shows that legal changes have not automatically been translated into a change in police practices (O'Donnell 1996; Pinheiro 1996; Holston and Caldeira 1998; Méndez, O'Donnell, and Pinheiro 1999; Oxhorn 2001).

This book addresses the conditions under which changes toward the protection of citizens' rights have occurred in Latin America, in particular transformations affecting the protection of citizens from police violence. This volume focuses on the impact that human rights advocacy groups have had on three levels: campaigns to increase public awareness about the topic (agenda setting), the promotion of legal reforms to guarantee a fair treatment at the moment of citizens' arrest; and advocacy groups' role in monitoring police practices. The study examines the cases of democratic Chile (1990–2002) and Argentina (1983–2002).

Even though I was originally motivated to exclusively focus on the human rights movement, soon after I began this project, I noticed that given the nature of the problem at stake, I had to study not only those who were challenging the status quo but also those who were resisting the reforms. Explaining the difficulties in implementing police reforms involves the study of macro-level conditions as well as the micro-level characteristics and strategies of the groups attempting to promote reforms and those promoting the status quo. I argue that the resistance to a restriction of police powers and the maintenance of police violence are due to a particular structure of incentives favoring those actors in society who want to maintain the status quo.

REASONS FOR OPTIMISM

In the last fifteen years, three factors have helped create opportunities for the advancement of citizens' rights in Latin America. First, there has been a progressive incorporation of international human rights norms into the domestic legislation of countries within the region. With the exception of Cuba, all countries in the region have progressively incorporated the 1966 U.N. Covenant of Political and Civil Rights and other international regulations into national legislation.[4] Second, the development of increasingly dense transnational advocacy networks, working locally and internationally, to monitor states' compliance with international norms has been a particularly important aspect of the globalization process. The international relations and social movements literatures have both emphasized the growing relevance of these networks in agenda setting, political debate, and even in changing state practices (Meyer et. al. 1997; Keck and Sikkink 1998; Dallmayr 1999; Samhat 1999; Forsythe 2000; Guidry, Kennedy, and Mayer 2000; O'Brien et al. 2000; Thome 2000; Khagram, Riker and Sikkink 2002). Finally, Latin American countries have progressively adopted democratic political systems since the 1980s. It has been argued that democratic settings are particularly favorable environments for the influence of advocacy networks because local authorities are usually committed to respect human rights and social groups have more options to publicly denounce and advance claims. Thus, countries more committed to international rules, a more dense civil society organized globally through transnational advocacy groups, and the process of democratization in Latin America should be considered as three favorable conditions for the advancement of citizens' rights. Even in cases in which local authorities close options for local activists to denounce police violence, theory tells us that advocacy networks can seek the support of international allies to overcome local resistance. This is the "boomerang effect" by which governments may face pressures from "below" and "above" to respect the rule of law (Keck and Sikkink 1998).

Empirical evidence shows, however, that few countries in Latin America have substantially improved the protection of civil rights since the re-establishment of democracy. As Guillermo O'Donnell has argued:

"[In Latin America] the more properly political, *democratic* freedoms are effective: uncoerced voting; freedom of opinion, movement, and association. But for large sections of the population, basic *liberal* freedoms are denied or recurrently trampled. The rights of battered women to sue their husbands and of peasants to obtain fair trial against their landlords, the inviolability of domiciles in poor neighborhoods, and in general the right of the poor and various minorities to decent treatment and fair access to public agencies and courts are often denied" (O'Donnell 1996: 186).

As O'Donnell and other scholars have argued, there is a significant gap between the enhancement of political rights and the enhancement of civil rights in Latin America (Shifter 1997; Zakaria 1997; Agüero and Stark 1998; Oxhorn 2001; Gitlitz and Chevigny 2002). Domestic conditions are key in explaining the circumstances that preempt the advancement of citizens' rights and the influence of local and international social actors within the policy process. The main goal of this book is to explain how and why domestic conditions affect the achievement of civil rights.

RESISTING CHANGE

This book demonstrates that police forces have continued to violate individuals' basic rights in Chile and Argentina since the re-establishment of democracy. Moreover, attempts to restrict police powers in these two countries have been poorly implemented or have been followed by policy reversals that have re-established some of the police powers. This seems to be a common pattern in other Latin American countries such as Peru, El Salvador, Dominican Republic, and Bolivia (NACLA 1996; Kincaid and Gamarra 1996; Holston and Caldeira 1998; Oxhorn 2001; Gitlitz and Chevigny 2002). In this context, human rights advocacy groups have in some cases influenced agenda setting but they have been less successful in affecting the political debate in Congress, monitoring policy implementation, and changing police practices.

What factors explain this resistance to change? A first, intuitive response is that authoritarian legacies, that is, the maintenance of police practices inherited from past military regimes with highly autonomous security forces, explain the persistence of police violence. Thus, police violence is explained by the institutional as well as the cultural characteristics of the police (Chevigny 1995; Méndez 1999; Neild 2000a). Other explanations are the existence of a tradition of authoritarianism in the region that influences political actors' values on the use of force (Wiarda 2001). Chaotic, violent, and lawless politics is explained by low levels of civic competence and democratic understanding on the part of mass constituencies and, equally importantly by high levels of corruption, mistrust, and abuse of power on the part of competing politicians (Diamond 1994). In this account, police violence and rules allowing it to continue are explained by certain authoritarian values prevalent within society.

One of the problems with these accounts is that they do not explain why democratic leaders, supposedly committed to protecting human rights, have not attempted to alter the status quo. In other words, if police autonomy explains the violence, it does not explain why policymakers in a democratic society do little to stop police misbehavior and reform police institutions. Moreover, if elites and masses maintain certain authoritarian values, it is difficult to explain why some sectors of society are trying to enact reforms.

Even though the historical legacy may explain a part of the story, I argue that a specific structure of domestic incentives favors those groups who want to maintain the status quo. First, citizens want to be safe from police abuse as much as they want to be safe from delinquency and, therefore, on this highly divisive issue, constituencies can be mobilized in two directions. They can be mobilized to promote police reforms if violence against citizens is detected and to increase powers if the perception of crime is rising. Second, governments are likely to rely on increasing police powers to control public safety, even in cases in which the record of security forces shows that police practices themselves are contributing to increased levels of violence. Third, those who defend pro-order views enjoy comparative advantages over those who defend civil rights views in terms of access to policymakers and available strategies. As "public safety" is highly valued by policymakers, the police and their allies in the political system have more room to maneuver over what policies are likely to be implemented. This study argues that advocacy groups may effectively impact agenda setting at some critical junctures, but that their impact on policy implementation and police practices are likely to be, at best, transitory. Put succinctly, the task of the enhancing individual rights is extremely hard given a structure of incentives that favors the status quo.

Explaining the persistence of police violence requires examining: (1) the structure of political opportunities in a given society, (2) the characteristics of the policy actors involved, and (3) the nature of the problem at stake. While the first two dimensions allow us to understand certain macro-and micro-level factors constraining or providing opportunities for social actors, the consideration of the nature of the problem at stake allow us to explain the incentives policymakers face to either maintain the status quo or enact reform to control the police.[5] The following paragraphs will briefly outline my argument and theoretical framework.

First, actors' decisions are contextually determined. In other words, the environment or context in which social groups interact imposes certain constraints and a repertoire of possibilities for social and political actors (Karl 1990; Mahoney and Snyder 1999). This political opportunity structure (POS) is defined by the nature of the transition to democracy, access to the political system, and the structure of the police. As will be seen below, these dimensions are defining the "rules of the game" in which social actors interact. In some cases, the POS provides more opportunities for social actors to influence the policy process but, in other cases, the POS constrains actors' choices, making it hard for them to influence the policy process.

Second, there are important differences between those who want to advance police reforms and those who want to block them. Those who want to protect individual rights (what I call the civil rights coalition) generally face serious problems in fostering collective action. Most people want their personal integrity to be protected from abuse by the authorities but few citizens are willing to expend personal resources in trying to collectively protect such rights. In contrast, those who want to maintain the status quo (what I call the pro-order coalition) are more likely to solve their problems of collective action due to the presence of a generally well-organized police institution that is itself willing to expend institutional resources to promote either a favorable status quo or an increase in police powers. Moreover, the police have the advantage of delivering a public good—public safety—that is highly valued by policymakers, which makes the latter to some extent highly dependent on the former. A close look at the characteristics and strategies of competing groups in society will allow us to understand why advancing the protection of individual rights is a more difficult task than maintaining the status quo.

Finally, governments in any democratic society face a difficult trade-off between maintaining public order and protecting individual citizen rights. This trade-off is particularly acute in developing countries where economic turmoil is more frequent and social inequalities more severe than in the developed world. Politicians thus generally view the protection of citizens' rights in zero-sum terms, that is, politicians tend to believe that what is earned in freedom and the protection of individual rights is lost in public safety. In countries in which the police have historically used their discretionary powers to violate human rights, the trade-off between protecting citizens' rights and maintaining public safety usually means that an increase in police powers is likely to result in more police violence against civilians. However, policymakers and citizens are also concerned about maintaining public safety, and one of the easiest ways to do it—besides increasing police budgets—is through the increase of police powers to cope with delinquency and social unrest.[6] As policymakers are concerned about maintaining public order and as the pro-order coalition has comparative advantages over pro-civil rights views, this creates a structure of incentives favorable to the status quo.

Drawing upon the new-institutionalism approach (Thelen and Steinmo 1992; Immergut 1998; Scharpf 2000), this study attempts to integrate structural, institutional, and resource mobilization approaches to explain policy results. I first examine macro-level contextual conditions constraining social actors' choices. Then, I observe micro-level internal conditions of social groups that make them more or less likely to succeed. By considering macro and micro levels of analysis, this study attempts to build a bridge between approaches that exclusively analyze the POS (Eisinger 1973; Tarrow 1994; Kriesi et al. 1995) and those that analyze groups' resource mobilization (McCarthy and Zald 1973; McAdam 1996).

The comparative study of macro and micro-level dimensions helps us to explain the conditions allowing social actors to successfully influence the policy process. For example, and as will be argued below, human rights advocacy groups are more likely to influence the policy process if they have more access to the political system, that is, when the balance of power favors leftist sectors and when the media is receptive to cases of police violence. Thus, the context provides a "window of opportunity" for social actors to influence the policy process.

I argue, however, that defining these macro-and micro level conditions is not enough because there is no guarantee that social actors will take advantage of such a window of opportunity. Indeed, the examination of advocacy groups trying to protect individual rights reveals that in several critical junctures they seem to "miss" opportunities for action. In this sense, the study of macro and micro-level conditions provides a useful but still static view of a given policy process. As policymakers face simultaneous challenges to both protect individual rights and maintain social order, it is very likely that they will face pressures from civil rights and pro-order groups to either protect citizens from abuse of power or increase police powers. Thus, understanding the advances and reversals in terms of the legal and actual protection of individual rights necessarily requires studying the context (POS), internal characteristics, and the nature of the policy issue at stake that will define actors' alignments and potential strategies. In brief, I argue that in Latin America resistance to changing practices of police violence can be explained by examining the comparative strength and strategies of pro-order and civil rights coalitions trying to influence the policy process. This requires understanding the POS that provides certain initial conditions for success or failure and explaining the characteristics and strategies of both coalitions over time.

In order to simplify reality, I make three assumptions related to the way actors respond to social challenges. First, I assume that on divisive issues, actors are likely to form coalitions. Second, these coalitions are not necessarily highly coordinated all the time, but they show more intense degrees of coordination at key junctures. Third, actors are likely to coordinate actions based on their beliefs and material interests.[7]

WHAT IS NEW?

This study aims to make four contributions: first, because most analyses regarding the protection of human rights have studied the influence of transnational advocacy groups over authoritarian regimes, the conclusions have tended to downplay the complexity of elements proper to a democratic regime. Indeed, when facing fragile established democratic regimes, advocacy networks confront new strategic challenges that have not been properly explored. The cases presented in this study provide evidence that even if alliances between domestic and international advocacy networks are active, the domestic configuration of power, the way the police force is organized, and the way citizens' rights are framed strongly influence whether governments are willing to address the issue of police brutality and push for police reforms.

While the conceptualization of the mentioned "boomerang effect" has been mainly applied to authoritarian contexts, this study suggests a more complex relationship between international and domestic forces in a democratic setting. First, even though democratic regimes are substantially more open than authoritarian regimes, democratic incumbents can still have *incentives* to block advocacy networks' influence. Second, in a democratic context *both* governments and advocacy groups may use international forums to advance their demands. For example, incumbents are likely to use international forums to respond to allegations of human rights, which—to some extent—may diffuse the initial impact of charges made by human rights groups. Third, if international actors want to support certain claims, local organizations *must* provide reliable and updated information to make the case of police abuses. This study aims to explain the strategic complexity associated with the enhancement of citizens' rights in a democratic context where multiple actors interact.

The second contribution of this study relates to the factors that explain the persistence of police brutality and policy reversals on formal police powers in Latin America. While some scholars have addressed the historical legacy of police autonomy and repression, I argue that the nature of the problem at stake and the characteristics of the policy actors involved are driving policy decisions. Given that governments rely on the police for public order, they face strong incentives to avoid disturbing their relationship with the police, making it more likely that they do not seek to improve mechanisms of internal accountability of the police. Moreover, citizens clearly want not only to be safe from police abuses but also to be safe from crime. Governments will respond to the pressures from those organized groups in society that are most successful in framing the issues, influencing them. According to my argument, the pro-order coalition has a structural comparative advantage over the civil rights coalition, making it harder for the latter to influence the policy process.

The analysis of the structure of incentives and power relations among actors challenge some explanations regarding the importance political actors' ideological commitment to certain worldviews. While we should expect center and leftist parties defending civil rights views, my argument suggests that this happens only under certain conditions and that policymakers are constantly facing a trade-off between the respect of citizens' rights and the maintenance of public order.

Third, this study challenges the pluralist idea that a change in objective conditions in society will automatically be translated into policy responses. In other words, increasing levels of crime or social protests do not necessarily imply that politicians will provide more powers to the police. At the same time, a reduction in the level of crime or an increase in the level of police violence does not automatically translate into a reduction in police powers. While objective social conditions may create incentives for action, I argue that an essential part of the story is how well organized are those who want to increase police powers and those who want to protect individual rights.

Finally, this study departs from a single-case study of one social movement—in this case the human rights movement—both by integrating the study of this movement within a broader political context in which competing groups in society attempt to influence policy outcomes and by examining three case studies over time (two in Argentina and one in Chile). The advocacy coalition framework is a useful analytical device because it allows us to consider the contextual conditions that define certain "rules of the game" as well as the comparative strength and strategies of competing groups in society—in this case, the pro-order and civil rights coalitions.

SHOULD WE CARE?

Studying the protection of citizens' rights is particularly relevant today. First, police violence is likely to occur in any political system, including the most developed and democratic societies. While some scholars argue that high levels of economic development reduce the incidence of police violence (Chevigny 1995: 249; Bayley 1996: 278),[8] several studies have documented persistent patterns of abuses in developed and fully democratic societies (Warren 1991; Chevigny 1995; Human Right Watch 1998b). The explanations given for the likelihood of police violence in any society are related to police discretion, the subjectivity of policing, and the difficulties in proving cases of police brutality.[9]

In modern societies, citizens give the police the power to legitimately use violence to maintain social order. Authorities provide a set of guidelines stipulating when the use of violence is legitimate, but there is always room for police discretion (Reiss 1971; Walker 1977). Police officers are "street-level bureaucrats" (Lipsky: 1980), generally badly paid who deal with problematical issues such as crime and social disorder. As police officers have some discretion over the use of force, their actions can lead to misconduct. Second, in many instances evaluations of police actions are based on *subjective* interpretations and, therefore, it can be difficult to draw a clear line between proper and improper behavior. Third, there is the practical difficulty of proving the existence of brutality after an arrest is made. As the collection of material evidence and witnesses is very difficult, accountability is obviously at risk (Chevigny 1969). Given that any society is likely to face problems of police violence, a key question is how different societies attempt to preempt police abuse and/or punish police misbehavior when this happens.

Another reason that makes this topic relevant is that police violence has continued in many developing countries despite democratization. Many newly democratic countries face simultaneous pressures to solve socioeconomic problems, reinforce the rule of law, and generate a more efficient state apparatus. Additionally, economic reforms initiated during the 1980s in many developing countries have tended to increase economic inequalities, which have created social pressures to address problems of unemployment and social marginality.[10] As these social pressures rise, governments may be tempted to use force to deal with internal conflicts. Moreover, high levels of unemployment and poverty have generally been associated with high levels of crime which, in turn, affect policies on the use of force to control crime.

Thus, while liberal democracies accept the inviolability of citizens' integrity as a core principle of democracy (Perry 1998), in reality there is a constant tension between citizens' inviolability and the actual use of force by the police. In an environment of growing inequalities and social conflicts, which is the case across Latin American countries, it is possible that levels of police violence may increase.

A third and related factor that makes this study relevant is the process of transition to democracy, particularly in Latin America and Eastern Europe. In theory, transitions to democracy imply dismantling antidemocratic forms of exercising power, changing the rules governing the distribution of power, the recognition and legal sanction of rights, and the internalization of such new rules among citizens (Jelin 1996: 102). New authorities have to deal with police institutions that were generally engaged in massive violations of human rights. In re-democratized Eastern Europe and Latin America reformists have attempted to curtail the excessive powers granted to the police to increase civilian control over the police, and to abolish the state security network that controlled society during authoritarian regimes (Frühling 1998b). The question here is to what extent this attempt has been successful, and what are the obstacles and opportunities for the enactment of reforms.

Finally, the issue of police violence must be considered within a broader debate about how democratic societies establish mechanisms of accountability. There are two, non-exclusive forms in which accountability can be enacted and maintained: citizens policing incumbents and incumbents enhancing the rule of law. Regarding citizens' policing, we know that controlling the state is difficult because it requires high levels of citizen coordination and access to information which is very unlikely on a day-to-day basis, and it requires all citizens to have similar interests in controlling the state, which is rarely the case because violating the human rights of one group often benefits another group (Weingast 1997).

The creation and use of mechanisms of accountability greatly depends on the distribution of power among competing groups in society, the level of citizens' coordination in demanding reforms, and the level of incumbents' control over the police. Thus, studying how societies attempt to establish mechanisms of accountability tells us something about citizens overcoming collective action problems and about elites dealing with conflicting interests in a democratic framework. Guarding the guardians can be understood as an ongoing struggle for power between citizens and politicians who have competing views and interests of what is best for society and for them. One of the objectives of this book is to provide a framework that allows us to make sense of this political struggle to enhance citizens' rights, explaining how societies achieve different equilibria according to the strength and strategies of competing groups in society.

ARGENTINA AND CHILE IN COMPARATIVE PERSPECTIVE

Using qualitative analysis, this study infers causal effects from the data observed. In order to do so, I have selected a set of attempts of policy reforms in newly democratized countries—Argentina since 1983 and Chile since 1990, tracing the role played by organized domestic groups in issues related to the legal, procedural, and behavioral protection of citizens from police abuse.

I observe legal reforms that have taken place in two regions of Argentina with independent police forces (Buenos Aires Province and Buenos Aires Capital in Argentina), and in Chile where the police is centralized. I originally selected to compare the Buenos Aires province and Chile because while both observed similar initial conditions and a dense network of human rights organizations, extensive legal reforms in Argentina seem to demonstrate a more relevant impact of Argentine advocacy groups than in Chile.

Given that Argentina is a federal political system with autonomous police forces in each region of the country, I incorporated a third case—the reform of police powers in the Buenos Aires Capital. Public safety in the Buenos Aires Capital is controlled by the more corporate Federal Police. By including this case, I can control for three crucial variables in this study—the nature of the transition, access to the political system, and advocacy groups' internal characteristics, allowing me to test whether police corporateness has an effect on policy outcomes in Chile as well as Argentina.

Selected countries share several macro-economic indicators of development including levels of poverty, education, life expectancy, and economic growth. Argentina has decentralized police forces and there is one police officer for every 270 inhabitants in the Buenos Aires province and one police officer for every 315 inhabitants in the capital. Chile has a centralized police force and there is one police officer for every 416 inhabitants. The average salary of police officers in Argentina is higher than in Chile. However, Chilean police officers enjoy extra-salary privileges such as access to institutional health care and subsidized housing.

As an average, homicide rates in Chile and the Buenos Aires Capital are relatively low (2.2 and 3.3 respectively) and the Buenos Aires province has higher homicide rates than the previous two cases (8.8).[11] However, in the Argentine case figures must be taken with caution for three reasons.

First, during the 1990s the Ministry of Justice improved the methodology to collect data on crime and, therefore, we should expect increasingly higher rates in all types of crimes and in all the country. Second, the Buenos Aires Capital observes low homicide rates in the first half of the decade (1.5 between 1990–1994) and significantly higher homicide rates for the second half of the decade (5.0 between 1995–1999). Finally, crimes against property and against individuals in the Buenos Aires Capital are dramatically higher than in the Buenos Aires province, particularly during the second half of the 1990s.[12]

Both countries share several features in terms of initial conditions. First, these two cases share a legacy of human rights violations, making the topic a first priority for new authorities. In both countries, incoming authorities showed an initial strong commitment to the human rights cause. Second, in both cases, police institutions enjoyed high levels of institutional autonomy. Police autonomy refers to formal and informal police independence from civilian authorities on key issues. In both cases, the police enjoyed high levels of freedom in conducting their affairs (Frühling 1998a).

Third, in both cases judicial mechanisms to solve claims of police misbehavior at the beginning of democracy were extremely weak. For instance, in both countries almost no case of police violence had ended with the officer's conviction in courts. Additionally, external mechanisms of accountability such as ombudsmen or citizen review boards did not exist in either Argentina or Chile (Frühling 1998b).

Fourth, in both cases the legal protection of citizens from the police was extremely low. Police officers could arrest people based on their suspicion that a crime was going to be committed, and individuals could be held under preventive arrest for 48 hours without charges in both countries. Moreover, police officers did not have to explain to citizens their rights at the moment of their arrest. Finally, if faced with an allegation of police misconduct, judges always considered officers' testimonies over citizens' version of the facts.

Fifth, both cases exhibit the continuation of police abuses after the transition, although several quantitative sources suggest a higher rate in Argentina than in Chile. But the important point is that in both countries police forces continued applying repressive tactics against citizens, activating human rights groups to demand reforms. Indeed, in both cases human rights organizations were seeking to address the topic of police violence just after the re-establishment of democracy.

In this context, we would expect that in both countries human rights advocacy networks would pressure new authorities to abolish old laws providing unrestricted powers to the police and enact new laws protecting citizens from abuse of power; reform police institutions to reduce their legal autonomy and to incorporate human rights views in their curricula; and create mechanisms of accountability to control police behavior. Finally, if police violence continues in both countries, we would also expect that advocacy networks would seek to monitor police institutions. Furthermore, we would expect social actors to increase protests and monitoring activities as levels of police violence increased in both countries during the 1990s.

The literature on social movements underlines the importance and strength of human rights groups in both countries during the military regimes and transition. Argentina has a dense network of human rights groups. After the fall of Argentina's last military government in 1983, some human rights organizations continued monitoring the behavior of police forces. At the end of the 1980s, CELS inaugurated an annual report on human rights, including the issue of police violence.[13] Moreover, four years after the transition a group of lawyers formed a NGO called "Coordination against Institutional Repression" (CORREPI) to provide legal advice to individuals affected by police violence. In Chile, at the beginning of the transition a dense network of human rights organizations existed, counting more than twenty six different organizations and more than five thousand volunteers across the country. Given the initial conditions described in here in both countries, potential advocacy networks were ready to respond to such challenges.

Following my argument, Argentina and Chile should follow two distinct paths after their democratization. In Argentina, we should expect advocacy networks to gain in public attention, in their ability to monitor police abuses, and in their capacity to influence the government to introduce some reforms. The political opportunity structure and the groups' internal characteristics should help these groups to gain allies within the political system and influence policy outcomes. Indeed, Argentina's context has allowed the civil rights coalition to possess comparatively higher possibilities to influence policy-making process than in Chile. This is due to the nature of the transition (by reform), the left-right balance of power in Congress favorable to the center-left, particularly after 1995, and the presence of a pluralist media. Additionally, the police in the different provinces show weak corporateness and, therefore, civil rights groups have more options to learn what happens inside police departments as internal struggles for power surface. Finally, advocacy networks enjoyed some favorable internal conditions in order to take advantage of the opportunities provided for the context. However, we should also expect a pro-order coalition trying to block initiatives and police institutions ready to preempt internal reforms. Comparing the Buenos Aires Province and the Capital, we should expect advocacy networks to have more difficulties in monitoring the Federal Police responsible for public safety, given its higher levels of corporateness.

In contrast, human rights groups in Chile should face a hard time trying to influence agenda setting, police reform, and policy implementation. Despite the existence of increasing trends in allegations against the police and the low level of case resolution against officers in courts, advocacy groups should not exert much influence given the unfavorable political opportunity for these groups. Moreover, we also should expect a pro-order coalition preempting those attempts to either restrict police powers or reform police internal mechanisms of accountability. The reasons explaining advocacy networks' poor performance in Chile are also related to the political opportunity structure and resource mobilization. Regarding the environment, in Chile advocacy networks faced a transition to democracy between pact and imposition, and a political system in which the balance of power was favorable to pro-order views and in which the media is owned by conservative sectors. Right-wing sectors controlled the discourse regarding public order during the 1990s, gaining the favor of police institutions and maintaining close ties between politicians and police institutions. Moreover, the police showed high levels of corporatism, which clearly limited the scope of possibilities for human rights groups to obtain information from inside and to contest an effective police public relation system.

But police legal autonomy, the absence of resolution of cases in courts, and the existence of continuous abuses should encourage citizens to ask for institutional and behavioral reforms. Why have advocacy networks in Chile not raised their voice more strongly? As chapter two will show, human rights groups have missed opportunities to influence the political agenda by not reacting when they had the opportunity to do so. I explain this lack of attention to the topic of police violence given a contextual factor, the nature of the transition, and two important internal characteristics of the groups: lack of leadership and the specific groups' social composition.

Drawing upon the new-institutionalism approach, this book aims to systematize the mechanisms by which certain contextual conditions affect social and political actors in their attempt to enhance citizens' rights. Chapter one discusses different approaches explaining the persistence of police violence in developing countries. Additionally, it introduces a theoretical framework that integrates the political opportunity structure and resource mobilization approaches to understand the factors promoting and inhibiting the advancement of citizens' rights in a democratic society.

Chapter two addresses the issue of police violence and legal reforms concerning police powers in democratic Chile (1990–2002). Chile is a puzzling case because, despite evidence suggesting constant police violence since the re-establishment of democracy, center-left civil authorities have adopted a defensive position that denies the existence of the problem. Moreover, institutional mechanisms to solve cases of police violence are weak and they tend to virtually always favor police officers. The first part of the chapter provides a general background including the legal status of the police, a qualitative and quantitative analysis of police practices, resolution of cases in court, and public opinion trends on issues of public safety and protection of citizens' rights. The second part explains why police violence is not a political issue in Chile, by analyzing contextual as well as internal characteristics of the pro-order and the civil rights coalitions.

Chapter three explains a legal reform that seems puzzling in Chile. We should not expect improvements of the legal protection of citizens' rights in an environment in which the pro-order coalition dominates the political scene and in which human rights advocacy groups are weakly organized. However, the Chilean case demonstrates precisely the contrary. In 1998 the Chilean Congress approved a bill restricting police powers and enacting, for the first time in history, *Miranda* rights for detainees. This outcome may challenge the explanation regarding "conditions for success." The examination of this particular bill helps to underscore the importance of pro-civil rights policymakers inside and outside the state as well as the importance of framing.

Chapter four examines the reform attempts of Buenos Aires Provincial Police in democratic Argentina (1983–2002). In this case, contextual conditions to influence the policy process are more favorable for Argentine advocacy groups than for those in Chile. However, by the end of the 1990s, several legal reforms had been reversed and police practices of violence continued. In the first part, I provide background information on the legal status of the police, a qualitative and quantitative analysis of police practices of violence, resolution of cases in court, and an analysis of public opinion trends on public safety and protection of citizens' rights. The second part addresses the factors that inhibit police reform by analyzing contextual as well as internal characteristics of the pro-order and civil rights coalitions, explaining the impact of the different strategies used by these groups.

Chapter five explores another case by considering the attempts to circumscribe the legal powers of the Federal Police in Argentina—which is the institution in charge of public safety in the Federal District of Buenos Aires (Capital). The examination of this case allows us to control for some variables such as the nature of the transition and access to the political system, and address whether different levels of police corporateness have an impact on certain outcomes. After examining two reforms in Argentina, I conclude that advocacy groups have faced enormous obstacles in trying to transform the Federal Police. I argue that this is due to the combination of facing a highly corporate police institution and the way the pro-order coalition has responded to attempts at reform.

Chapter six concludes by systematizing the evidence presented in previous chapters in terms of macro and micro level conditions. Additionally, I examine coalitions' strategies and incumbents' incentives to adopt one or another policy. Finally, I outline some theoretical and policy implications of this study.

Chapter One

Guarding the Guardians

Daniel is a young man who lives in a poor neighborhood in Santiago, Chile. He is 23 years old and has a job in the construction sector. Like many other young people, he likes going out and drinking with his friends on weekends. During the year 2000, the police detained and beat him twice. The second time, he was walking on a dark street and a police car stopped him to ask for his ID. After having an argument, he refused to show his ID and the police beat him. The medical report stated that Daniel suffered severe contusions in his head and body. But Daniel did not take legal actions against the police because he knew the judge would not believe him, and the likelihood of obtaining a favorable judgment were minimal.[1] Indeed, in Chile, less than 0.2 percent of these cases end up with an officer being convicted of brutality or excessive use of force.

José Luis is also a young man who lives in Buenos Aires, Argentina. His story is a little different from that of Daniel. After having been severely beaten by the police, José Luis contacted the *Centro de Estudios Legales y Sociales* (CELS), a human rights organization that provides legal support in cases of police violence. The case was widely publicized by the press thanks to CELS' connections and reputation. Several months later, José Luis was severely attacked again and received threats from unknown people. His lawyers had to ask for special protection for him. He had to move from his old neighborhood and look for a new job. Several months later, after a number of failed attempts to obtain justice, José Luis decided not to pursue the case anymore (CELS 2001).

These two stories have something in common: in both Chile and Argentina the chances of obtaining justice in cases of police violence are minimal. Police violence is a common practice in many developing countries and, as in the stories of Daniel and José Luis, it usually goes unpunished because either citizens perceive they do not have access to justice or citizens do not have the legal tools to protect themselves from abuses.

As these two stories show, one of the crucial questions in a democratic society is who protects citizens from those in charge of protecting society—"Who guards the guardians?" The modern concept of democracy implies that every human being has certain rights, that governments must protect these rights, and that this protection is a necessary condition of governmental legitimacy. Since this social contract allows the state to monopolize the use of force to maintain social peace, a fundamental right is the protection of the physical integrity of individuals from the abuse of state power. Even though in theory this right is guaranteed by the existence of checks and balances within and outside the state, in practice many democratic regimes face a daily struggle to guard their guardians.

The central concerns in this book[2] are (1) how post-authoritarian societies in developing countries attempt to reduce and eventually prevent police abuses, and (2) what are the principal factors inhibiting an improvement of citizens' rights in legal and actual terms.[3] I assume that protecting citizens from police abuse in re-democratized countries requires: creating a legal framework granting citizens basic rights; establishing procedures for the police to deal with citizens in the streets; instituting mechanisms of internal accountability within police institutions; and generating mechanisms of external accountability to control police compliance with rules.

This chapter begins examining certain potentially favorable conditions for the enhancement of citizens' rights. According to some authors, the establishment of democratic regimes and the incorporation of international standards into domestic laws are pre-conditions for the protection of citizens' rights. As international norms have weak enforcement mechanisms, transnational advocacy networks play a key role pressuring states to adopt universal principles and monitoring policy compliance. Thus, the diffusion of international norms, expansion of advocacy networks and democratization are usually considered a 'virtuous cycle' helping to enhance citizens' rights.

Nevertheless, in many developing countries transitions to democracy and enactment of laws have not necessarily been translated into a substantive improvement of citizens' rights (O'Donnell 1996; Pinheiro 2000). How can we explain the gap between the universal acceptance of human rights principles and the poor performance by states to respect such norms? I suggest that this gap is more than a problem of social actors not being aware of their rights, or of powerless social actors not ready to fight for their rights. Protecting individual rights is a complex problem involving political actors who want maintain social order and maintain their prerogatives, and other actors who want to protect citizens from abuse.

THE "VIRTUOUS CYCLE" OF RECOGNITION, ADVOCACY, AND DEMOCRACY

Before the 1960s, if a police officer brutalized an African American in the United States, this would probably not make the news of the day. If a police officer acts in the same way today, however, it is more likely that the injured person will file a complaint in court; that the press will report on the case; and that civil rights groups will protest against the police. What has happened in the United States and in many other societies is that the protection of individuals' physical integrity from illegitimate abuse of power has become an essential principle of democratic life.

Political scientists and lawyers have noticed an enormous progress on this issue from the pre-World War II era until current days. Beginning with the 1948 United Nations Universal Declaration of Human Rights, international and domestic laws have incorporated the protection of individuals' integrity as a fundamental element in a democratic regime. Scholars recognize that international human rights have become part of the collective understanding of world politics and, therefore, a constitutive element of modern and 'civilized' statehood (Boli and Thomas 1997; Meyer at al. 1997; see discussion in Risse and Ropp 1999).

Indeed, over the past several decades the international system has been an important source of legitimacy to the existence and respect of basic political and civil rights. Gradually, the international community has extended legitimacy to national governments by accepting them as independent and autonomous political entities, by establishing international rules that have progressively been incorporated domestically, and by monitoring state behavior. The 20th century witnessed a change in international law "as a result of which the legitimacy of each government someday will be measured definitively by international rules and processes" (Franck 1992). In this context, the entitlement to democracy in international law has gone through both a normative and a customary evolution. According to Franck this evolution has occurred in three phases: "first came the normative entitlement to countries' self-determination. Then came the normative entitlement to free expression as a human right. Now we see the emergence of a normative entitlement to a participatory electoral process" (Franck 1992: 90). In other words, all states are facing more constraints than ever before regarding their domestic behavior, as limited and partial are these rules still be.

As the international system has moved toward a democratic entitlement, the international system expects countries to adopt the basic "system of rights" provided by the United Nations (UN) conventions. The progressive internalization of international rules is a good example of this trend. Indeed, Latin American countries have progressively ratified different conventions and protocols on human rights, including the UN Covenant on Civil and Political Rights (1966), the optional protocol on Civil and Political Rights that recognizes the competence of the UN Human Rights Committee to consider individuals' allegations; the second optional Protocol related to the abolition of the death penalty (1989) and the Convention Against Torture and other Form of Cruel, Inhuman or Degrading Treatment or Punishment (1984).

Countries have different incentives to accept these norms. First, societies may internalize certain ideas about what is a 'modern statehood.' According to this argument, authorities follow certain rules not because of the potential tangible or non-tangible benefits, but because they believe these rules constitute something 'proper' or 'expected.' Norm internalization occurs when rules are socially accepted and individuals do not question existing principles. As individuals interact with others, they learn certain social norms that are beneficial for the maintenance of the group, creating a natural self-containment. If we extend this argument to states' behavior, we should expect to see that countries respect certain principles because policymakers have internalized central aspects of the "Western civilization" in their national identity.[4] Countries that have not internalized the Western discourse of human rights are more successful in trying to resist international pressures by creating a national identity linked to particular beliefs—i.e. Asian values (Keck and Sikkink 1998: 118; see also Risse and Ropp 1999).

But countries may also follow those rules because of the tangible and non-tangible costs of not respecting human rights.[5] International agencies and other states may use economic and military sanctions to pressure other governments to behave in certain ways. Moreover, not respecting some rules may affect the state's participation in other international regimes, which is in fact a powerful incentive to follow an internationally accepted pattern of behavior (Keohane 1984; Thomas 2002).

Additionally, states may face less tangible but still important reputation costs. For instance, countries that are considered part of the "Western culture" do not want to lose their status as such. As this "Western culture" has progressively established what is expected from a democratic state, democratic regimes will adopt international regimes to acquire full membership from this civilized and also economically powerful world. If countries do engage in unlawful practices, they may face political and symbolic sanctions from the international community, which in fact may deter those actors from using illegitimate mechanisms to repress citizens.[6]

Despite the incentives to incorporate international laws into domestic law and to respect human rights, states still violate human rights. Three factors may explain this fact: first, strategic calculations lead powerful countries to decide not to enforce certain rules when they affect potential allies. This was the case of the United States when it supported the emergence of repressive military regimes in Latin America, subordinating human rights principles to security concerns. Second, in comparison to domestic laws, enforcement is difficult to achieve in the international arena. Many times, strategic interests tend to reduce the impact of collective sanctions over some target states.[7] Finally, monitoring countries' compliance with rules is expensive and hard to accomplish.

This enforceability problem makes the role of transnational advocacy networks crucial. Advocacy networks are "forms of organization characterized by voluntary, reciprocal, and horizontal patterns of communication and exchange" (Keck and Sikkink 1998: 8). Scholars have argued that these networks are relevant because they can influence: (a) issue creation and agenda setting, (b) institutional procedures, (c) the discourses of states and international organizations, (d) policy change in 'target actors,' and (e) state compliance with new rules (Keck and Sikkink 1998: 25; Friedman, Hochstetler, and Clark 2001).

Transnational advocacy networks have grown exponentially in the last 50 years.[8] While in 1953 the Union of International Associations registered 56 human rights, peace, women, and environment organizations, in 1993 this figure was 378, a 675 percent increase.[9] In the context of a more interdependent world, non-state actors and the transnational links among them have achieved particular significance, transforming global governance (Lipschutz 1996; Shaw 2000; Evans 2001; O'Brien et al. 2000; Khagram, Riker, and Sikkink 2002).

Keck and Sikkink argue that when channels between the state and its domestic actors are blocked, a "boomerang" effect is likely to emerge: "domestic NGOs bypass their state and directly search out international allies to try to bring pressure on their states from outside" (Keck and Sikkink 1998: 12). Thus, when states refuse to recognize rights and when the channels between the state and social actors are blocked, domestic NGOs will bypass their state and directly search for the support of international allies in order to bring pressure on their states from outside. The recent reduction of costs and expansion of communications can amplify domestic groups' demands, increasing the power of domestic groups vis-à-vis the government and other domestic forces (Keck and Sikkink 1998: 12–13).[10] In other words, "international human rights pressures contribute to changing understandings about how state should use their sovereign authority over their citizens and to changing specific human rights practices" (Sikkink 1993: 435).

Given the highly constrained domestic environment with tightly controlled political opposition and mass media, activists are likely to contact inter-governmental organizations and international human rights organizations to pressure governments from abroad (Weissbrodt 1984; Hutchison 1989; Sikkink 1993; Garretón 1996; Dassin 1999; Ropp and Sikkink 1999; Samhat 1999; Hawkins 2002).

In Latin America, the legitimacy of expansion of international norms and the rise in transnational advocacy activism have been accompanied by the parallel process of transitions to democracy. By the early 1990s and for the first time in history, all Latin American countries except Cuba had democratic governments elected in relatively fair elections. The absence of military coups in a context of severe economic crises during the 1990s led some scholars to be surprised by the resilience of democratically elected governments. Mainwaring (1999) concludes that "more political actors are now committed to democracy than ever before." Indeed, transitions to democracy in Latin America have brought new authorities to power who have promptly adopted international human rights norms.

Transnational advocacy networks should find in a democratic regime a fertile environment to influence policy making because (a) democratic authorities are usually committed to principles of rule of law and respect of human rights, (b) checks and balances across state powers (horizontal accountability) provide citizens with greater ability to control public authorities, and (c) democratic political systems open opportunities for the expression of different views and, therefore, citizens have more freedom to pressure incumbents (vertical accountability).

In sum, the 'virtuous cycle' of human rights includes international rules that progressively constrain states' behavior, increasing monitoring activities by transnational advocacy networks, and the expansion of democracy that should open opportunities for organized citizens to influence governments.

THE 'VIRTUOUS CYCLE' REVISED: EXPLAINING THE MAINTENANCE OF POLICE VIOLENCE

The evolution of political and civil rights in Latin America in the last 15 years, however, does not show a linear relationship between the diffusion of the rule of law and the actual protection of citizens' rights. In this sense, the adoption of international norms, the expansion of advocacy networks, and democratization processes have not automatically been translated into an improvement of citizens' rights (Agüero and Stark 1998; O'Donnell 2001b; Oxhorn 2001).[11] For instance, considering the Freedom House Survey on political and civil rights, an increasing number of Latin American countries have improved political rights, going from four to eleven those countries where political rights were fully respected between 1976 and 2001. However, if we consider the respect for civil liberties—which includes the protection from abuse of state power, while in 1976 four countries enjoyed full respect for civil liberties, in 2001 only five countries observed a full respect of such rights. In other words, while citizens in Latin America can currently elect authorities fairly and freely, they still suffer mistreatment and abuse of authority.

Several sources recognize persistent patterns of police violence in Latin America (Amnesty International 2002; Human Rights Watch 2002). While new democratic authorities do not illegally detain, torture, and make people disappear, police violence is a daily practice that remains unchecked in several 'democratic' countries (NACLA 1996; O'Donnell 1996; Holston and Caldeira 1998; Méndez, O'Donnell, and Pinheiro 1999). This does not mean the absence of change. In fact, some governments in the region have attempted to reform police institutions, provide new legal frameworks to protect citizens' rights, and create mechanisms of accountability such as ombudsmen and citizens review boards. However, all these initiatives have been strongly resisted by political sectors and the police, are difficult to implement, or are followed by increasing police powers.

Thus while social actors are more interconnected than ever to demand the protection of citizens' rights locally and internationally, certain domestic forces preempt such an influence and inhibit substantive changes.[12] As transitions to democracy have facilitated the expression of civil society, the political process has also facilitated the development of counter-balancing influences. Neither have transitions to democracy implied an automatic improvement of citizens' rights.

Thus, if the development of international norms, the existence of transnational advocacy networks, and the democratization process are not sufficient conditions for the protection of individual rights, we need to observe the domestic factors which inhibit improvements in respect for human rights. What are the factors explaining the gap between the recognition of international norms of human rights and the actual performance of governments in terms of protecting citizens' rights? Explaining the domestic resistance to change is the goal of the following paragraphs.

There are several alternative explanations for why is so difficult to improve citizens' rights in developing countries. The first suggests that the perception of injustice is a pre-condition for change. If a significant number of citizens do not perceive they are being treated unfairly by police forces, collective action is unlikely. Contrary to a traditional pluralist approach, however, deprivation, frustration, and anger are not directly translated into social organization and policy change.[13] Citizens who are facing disadvantageous circumstances or who perceive the police is unjust do not always engage in active mobilizations to end injustice. For example, if police violence was a problem in several U.S. urban cities during most of the 20th century, we should expect those citizens (particularly African Americans) to pressure the government to change this situation; yet, this did not happen until the early 1960s. Thus, the question is when and under what circumstances do citizens respond to unfair treatment individually and collectively.

If grievance alone does not explain change, one important feature is related to the structure of power among political and social actors.[14] According to this view, police violence in Latin America can be explained in part by the uneven distribution of power among those who control resources of power (the means of production, the state apparatus) and the rest of society. For instance, economic elites may influence policymakers to repress workers who are not willing to accept new rules of the game. Those elites may influence policymakers to punish those who attempt to violate private property as well. In this context, the police would play their assigned role by repressing those groups and individuals who threaten the elite.[15]

Even though this structural, power-based analysis highlights an important feature of social relations, social actors' distribution of power, it provides an incomplete picture of the problem. First, analyses that only take into account actors' distribution of power are not well suited to predict outcomes.[16] If the balance of power among social actors defines the structure of a system, then we should not observe major changes after powerful actors impose certain conditions and rules. For instance, if upper classes dominate national security forces, how can one explain new restrictions on police powers in some Latin American countries during the 1990s?[17] For structuralists, the only possible explanation for such change is variation in the balance of power among actors; however, these theories do not explain why such an alteration in power was possible or has occurred.

Moreover, structuralist approaches portray institutions as an equilibrium solution to social actors' conflicting interests; in other words, institutions reflect the power distribution among different groups in society. For example, power-based analyses consider the police to be a reflection of the interests of the powerful. But even though police institutions may reflect an initial distribution of power, they incorporate historical experience into rules, routines, and procedures, which persists beyond the initial historical moment and conditions.[18]

A subset of structural arguments contends that changes in the structure of the global economy (a greater openness to trade, increasing investment), may lead to lower levels of human rights violations and policy reforms. First, as global markets and organizations guide governments' policies, they may impose limits on what is a "legitimate" state behavior. Second, investors and international financial organizations value stability, requesting local elites to respect the rule of law and enhance institutions such as the judiciary (Richards et al. 2001). Finally, participation in global markets stimulates growth, which promotes the development of a middle class that would demand more protection of essential rights (Winston 1999).

However, quantitative and qualitative analyses show contradictory evidence regarding the relationship between economic globalization—measured in terms of trade and investment—and protection of human rights. In a systematic review of quantitative works, Emilie Hafner-Burton (2002) concludes that this research program suffers from inconsistent findings and fragile correlations between trade and investment indicators and human rights. Conceptual, methodological, and measurement problems make it very difficult to draw conclusions about such a relationship.[19] Moreover, qualitative studies have shown that the neo-liberal trend of economic reforms has been accompanied by the reduction of state agencies that attend social needs, which weakens the capacity of incumbents to implement certain policies. Conditions attached to the process of economic liberalization may increase options of social conflicts, particularly when such a process has not fostered economic equality (Pinheiro 1996; Oxhorn 2001; ECLAC 2002).[20]

The inconsistency of these studies suggests the need to explore domestic conditions affecting trends in the protection of citizens' rights and a first intuitive argument is related to governments' economic performance. According to this argument, periods of economic emergency increase the likelihood of police violence because of raising levels of social discontent and policymakers' incentives to maintain public order. Policymakers may increase police powers in periods of economic crisis to contain social unrest. Thus, we should expect lower levels of police violence in good economic periods and, therefore, lesser incentives for policymakers to use the police to repress social actors.

While several studies have shown a strong association between economic backlash and police violence (O'Donnell, Méndez and Pinheiro 1999; Oxhorn 2001), these studies cannot account for the maintenance of police violence after the national economy has been stabilized. Moreover, highly repressive police behavior in times of crisis may open a window of opportunity for those who defend civil rights, generating institutional changes that attempt to control police behavior.[21] These contradictory findings have led scholars to explore two domestic conditions often hypothesized to explain the maintenance of police violence in post-authoritarian societies and the resistance to institutional changes: political culture and institutions.

Concerning the political culture argument, in the 1960s modernization theory suggested that the main problem in Latin America was the lack of a 'modern man,' that is, the lack of essential modern values. This argument may explain persistent patterns of police violence in Latin America. For instance, some authors have claimed that Latin American countries are caught in a clientelistic and authoritarian social system inherited from colonial times, allowing certain elites to maintain the status quo. In this interpretation, an inherited traditional value system inhibits the notion that all citizens are equal and must be treated as such. Feudalistic social interactions have evolved to establish hierarchical, patron-client relationship, inhibiting social actors from advancing a civil rights agenda.[22]

The cultural argument makes three assumptions: first, political culture understood as people's predominant beliefs, attitudes, sentiments, and ideas (Almond and Verba 1963; Diamond 1994) shapes political outcomes. People's beliefs and ideas filter, shape, and mediate political processes by establishing certain parameters from which individuals observe and take decisions, and by affecting and shaping institutions (Wiarda 2001). Second, the central conceptions of the Latin American 'culture'—Catholicism, elitism, patrimonialism, corporatism, and organicism—have become embedded in political and social institutions. Finally, these institutions "have generally proved sufficiently flexible to absorb new rising currents, and co-opt them in" (Wiarda 2001: 354). In other words, traditional institutions have generative mechanisms keeping them from transforming themselves.

Some authors have linked Latin American 'traditions' or 'culture' to the maintenance of police violence. Chevigny, for example, suggests that police violence in Buenos Aires is not simply a hangover from the military regime, "but instead shares with the dictatorship common roots in an old authoritarian tradition, derived from political ideas that predate modern practice in criminal justice" (1995: 185). Bolívar suggests that police violence is more likely to be socially accepted and applied against the population in Latin

America because this region has inherited a culture deeply rooted in colonial authoritarian patterns (Bolívar 1999: 42).

This cultural argument has several problems. First, it is puzzling why some societies that have escaped from "traditional" values, becoming modern in terms of industrialization, urbanization, levels of literacy, etc., nevertheless experienced authoritarian regimes.[23] Second, if the authoritarian culture is embedded in the value system and institutions, we should expect citizens to defend those traditional values. However, empirical evidence has demonstrated that even in countries with a long history of authoritarianism (i.e., Nicaragua and Mexico), citizens still favor civil and political liberties (Booth and Seligson 1994). Waisman makes the same point regarding the capitalist, profit-maximizing behavior of the Argentine elite as opposed to "traditional" or "anti-capitalist" attitudes that we should expect in those societies (Waisman 1987).[24] Moreover, as culture change slowly, this argument is neither a good explanation for abrupt changes. Finally, even if Latin American societies tend to be authoritarian, it is not clear whether certain inherited "values" are the cause rather than the effect of other social, economic, and political conditions.

Another way to approach the subject of the persistence of police violence is to consider the role of institutions and how they shape political outcomes. Institutionalists believe that formal rules and standard operating procedures have an independent effect on political actors.[25] Institutionalism observes power relations influencing the creation of certain formal and informal rules and how they have evolved.[26] It is argued that institutions have a constraining effect on social interactions, limiting actors' alternatives (March and Olsen 1984).

Here we could make two intuitive institutional arguments: first, institutional arrangements at the beginning of the transition to democracy may have an enormous impact on future political outcomes.[27] Transitions to democracy are a critical juncture in which power realignments take place, but new democratic authorities may inherit constraining rules allowing high levels of police autonomy from civilian rule, low levels of accountability over police practices, and institutional arrangements that make it difficult to change existing rules.[28] Police institutions continue using repressive strategies learned during the military regime to maintain public safety. In this gridlock situation, democratic authorities have no other choice than attempting to shift the balance of power through democratic means.

But focusing only on inherited constraining rules has two problems. First, one should not make the assumption that new democratic authorities will always attempt to advance civil rights and, second, this approach is not able to explain why some Latin American countries have either increased or restricted police powers while no apparent change in the political balance of power took place.[29]

Other authors have argued that specific features of police departments may explain police abusive behavior. In this case, rather than studying the social and political factors inhibiting police reforms, the main question is usually why police abuses persist. The main response is that some institutional features of the police encourage violent behavior against citizens. Low pay rates, imperfect training, low recruitment standards, bureaucratic routines, and vocational incentives are seen as crucial factors allowing the persistence of police violence (Ahnen 1999).

Two additional institutional arguments have been developed to explain persistent patterns of police violence. Some scholars have argued that police violence can be explained by the maintenance of certain institutional features characteristic of a military regime (Neild 2000a; Chevigny 1995; Méndez 1999). Indeed, according to David Bayley, "the military dominates policing in Latin America more than in any region of the world" (Bayley 1993: 11). Examples of such militarization are the placement of police institutions within ministries of defense in several countries including Brazil, Chile, and Colombia, the prosecution of police crimes under special military courts, and the assignment of military officers to police tasks. Moreover, as the police's main task in the past was to defend the regime from "enemies," national security doctrines blurred the distinctions among criminals, terrorists, political opposition, and poor sectors of society (Holston and Caldeira 1998; Neild 2000a).

Overall, authoritarian legacies have reinforced repressive and social control functions of the police and weakened the rule of law. Police institutions are often considered as *insulated corporate institutions,* resisting any reform attempts: "a major contributing factor to the lawless state of violence [in Latin America] is, then, the twin effect of a legacy of authoritarianism and the ingrained habit of law enforcement bodies of resisting all attempts to bring them under democratic controls" (Méndez 1999: 22). Unchecked security forces with inherited institutional and legal privileges from past regimes may explain the maintenance of police violence.[30]

A complementary argument suggests another causal mechanism. Here, police officers and incumbents are embedded in unlawful and *patrimonialistic* behavior; that is, both public authorities and police officers use their position and authority to achieve private benefits, creating a complex network of patronage (Hartlyn 1998b, Bratton and van de Valle 1997).[31] Chaotic, violent, and ruleless politics is explained by low levels of civic competence and democratic understanding on the part of mass constituencies and, equally important, high levels of corruption, mistrust, and abuse of power on the part of competing politicians (Diamond 1994: 244).

An example from Argentina may illustrate this point. Several studies, including my own research, demonstrate continuing practices of police violence after Argentina's transition to democracy in 1983 (CELS 2001; Dutil 1997; Oliveira and Tiscornia 1997; Saín 2001). One may argue that this is due to a combination of factors such as weak mechanisms of accountability over police institutions, so officers perceive they will not be punished, and incumbents not willing to punish abusive police officers given the mutually beneficial relationship between those incumbents and corrupt officers. Indeed, several sources have documented the existence of a network of illegal activities (gambling, prostitution, stolen car trafficking, drugs) that are maintained thanks to a complex chain of patrimonial relationships that involve police officers, party chieftains, state bureaucrats, and even high-ranking politicians. Thus, the status quo is explained not by the existence of legal provisions allowing police autonomy, but by a given social equilibrium favorable to certain groups of society. The lack of accountability is the mechanism allowing the persistence of such patterns.

While the analysis of security forces' historical development and internal features may help us to understand the factors motivating police violence, it does not help us to explain the political process that allows police officers to continue violating citizens' rights. Moreover, studies on police bureaucracies have produced contradictory findings regarding the relationship between the level of 'professionalism' and violence.

The historical process of police reform in the United States illustrates this point. In the early 20th century, professionalization of the police was seen as the best solution to end practices of political co-optation and to reduce police violence in the streets. Ironically, while the northern cities of Boston and New York created police departments to control increasing social disorder in the 1830s, police institutions' systematic corruption and non-enforcement of laws made politicians propose internal reforms to protect citizens by the turn of the 20th century (Walker 1977: 3–31). Reformers believed that by changing the administrative structure and processes within police departments, police corruption and violence would be reduced. Professionalization essentially implied the centralization of command, the development of a 'culture' of public service, the improvement of training and recruitment selection, the creation of promotion incentives related to merit rather than political connections, and the establishment of standard operating procedures to avoid misbehavior.

Despite the efforts to make these institutions more professional, several well-publicized cases of police brutality in New York and Los Angeles in the early 1990s demonstrated that highly trained officers who follow standard operating procedures may be willing to commit abuses precisely because those bureaucratic procedures protect such officers.[32] Thus, even though the institutional framework is important, we need to go beyond that to understand the political incentives that allow certain police routines to persist over time.

EXPLAINING THE RESISTANCE TO CHANGE: STRUCTURED CONTINGENCY[33]

While the uneven structure of power and particular institutional features may be important determinants of the maintenance of police abuses in Latin America, additional mechanisms keep these societies from enacting reforms to protect individual rights. Understanding these mechanisms will allow us to explain why advocacy networks are less influential than one may expect. I organize my argument as follows: what explains resistance to change in police practices and institutions is a structure of incentives favoring those sectors that want to maintain the status quo. First, citizens want to be safe from police abuse as much as they want to be safe from delinquency and, therefore, constituencies can be mobilized to both promote police reforms if violence against citizens is detected and to increase powers if the perception of crime is rising. Second, governments are likely to rely on increasing police powers to control public safety, even in cases in which the record of security forces show that police practices are contributing to increased levels of violence.

In order to understand this structure of incentives, we need to examine three dimensions: First, it is important to observe the context or political opportunity structure (POS) because it may constrain or open possibilities for social groups to influence the political system. I argue that three contextual variables are relevant: the nature of the transition, access to the political system, and the structure of security forces. Second, it is necessary to examine social groups' resource mobilization, including issues of leadership, social networks, and ability to obtain resources. Finally, it is important to clarify what is the nature of the policy issue at stake. This is particularly relevant because in the issue under scrutiny—the protection of citizens' rights from police abuse—policy reforms directly affect those who have the monopoly of force in the country.

I argue that in this highly divisive issue, it is very likely that actors will act in coalition to either protect individual rights (what I call the civil rights coalition) or increase police powers (what I call the pro-order coalition). As security forces are the institutions more directly affected if individual rights are enhanced, we should expect the pro-order coalition enjoying comparative advantages over those who defend pro-civil rights views because of the access to institutional and political resources as well as a set of strategies that the civil rights coalition can hardly access. As "public safety" is highly valued by policymakers, the police and their allies in the political system have more room to maneuver over what policies are likely to be implemented. This particular structure of incentives favorable to the enhancement of police powers explains why is hard to reform police institutions and why police violence is likely to prevail.

As was suggested above, some scholars have convincingly argued that the status quo would continue if policymakers and police institutions have mutually beneficial relationships (*patrimonial polity*) or police institutions remain unaccountable (*police corporate insulation*). My study adds an additional mechanism: If the pro-order coalition has the power and ability to frame and influence the government on the need to make anti-crime policies a top-priority and to solve this problem by increasing police powers, then, incumbents will hardly accept changing the status quo. If the pro-order coalition succeeds in this task, governments will not be willing to pursue costly police reforms that have long-term effects and unexpected results. Instead, if the civil rights coalition has the power and ability to frame and influence governments on the need to protect individual rights because it is a major social concern and because the lack of police reform is part of the problem of general social violence, then governments may pursue reforms.

But reforming the police (by protecting citizens from abuse) is costly, and there are no immediate or short-term benefits. As police institutions generally resist change, these institutions will attempt to influence the policy process, suggesting that any increase in crime is the direct result of those "ineffective" reforms. Restricting police powers are seen as an obstacle to law enforcement. Because the civil rights coalition has more problems of coordination than the pro-order coalition, the chances are high that reforms will not advance or will provoke a reversal. In short, the structure of incentives driving this policy issue and the way social actors are likely to form alliances is a crucial element explaining the status quo.

Political Opportunity Structure (POS)

I assume that actors' decisions are contextually determined. Social and political actors take decisions according to the structure of opportunities provided by the context (political opportunity structure).[34] In other words, elements in the environment impose certain constraints and a repertoire of possibilities for social and political actors.[35] According to this reasoning, social and political structures set a given equilibrium in a society that is difficult to change because of the self-enforcing nature of political institutions (March and Olsen 1989; North 1990; Pierson 2000). However, in certain *critical junctures,* social actors can alter the existing status quo by taking advantage of opportunities for action. As these critical junctures generate opportunities, the actual transformation of the status quo ultimately depends on organized social actors' capacity to observe the opportunities and promote change.[36]

Thus, the first task is analyzing what are the contextual conditions constraining actors' choices—the political opportunity structure. The literature has offered a wide range of contextual variables defining the political opportunity structure.[37] I suggest three critical contextual variables affecting actors' choices: the nature of the transition, access to the political system, and police autonomy impact groups' ability to influence the political system.

Concerning the nature of the transition, the literature on democratization has linked the mode of transition to future political outcomes (Agüero 1999; Karl and Schmitter 1994; Karl 1990; 1995). The nature of the transition refers to a set of arrangements among the elites who take part in the transition process. These new arrangements define the power different actors will have in the future. Transitions to democracy are seen as windows of opportunity for establishing new rules. However, political actors may or may not take advantage of them. The way actors respond depends on: a) structural and institutional factors that help to determine the transition mode itself (e.g., the strength of the military vis-à-vis other actors), b) new institutional realities generated by the transition process itself, and c) junctures opened up by the transition (Hartlyn 1998a). Transitions to democracy are a crucial moment, generating a new set of constraining conditions.

Scholars have identified three types of transition that are relevant to this study: imposition, pact, and reform (Karl 1990; Karl and Schmitter 1991). In democratization by imposition, ruling sectors define unilaterally the conditions of a given transition. Transitions by pact are those in which there is a compromise on the basis of mutual guarantees to respect certain the vital interests of both the governing regime and leaders of the opposition. Transitions by reform are the result of mass-based mobilizations that end in a compromised outcome without resorting to violence.

There are two mechanisms by which the mode of transition affects social groups. First, institutions and rules inherited from military regimes may favor the maintenance of the status quo over institutional and legal transformations. Rules that are hard to reform and institutions that are legally protected from civilian rule impact social groups differently. For instance, those groups that want to maintain police powers after the transition will have a comparative advantage if the mode of the transition allowed high levels of police powers, as often occurred in democratizations by imposition and pact. Several authors have mentioned how new institutional as well as power constraints restrict political actors' choices.[38] In transitions by reform, we should expect to find fewer inherited constraints favoring, for instance, security forces.

A second way by which transitions affect social groups is related to the salience of the human rights legacy.[39] The mode of the transition will define the space new authorities will have to deal with the past, which in turn will strongly affect human rights groups' agendas by defining the salience of the legacy vis-à-vis emerging conflicts in society. One should expect that in transitions by imposition and pact outgoing regimes' authorities will have more options to restrict new authorities' ability to punish crimes committed during the military regime. As the human rights legacy is not solved, human rights organizations may focus their scarce material and human resources on dealing with the legacy.

If new authorities have more freedom to address the issues of the past by bringing those responsible for past human rights violations to justice, as occurs in transitions by reform, then, human rights organizations have to spend less material and human resources on solving the legacy. In other words, the nature of the transition will determine the salience of the human rights legacy, which in fact will affect the priorities different social and political actors will have regarding the resolution of past human rights violations vis–à-vis emerging social conflicts.

A second contextual element is the extent to which actors in the political system (including political parties, policymakers, and the media) are willing and able to respond to different groups of society. I argue that access depends on three main elements: the balance of power among political parties, the existence of veto points, and the level of mass media pluralism.

Parties play a pivotal role as mediators between social demands and the state. In this case, party intermediation acts as a facilitating condition for social groups' success, while lack of it acts as an inhibiting condition of groups' success. As a general rule, the civil rights agenda has tended to be associated with centrist/leftist sectors, while pro-order positions have been supported by right-wing sectors. Thus, the stronger the center/left, the more chances for human rights groups to influence the political system; the stronger the right-wing sector, the more chances for pro-order positions to succeed.

Veto points are institutional devices used by politicians to block certain policy decisions (Immergut 1992:31). Interest groups, associations, and other institutions in society may attempt to influence those politicians who have the ability to block certain undesired policy decisions. In other words, the existence of veto points increases the possibilities for social groups to influence key policymakers.[40] The study of veto points is closely related to the balance of power among actors. It is the balance of power among political actors that will define the direction a given veto point will take. For instance, if right-wing sectors are able to block policy decisions, then, we should expect those actors using veto points to preempt restrictions of police powers. In order words, actors but not institutions produce political action. Veto points are a set of rules that provide the context in which social and political actors interact.

But gaining access to the political system also depends on whether the media pays attention. In this regard, the existence of a pluralist media will increase the chances for a diversity of social groups to gain social visibility and influence the political process. Alternatively, in countries in which the media is highly concentrated in few hands, groups that are not close to those conglomerates will face more difficulties to getting their voice heard.

Finally, another contextual factor is the structure of the police. Police institutions are in charge of a country's public safety, which is generally considered as the top priority of state officials and society. Thus, police institutions always have some leverage vis-à-vis political authorities to defend their interests in exchange for effective public safety. If their leverage is constant across countries, the main difference among police institutions is their capacity to respond to external influences in a coherent and centralized way. In a fully democratic system, the capacity to respond to external shocks mostly depends on effective mechanisms of accountability. If a citizen alleges torture, police institutions can respond by external and internal—transparent—investigations as well as on the later punishment of those responsible for committing unlawful actions.

However, in many developing countries external and internal mechanisms of accountability are weak or non-existent. In this case, what we need to observe is the type of responses police institutions are able to articulate once allegations of police brutality are made public. I argue that the type of responses depends on the internal organization of police forces. A highly corporate police is one characterized by prolonged training, a system of internal administration, and group identity. Police officers are committed to a career service with an "expertise" in public safety. From this commitment comes a sense of group identity or "corporateness."[41] A weakly corporate police is one in which discipline and training systems are poor, internal systems of accountability are weak, and police officers observe relatively low levels of loyalty toward hierarchical authorities.

More corporate institutions do not necessarily imply more respect for human rights. In studying institutions, some authors distinguish between *professional* and *non-professional* institutions, considering the same indicators (training, discipline, corporateness) plus the sense of social responsibility, that is, the idea of institutions serving some social and morally accepted purposes (Huntington 1959: 9–10). Studying the development of military institutions, Janowitz (1960) suggests that is highly problematic to define the criteria of professional responsibility. The Nazi army, for instance, has been considered as highly *professional* because of its training, discipline, administrative structure, and sense of identity. However, it devoted its skills to—mildly speaking—antisocial purposes. To avoid a misunderstanding, I define police corporateness with specific sociological and institutional characteristics related to the establishment of internal rules of administration, training and education, and the development of a sense of organic unity.

There are several examples of highly corporate police institutions (well-trained, highly bureaucratic, and with a strong sense of identity) that have engaged in unlawful practices. During the 1950s, for instance, William Parker reorganized the Los Angeles Police Department's (LAPD) bureaucracy, recruitment, and training under the assumption that *professionalism* would solve police corruption scandals (Woods 1993). Thirty years later, the Warren Commission (1991) showed that the *professional* model of policing was primarily concerned with maintaining a well-disciplined, highly trained, and technically sophisticated force insulated from political influence but not necessarily respectful of citizens' rights. The LAPD model tended to create a strong sense of mistrust and confrontation with the public and strong defensive/corporate reactions when police officers were under public scrutiny (Warren 1991).

Given the lack of mechanisms of accountability over police institutions in many developing countries, the main difference becomes the degree of police corporateness. Highly corporate police institutions are more likely to have a very efficient system of public relations to respond to potential criticisms, independently of whether they solve cases and punish the responsible. Moreover, these police institutions have the resources to establish and defend their 'reputation' through public campaigns. Finally, the highly centralized nature of police institutions permits top-ranking officers to have tight control over internal investigations, reducing the chances for external actors to know about allegations of police misbehavior. Facing corporate police institutions, human rights groups should face more difficulties given the more efficient management of public relations and the capacity of police to manipulate information.

Less-corporate institutions have more problems coordinating responses, gathering information concerning specific allegations, and responding to allegations of police violence. As officers are less subject to accountability, they tend to use their positions to obtain private benefits by engaging in illegal activities. As police officers are sometimes loyal to 'bosses' other than the central authority, disputes among them open opportunities for actors from civil society to obtain internal information that may favor one group or another. In this context, human rights groups have more options to obtain information from inside police institutions and more options to contest top-ranking responses.

To summarize, before observing how social actors interact, we need to consider how contextual elements affect both civil rights and pro-order coalitions. The specific influence of advocacy networks will strongly be affected by certain contextual conditions. First, we need to observe how the mode of the transition (whether it is by pact, reform, or collapse) impact social actors and in what ways. In countries that faced controlled transitions, advocacy networks are less likely to influence the policy process given the salience of the legacy. Second, we need to observe whether the political system is open for the expression of advocacy groups' agendas. In countries in which right-wing sectors are stronger in controlling the media and in political terms, there are fewer chances for groups to influence the policy process. Finally, we need to observe the degree of police corporateness. We should expect to find that human rights advocacy networks' influence is less likely in cases with higher levels of corporate police institutions.

Resource Mobilization

If the context provides certain facilitating/inhibiting conditions for groups' success, groups' internal characteristics are crucial for an effective and enduring influence within the policy process. Scholars have recognized that specifying structural factors and necessary conditions is not enough to explain processes of political change (Tarrow 1994; McAdam 1996; Abelson 2002). In this sense, political opportunity structure approach suggests that while the context provides a set of constraints and opportunities for action, individuals can take advantage of such opportunities for action at a given time.[42]

What are the factors that make some social actors more likely to take advantage of a given opportunity? As Olson (1971) recognizes, actors are not willing to engage easily in collective action given the costs of involvement in a process of change and the free-ride effects related to public goods. The literature on interest groups and social movements has underlined three ways by which social actors have solved this problem: (a) the existence of leaders who visualize opportunities, (b) specific features of social organizations, and (c) the availability of resources (Salisbury 1969; Chong 1991; Tarrow 1994; McAdam 1996; Kollman 1998; Baumgarther and Leech 1998; Abelson 2002).

The literature on social movements and interest groups emphasizes the role of policy entrepreneurs in contributing to social change and groups' success. Policy entrepreneurs are individuals who are capable of visualizing and taking advantage of the opportunities that the social and political context provides. They overcome obstacles to group formation and—particularly—to survival over time. Using inputs from economics, Salisbury (1969) defines entrepreneurs as those individuals who "invest capital to create a set of benefits which they offer to a market of potential costumers at a price." Entrepreneurs are individuals who pursue material or nonmaterial rewards and who take advantage of opportunities to make an issue noticeable, attract public attention, and engage citizens in the defense of certain principles and ideas (Chong 1991; Sabatier 1992; Kollman 1998). Policy entrepreneurs call attention to certain issues and even "create" new issues by framing a problem in an innovative way (Finnemore and Sikkink 1998).

The maintenance of a movement and its eventual success depends on its leaders' capacity to choose creative strategies and to present the problem within an appealing frame that attracts the public's attention (Tarrow 1994). Frames are defined as "interpretive schemata that simplify and condense the 'world out there' by selectively punctuating and encoding objects, situations, events, experiences, and sequences of actions within one's present or past environments" (Snow and Benford 1992: 137). Collective action frames are devices that help social movements encapsulate and underscore the seriousness and injustice of a given social condition. At some point, collective action frames become powerful mobilizing resources, as policy entrepreneurs convert such abstract notions into strategies, tactics, and ultimately actions (McAdam 1996).

On the other side of the coin, sometimes leaders keep doing what they have learned in the past without considering eventual changes in the context that make such old form of collective action outdated. Sheri Berman (1998) suggests that while structural factors may constrain actors' decisions, internal cognitive choices bound social actors' choices as well. In other words, many times leaders reproduce forms of collective actions learned from the past.

A second relevant feature is the existence of social networks linking different small groups to each other and linking leaders with their followers (Hardin 1993: 38–49, Tarrow 1994: 136). In this sense, since a movement is a web of social networks loosely linked to one another (Tarrow 1994: 22), what matters is the structure and composition of such social networks (McCarthy 1987). In economic terms, the preexistence of social networks "lowers the social transaction costs of mounting demonstrations, and holds participants together even after the enthusiasm of the peak of confrontation is over" (Tarrow 1994: 22). For instance, we should expect that in countries in which social networks are broad—including multi-class and multi-ethnic alliances—the chances for success are higher than in those that are sectoral because groups have more options to mobilize different sectors and to maintain fluid contacts, transmitting information from the top to the bottom and vice-versa.

Resources involve the *availability* of resources, *actual* organizational resources, and groups' internal *ability* to obtain resources. As the availability of resources is exogenous to social groups, I will consider this component within the analysis of the contextual balance of power among social groups. Availability of resources includes access to funds from business and philanthropy, donations, etc.

The actual organizational resources are endogenous to social groups. They are measured by the number of organizations, group-membership, and annual budget. The ability to obtain resources is also endogenous and focuses on technical expertise and the presence of "development and research" areas within the organizations, among other elements.

FROM INITIAL CONDITIONS TO COMPETING COALITIONS

The political opportunity structure and resource mobilization define certain necessary conditions for social groups' success. If faced with police violence, we should expect a more successful outcome for the protection of individual rights in a country in which the transition was by reform, a system in which the balance of power favors leftist sectors, in which the media is pluralist, in which few veto points exist, and in which police corporateness is low. As internal characteristics of the groups also matter, we should expect that groups with pro-active leaders who develop skills to obtain resources, who frame the debate in innovative ways, and who are making cross-class alliances are more likely to succeed.

I argue, however, that defining the conditions of success or failure for one group, in this case, human rights advocacy groups, provides an incomplete picture of reality. Analyzing the shifts in the protection of individual rights requires a focus on competing groups of society attempting to influence the political system. Thus, a first task is to observe the nature of the policy problem at stake and how this will affect alliances among different groups in society. Indeed, protecting citizens' rights is part of a broader agenda involving the way authorities try to deal with problems of public safety and social control. The political debate about citizens' rights usually involves a tradeoff between liberty and security—between individual rights and police powers. [43] Politicians tend to see the problem of public safety as a zero-sum game, that is, what citizens gain in security by increasing police powers they will lose in liberty by restricting individual rights.[44] Note that in this debate, increasing police powers are seen as increasing the likelihood of police discretion and, therefore, increasing the likelihood of police abuse.[45] On the other side of the coin, competing actors see the reduction of police powers as an obstacle to public order.

I argue that on this highly divisive and controversial issue it is more realistic to assume that social actors will tend to act in coalition with other actors outside and inside the state to advance their particular agendas. [46] Coalitions are defined here as "people from a variety of positions (elected and agency officials, interest group leaders, researchers) who (1) share a particular belief system—i.e. a set of basic values, causal assumptions, and problem perceptions—and who (2) show a non-trivial degree of coordinated activity over time" (Sabatier and Jenkins-Smith 1999: 138).

The two coalitions examined in this study are defined as follows: *Civil Rights coalition.* The goal of this coalition is to improve the legal as well as actual status of citizens' rights. Lawyers, human rights organizations, politicians generally identified with liberal and leftist ideas, and some career state officials are likely to support the notion that every citizen has basic inalienable rights, even in cases in which a society is dealing with crime, terrorism, and social disorder. Certainly, the more active groups are human rights advocacy networks attempting to convince other social and political actors of the need to advance people's rights. Advocacy networks are defined here as organizations characterized by voluntary, reciprocal, and horizontal patterns of communication and exchange including international and domestic nongovernmental research and advocacy organizations, local social movements, foundations, the media, parts of regional and international intergovernmental organizations and parts of the executive and/or parliamentary branches of governments (Keck and Sikkink 1998).

Pro-order coalition. The other side of the coin is the pro-order coalition, whose primary concern is the maintenance of social order. In many countries the police, intelligence agencies, some state officials, more conservative political parties, and some sectors of civil society tend to champion this view. These actors will seek to provide police institutions with wide legal tools to preempt social disorder, terrorism, and crime. Those sectors do not reject the existence of individual rights, but they emphasize that such rights should be circumstantial and that authorities must restrict citizens' rights and widen police powers in order to maintain social peace.

I make four assumptions related to the characteristics of the two coalitions:

(i) Coalitions are not highly coordinated. The two coalitions are not necessarily unified and highly coordinated. These coalitions are usually held together by informal ties among actors and groups of society that share a common view. What is important here is the observance of some minimum level of coordination among those actors who hold common views. These actors are generally tied by past experiences and/or membership in specific organizations. It is expected that latent interests achieve greater coordination in crucial junctures, such as when a case achieves public notoriety, or when a prominent bill affecting these groups is debated in Congress.

(ii) Not all actors are part of a specific coalition. I do not assume that all social and political actors are part of one or another coalition. In this sense, this is a three-player situation, with incumbents generally adopting one or another posture according to the strength of each coalition. For instance, a minister of the Interior who defends positions close to the 'civil rights' coalition cannot be considered part of this coalition unless there is specific evidence tying this politician to a given group. These ties may be continuous communications with human rights groups, a persistent pattern of defending certain positions over time, and the politician's history of linkages to human rights groups, among other elements. In other words, defending a position in a given time does not make an actor an automatic supporter of a coalition. As we will see in subsequent chapters, it is relatively easy to establish those who belong to a given network or coalition and those who do not.

(iii) Pro-order coalition has the advantage. There are three reasons why the pro-order coalition has a comparative advantage over the civil rights coalition. First, coordination for the pro-order coalition is easier than for the civil rights coalition given the support they have from an established institution—the police. The civil rights groups are less likely to have bureaucratic institutions defending their position.[47] Bureaucratic institutions such as the police have comparative advantages over voluntary organizations, because they can use the financial resources they receive to lobby and the costs of mobilization are lower than voluntary organizations (Lowery, Gray and Fellowes 2002).

Second, in terms of policy implementation, it is always harder to put into practice reforms regarding the protection of citizens' rights than regarding increasing police powers. The protection of citizens' rights requires creating institutions, transforming institutional practices, and monitoring new rules. Increasing police powers just requires an internal administrative order within the police.

Finally, there is always the problem of proving police abuses. First, evidence of police abuse must be collected in a short period of time (before 72 hours) otherwise it tends to vanish. Second, in many developing countries police institutions have the double role of controlling public safety and helping judges in the process of collecting evidence, which increases the opportunities for altering evidence. Third, several comparative studies have shown an intense peer loyalty among officers, building a code of silence regarding illegal practices and misbehavior (a summary of these arguments in Waddington 1999).

(iv) Available strategies favor the pro-order coalition. The pro-order coalition has also comparative advantages over the civil rights coalitions regarding the strategies they can rely on. First, both coalitions use the issue of police powers to mobilize citizens. We tend to observe citizens demonstrating against the police after episodes of police violence. However, social groups may also organize mobilizations to demand increasing police powers. Moreover, when crime and police violence become a relevant public concern, it is likely that politicians use this topic in their electoral platforms. For instance, proposing increasing powers can be perceived by the public as a tangible offer to cope with delinquents. Finally, both coalitions may attempt to develop media campaigns to promote their agenda.

Regarding the actual policy process, the pro-order coalition has more strategies available than the civil rights coalition mainly because the implementation of many measures depends on the security forces. For example, the police have the potential ability to develop a tough anti-crime strategy, magnifying certain events at a given juncture in order to pressure for some changes. As the police are in control of public safety, the deployment (or lack thereof) of forces in the city can be used as a tool to advance certain demands. Moreover, the police can block the implementation of certain undesired reforms by using internal bureaucratic procedures or by simply interpreting the meaning of ambiguous rules how they want.

There are two strategies that are potentially open to both coalitions: the use of veto powers and the influence of policy experts during the debate on a given reform. As veto powers depend on who is in charge, both coalitions may have the opportunity to lobby policymakers to use (or avoid using) such veto powers. However, since the pro-order coalition is supporting the status quo, their access to veto powers is more important. Other strategy available to both coalitions is the establishment of alliances with key "professionals" or "experts" to advance their agenda. Technical experts are relevant because they ultimate translate an idea into a specific proposal.

Another option is the use of illegal strategies to achieve certain objectives. Given the fact that the police enjoy a monopoly of force and have an intelligence apparatus, they may use illegal tactics such as threats, extortion, and the threat of disruption of police services to preempt reform of the status quo.

Finally, both coalitions may use international networks and institutions to advance their demands. Civil rights activists generally seek for allies abroad to advance human rights locally (Keck and Sikkink 1998; Khagram, Riker, and Sikkink 2002). However, we could plausible argue that supporters of pro-order views may have the same incentives to seek for allies abroad. As regards international institutions, both coalitions may use international forums to advance their demands. We are used to reading about the specific influence of human rights advocacy groups over international institutions such as the United Nations and the Organization of American States. However, in a democratic context governments—and even police institutions—can also use forums to respond to allegations of police violence and corruption.

SUMMARY OF THE ARGUMENT

In explaining persistent patterns of police violence in democracies, scholars have usually mentioned how some political systems that lack mechanisms of accountability are able to reproduce certain insulated and/or patrimonial patterns. In the first case, police institutions are highly autonomous and they can manipulate information and effectively respond to external complaints. As the system lacks accountability mechanisms and as authorities want to maintain a good relationship with those in charge of police safety, the status quo is likely to be maintained. In the patrimonial model, corrupt incumbents have a personal interest in maintaining a mutually beneficial relationship with the police. Because police officers are hardly accountable for what they do, police violence is likely to continue.

My study does not reject this logic, but it adds complexity to the account. I argue that the debate on police violence has to do with a broader debate on the maintenance of public order vs. protecting citizens' rights. In which direction policy will shift depends on the comparative power of the civil rights and pro-order coalitions. The power of these coalitions depends on both the contextual and individual factors mentioned above.

In a democratic setting, incumbents face pressures to simultaneously reduce crime, maintain the stability of the country, and protect citizens' rights. Moreover, governments want to keep themselves in power by advocating policies that are appealing to their electorate. If the pro-order coalition has the power and ability to frame delinquency and crime as main concern of society, the status quo is likely to prevail. In contrast, if the civil rights coalition has the power and ability to frame the protection of individual rights as a main social concern and the issue of police violence as a part of the problem of social violence, then, governments will engage in reforms to transform the police.

If governments do engage in reforming the police, this will open a new set of dilemmas for both coalitions. Police reforms tend to be costly, they are not likely to show short-term political and social benefits,[48] and police institutions are likely to manipulate the results of a reform. Police institutions will attempt to influence politicians and the general public, suggesting that any increase in crime is the direct result those "ineffective" reforms. If the perception of public insecurity rises, governments are more willing to listen to police institutions, increasing the chances of a restriction in the scope of the reforms and/or a re-establishment of police powers. Because the civil rights coalition has more coordination problems than the pro-order coalition, it is hard for them to articulate an immediate response to this proposed new wave of counter-reforms. Given the inequality of resources of power resources between these two coalitions, we should expect that even in cases in which governments accept reforms, they tend to be mild and face serious problems of policy implementation.[49]

In this context, the influence of advocacy networks in a democratic context is mediated by a complex set of power relations among social actors and governments' priorities. First, advocacy networks have to overcome contextual constraints such as inherited rules, an unfavorable balance of power, the lack of a pluralist media, etc. But if they face favorable conditions, they still have to deal with active groups of society seeking "tough" measures against crime. If advocacy networks succeed in influencing reformist

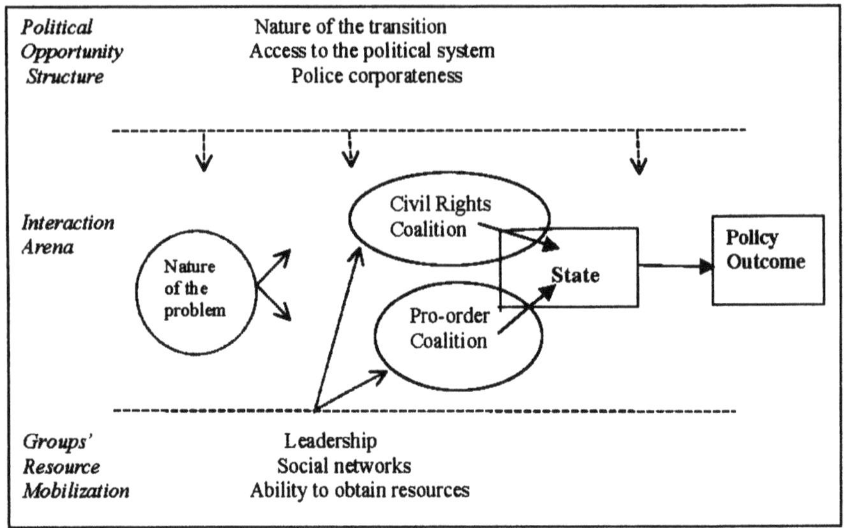

Figure 1.1 Diagram: Explaining Policy Influence

sectors to advance changes, then, they have to make the case that an eventual increase of crime has nothing to do with restricting police powers. Even in cases in which the police is perceived as corrupt and inefficient, governments are likely to re-establish police powers if they perceive that increased "public safety" is highly valued by the population.

Figure 1.1 summarizes the main variables considered in my argument. While the political opportunity structure defines the context in which actors interact, resource mobilization defines certain internal characteristics of the groups. While contextual conditions are conceptualized as antecedent or more distant causes, actors have been assumed to be the proximate causes of policy outcomes. Moreover, the policy problem at stake is likely to create incentives for the formation of coalitions. These two coalitions start from a very different point of departure and, therefore, one should expect the pro-order coalition to have comparative advantages over the civil rights coalition.

If citizens do not respond to unfair treatment in an automatic or spontaneous way and if the distribution of power is not the only determinant of political outcomes, under which conditions is policy change possible and why do some social groups perform better than others in obtaining their demands. Conceptually, one needs to determine the nature of the problem, the external conditions constraining actors' behaviors, and groups' internal characteristics making a policy change more or less likely.

As two coalitions are likely to emerge in dealing with the protection of citizens' rights (pro-order and civil rights), we need to observe the comparative strength and strategies of both coalitions. The analysis of the institutional and political resources and strategies available to these coalitions allow us to infer that the pro-order coalition often has a comparative advantage over the civil rights coalition. Thus, we should expect the civil rights coalition to have a difficult time trying to coordinate policy initiatives and the pro-order coalition quickly responding to challenges to the status quo. In the next chapters, I will test the hypotheses regarding the structural and internal conditions for success in post-authoritarian Chile (1990–2001) and Argentina (1983–2001).

Chapter Two

Chile: The Denial of Police Violence

On May 28, 2002, Amnesty International (AI) released its annual world report on human rights. The chapter on Chile states that: "Police reportedly used excessive force in a number of incidents, including several police operations in the South of Chile where indigenous people maintain a longstanding land conflict." The report includes five cases in which police officers violated essential citizens' rights (Amnesty International 2002).

The same morning, Chile's police force (the *Carabineros*) unsurprisingly rejected the report, stating that "the Chilean judicial system is the only competent institution to investigate and rule on alleged police abuse. Police actions are carried out in agreement with technical criteria established by legal norms and institutional rules."[1] A few hours later, the Chilean undersecretary of the interior, Jorge Correa, also rejected the AI report, stressing that "with few exceptions, AI reported allegations have not been documented in Court." The civilian authority added that the use of force in Chile "is proportionate to maintain order," and that in the case of indigenous people "the police have acted in self-defense."[2]

These reactions are not uncommon in Chile. A close look at the government's responses toward international reports since the re-establishment of democracy in 1990 reveals that civilian authorities have generally rejected international allegations of excessive use of police force: of 16 international reports denouncing police abuses in Chile between 1994 and 2002, in 8 cases civilian authorities explicitly rejected allegations, in 2 cases the government underlined positive aspects of the report without addressing the report's criticisms, and in the remaining 6 cases there was no public response at all. Authorities have argued that Chile has judicial mechanisms to solve such allegations and that the government promotes human rights. Additionally, civilian authorities have rejected the idea of other governments intervening in domestic affairs[3] (Appendix 1).

While one should expect a defensive reaction from the police, it is interesting to see civilian authorities taking defensive positions as well. Since the re-establishment of democracy the government has opposed the high levels of police legal autonomy from civilian rule. These incumbents have also rejected that police officers can only be prosecuted by military courts, regardless of the crimes they have committed and whether they were in active service or not. And many of these civilian authorities had personal commitments to the defense of human rights during the previous authoritarian regime. Why, then, do politicians—who, in many cases, are committed to human rights—now reject international reports? What is also puzzling in this story is that no local human rights organizations or leftist politicians reacted to the 2002 AI report.

This chapter aims to answer these questions. I argue that the political opportunity structure favorable to the pro-order coalition and the weakness of the civil rights coalition have made incumbents disregard the topic.

BACKGROUND: INSTITUTIONS, PRACTICES, AND PUBLIC PERCEPTION

This part provides a background concerning the legal status of the police, legal reforms concerning citizens' rights after the transition, trends of police violence in Chile since the re-establishment of democracy, and public opinion regarding public safety.

Police Legal Prerogatives

The Chilean state is centralized and maintains two security forces: a national police (the *Carabineros*) in charge of public safety, which is a military organization with approximately 33 thousand police officers, and a civilian investigative police (*Investigaciones de Chile*) in charge of criminal investigations with approximately five thousand officers. Because the *Carabineros* is the main institution in charge of public safety, I will focus on this institution, unless otherwise indicated.

Since its independence, Chile has followed what is called an "inquisitorial system of justice," that is, a system in which prosecutorial and jurisdictional powers are concentrated in a single professional judge. In Chile, the same judge conducts the investigation, formulates charges against the defendant, and dictates the verdict.[4] The police provide help by responding to judges' requests during the investigative phase of the trial.[5] Thus, the police play a key role in maintaining public safety, collecting evidence immediately after a crime is committed, and helping judges during the trials. Moreover, in twelve years of democratic rule (1990–2002), the legal status of the police has not drastically changed. A center-left coalition

(*Concertación*) has won three consecutive presidential terms (1990–1994 President Patricio Aylwin, 1994–2000 President Eduardo Frei, and 2000–2006 President Ricardo Lagos), and these governments have not interfered with one of the most autonomous and politically powerful police forces in the hemisphere.[6]

In terms of autonomy, the previous military regime prohibited the President from removing the director of the Police or any officer within military and police institutions without consulting the National Security Council, in which the armed forces and the police have 50 percent of the votes. These norms have not changed since the re-establishment of democracy in 1990. If the government questions the behavior of any officer, civilian authorities have to request the resignation of such an officer from the Director of the Police, who has the ultimate power to dismiss officers.

The police also have a military justice system that applies a broad interpretation of a 'military crime.' If a police officer is accused of any crime—in service or not—he or she has to be prosecuted by military courts. A military judge is in charge of the investigation and he is the only person who can request secret documents. Furthermore, lawyers involved in a judicial review are not allowed access to any documents during the investigative part of the trial. According to the military judicial system, the investigative part of the trial (*sumario*) is secret.

Another source of legal autonomy is the lack of external mechanisms to control internal police investigations. The government can recommend an internal investigation in cases in which police officers are accused of violating citizens' rights, but the police control internal investigations and no independent institution within the state or outside the state, such as the Ministry of Interior or Congressional Commissions, are allowed to verify the information provided by the police. Ministerial reviews are prohibited (Quintana 1998).[7]

Finally, until July 1998 the police enjoyed high discretionary powers to detain individuals. Citizens could be held in custody for up to 24 hours if caught committing a crime or offence, and up to 48 hours otherwise. This time was increased to 15 days when terrorist offenses were being investigated. Police could interrogate witnesses and detainees before placing them at the disposal of a judge. Police officers did not have the obligation to inform citizens of their rights, and lawyers were not allowed to visit detainees, who were held incommunicado. Additionally, the 1990 Penal Code included the provision of "arrest on suspicion," which meant that police were authorized to arrest "anyone who is disguised or who in any way makes it difficult to ascertain or conceals his true identity and refuses to identify himself," as well as "anyone who is present at an unusual time or at a place or in circumstances that give grounds to suspect malicious intent" (República de Chile 1996). Statistics show that more than 300,000 citizens were arrested under this provision between 1990 and 1992.

In terms of political power, the Constitution enacted by the military regime established nine appointed senators, four of them former generals and former directors of the police. In 1990 and before leaving office, Gen. Pinochet appointed all of them, providing the right-wing opposition with the necessary votes to have a majority in the Senate. Thus, the police have a semiformal representative and voting on their behalf of the police in the Senate.[8]

Legal Changes

Since 1990, three main legal changes have been implemented in Chile regarding the protection of citizens' rights: ratification of international treaties concerning human rights (1990–1992); legal reform regarding prisoners' rights (1993); and the abolition of the "arrest on suspicion" clause and the establishment of the equivalent to the *Miranda* rights for detainees (1998). In these three cases human rights advocacy groups have exerted some influence in agenda setting, but low influence in the political debate and policy implementation.

From the beginning of his administration, President Patricio Aylwin had a strong commitment to ratify international treaties that had been postponed by the previous regime and by 1992 the Chilean government had ratified several international treaties related to human rights, including the Covenant on Civil and Political Rights, the additional Protocol of the Covenant allowing individuals to file petitions of grievance with the UN Human Rights Committee, and the American Convention allowing the Inter-American Court of Human Rights to have compulsory jurisdiction over Chilean territory. In this context, there was no need for civil rights groups to lobby because of the government's commitment, although the civil rights coalition played an indirect influence through the presence in government of several lawyers with previous experience in the human rights network.[9]

In terms of policy implementation, the ratification of these treaties has had no impact on police behavior. The new Penal Code approved in 1998 incorporated the U.N. concept of 'torture' as a crime. However, because police officers are ruled by the Military Penal Code, they are still prosecuted by the charge of 'unnecessary violence,' which implies lighter punishment than in civil courts. As of December 2002, no attempt has been made either by the government or by leftist parties to reform the Military Penal Code's definition of what is considered a military crime and its definition of torture.

The new democratic government also had to deal with the more than 350 political prisoners who were a waiting trial or who were already sentenced.[10] As one of his first acts, President Aylwin pardoned 47 political prisoners and sent a bill to Congress to improve the legal conditions of prisoners, particularly in cases where terrorist crimes were committed. The package sought to eliminate the death penalty, to amend the anti-terrorist law, to reduce penalties, and to reexamine offenses set out in the various laws. Moreover, the proposal included some basic guarantees of decent treatment for detainees. In 1991, the Congress approved some reforms regarding citizens' rights, including limiting detentions to a maximum of 48 hours,[11] requiring judges who order an extension of incommunicado detention to appoint a doctor to carry out a medical examination of the suspect, guaranteeing detainees held incommunicado the right to have a lawyer check the physical conditions of the detainee, and explicitly requiring judges to satisfy themselves that the detainees have not been subjected to torture or threats before giving statements, and to ensure that they are protected from abuse.

The government was interested in solving the prisoners' rights issue for two reasons.[12] First, authorities had a strong commitment to re-establish the rule of law in the country, and probably one of the most evident cases in which the principle of due process was violated during the previous regime was concerning political prisoners.[13] In this sense, the government aimed to pardon all prisoners except those who had committed homicide, serious assault, kidnapping or the abduction of a minor. Thus 250 political prisoners were released in the first 18 months of democratic rule. Most of the prisoners were released on bail, were paroled or saw the charges against them dismissed, and 80 received pardons from President Aylwin (International Commission of Jurists 1992).

A second reason for the government's concern was that human rights organizations were particularly active in trying to solve the problem of political prisoners by lobbying the government, the Congress, and international actors. In this case, human rights groups played three important roles: first, they made this issue noticeable before public opinion by constant demonstrations by relatives and sympathizers outside Congress. The campaign was stimulated by hunger-strikes, prison occupations and demonstrations, some of which were violently repressed by the police (CODEPU 1994). Second, human rights groups played an important role in holding the government accountable to its agenda. After the government sent the proposed reform package to Congress in 1990, the opposition tried to negotiate an agreement with the government that traded reduction of sentences for political prisoners for similar measures of clemency for military officers involved in human rights violations.[14] The governing coalition agreed to begin conversations with the opposition in Congress, but was strongly challenged by human rights organizations, which pressured allies in Congress not to accept such negotiations. After three weeks of pressure, the deputies of the governing coalition abandoned these negotiations, going against even the President's desire to achieve an agreement (International Commission of Jurists 1992: 179). Finally, human rights organizations actively denounced political prisoners' imprisonment and legal conditions before the international community, with local advocacy groups providing information to the U.N. Committee against Torture and to several international non-governmental organizations in order to obtain international support for their campaign. In turn, international organizations such as Human Rights Watch, Amnesty International, the International Commission of Jurists, and the Centre for the Independence of Judges and Lawyers published well-documented information regarding the status of political prisoners in Chile.[15] But probably the most important achievement of these human rights groups was the visit to Chile of a special U.N. Rapporteur in 1995.[16]

The legal change with most significance in terms of police behavior has been the abolition of the 'arrest on suspicion' clause and the establishment of an equivalent to the U.S. *Miranda* rights for detainees. Until July 1998, the Chilean Penal Code stated that the police had the power to arrest individuals based on their physical appearance, and Article 260 of the Code of Penal Procedure stated that police officers were authorized to detain "anyone who is present at an unusual time or at a place or in circumstances that give grounds to suspect malicious intent" (República de Chile 1996). Since the re-establishment of democracy, groups from civil society coordinated by the Commission for the Rights of Young People (CODEJU) initiated a campaign to eliminate this legal provision. Human rights organizations claimed that the 'arrest on suspicion' clause allowed the police to arrest people—particularly youth—without justification, generating propitious opportunities to violate citizens' rights. Given the increasing number of complaints received between 1991 and 1993, CODEJU decided to coordinate a national campaign to abolish this clause. According to one leader of this movement, the most effective way to influence the government was through public mobilizations to make the issue noticeable to authorities and the public, and through the establishment of a strategic alliance with key actors within the government.[17] Essentially, CODEJU's strategy was to build a broad "civil rights" coalition to lobby the government to enact legal reforms.

While not massive, the mobilizations were constant. Generally, no more than 20 to 50 people peacefully protested in front of the police headquarters in Santiago's center at least twice a month from 1990 until 1993. They were led by the director of CODEJU, José Sabat, who brought letters to the Director of the Police authenticating cases of police abuses. They received press attention—CODEJU recognized the importance of good public relations, and established contacts with journalists before any public activity and provided reporters with information concerning the subject.[18] At the same time, human rights organizations established alliances with key government officials. The government agency for the Youth—National Institute for the Youth (INJ)—supported eliminating the 'arrest on suspicion' clause and favored the creation of the committee against this clause in 1992.[19] Soon after the establishment of this alliance, a group of deputies introduced a proposal in Congress to eliminate the 'arrest on suspicion' clause. The project also included several proposals regarding the protection of detainees' rights.

Thus, CODEJU and other groups of society played an important role in setting the agenda for the debate on this issue. As a culmination of this process, the President invited these organizations to participate in the principal act commemorating the third anniversary of the re-establishment of democracy, on March 11, 1993. In this event, the President promised executive support for the elimination of the 'arrest on suspicion' clause.[20] Later on, CODEJU was invited by the Director of the police to talk about this issue and, a week later, the President of the Chamber of Deputies announced that he was personally asking the executive to give the bill urgency status, after receiving in his office the representative of the committee against the 'arrest on suspicion' clause.[21]

Pressure by human rights organizations partly explains the steady decline of arrests on suspicion practiced by police forces since 1993. As human rights organizations achieved prominence and found allies within the government, the issue came to be considered an important priority by top-ranking authorities. Soon, the government pressured the police to stop such practices.[22]

Nevertheless, the constant decline cannot be solely explained by activists' pressures. While human rights organizations discontinued mobilizations and campaigns against arrests on suspicion after 1993, detentions have continued to decline. Conscious of the negative public impact of these arrests and the government's concern, the police used internal procedures to reduce arrests on suspicion.[23]

As figures of arrests on suspicion were drastically declining from over 127,012 in 1991 to 5,465 in 1997, the overall number of detainees was not diminishing proportionately. In fact, other causes of detention such as misdemeanor, public disturbance, and drinking in public places abruptly increased during 1994 (Graph 2.1). In part, the police simply shifted tactics by resorting to other legal tools to arrest people.[24] Interestingly, this was not an issue picked up either by human rights organizations or by the government.

The approval of the bill eliminating the 'arrest on suspicion' in 1998 seems unexpected. Human rights groups had stopped their campaign after Congress began the debate on the project in 1993, the police had reduced the number of detainees on suspicion, the government had rejected the Congress' petition to give urgency status to the project, and the right-wing opposition in Congress, with the strong support of the Police, opposed any modification of this clause at least until 1996.

Nonetheless, with the support of moderate conservative sectors, in July 1998 the Congress approved the initiative. The new law established three innovations: (a) for the first time in Chilean history the police had the obligation to read detainees their rights; (b) the police could detain persons only when the police had a judicial notification to do so or when individuals are in the process of committing a crime (probable cause principle), eliminating arrest on suspicion; and (c) in cases in which individuals cannot prove their identity with a legal document, the police could take them to the closest police station in order to allow individuals to provide a satisfacto identification by establishing an address or by paying a bail depending on the offense they were accused of committing.

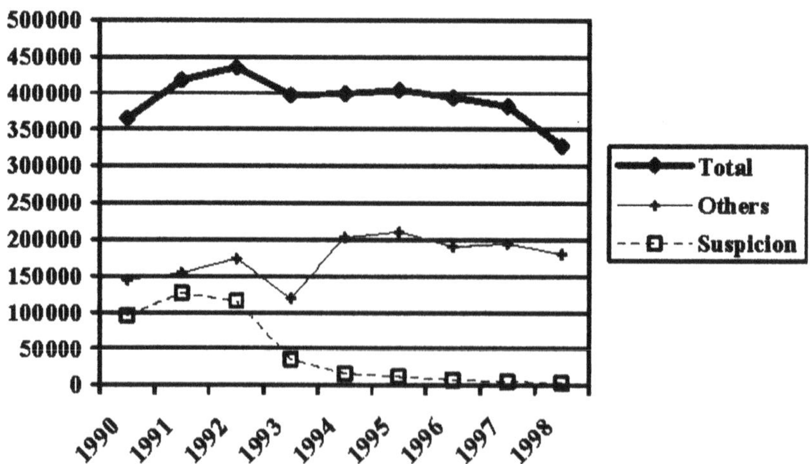

Graph 2.1 Chile: Detentions Practiced by the Police, 1990–1998 (Others: Misdemeanor, drinking in public places, street disorder)

Source: Carabineros de Chile and INE, 1999

Human rights organizations recognize their insignificant role in lobbying Congress. As the director of CODEJU admitted, "the burden of following this topic in Congress was on the INJ." In general, human rights organizations did not develop technical capacities to systematically lobby in Congress. Moreover, the "Committee Against Arrest on Suspicion" confined its work to providing political support for the presentation of the 1993 motion in Congress, but disbanded after the bill was presented to the Chamber of Deputies. As CODEJU leaders suggested, "This committee provided nominal but not real support to specific leaders. No more than three or four people actually tried to convince the government to change the arrest on suspicion clause. And these people were in the INJ."[25]

The main reason for the bill's approval can be found in a parallel process that will be analyzed in detail in chapter three—the reform of the judicial system. In general, most legislators agreed with the idea of eliminating arrest on suspicion because of the need to provide a coherent framework of principles for the new Penal Code.[26] The final project that was approved followed most of the recommendations made by the government at the beginning of 1998.

However, once the new Penal Code was implemented, the police lobbied the government and its allies in Congress to re-establish the 'arrest on suspicion' clause, arguing that increases in crime were due to the elimination of the clause.[27] Responding to this pressure, [28] the government agreed to introduce an amendment that was approved by Congress in April 2000, allowing police officers to detain individuals who do not carry their official ID and those who may know something about a crime and who happen not to have an ID. A new reform was introduced in January 2002, allowing the police to search suspects. In both cases, no major opposition was registered by civil rights groups or leftist politicians.[29]

Police Practices

In terms of police practices, Chile has earned a reputation for having one of the least corrupt police institutions in the region, and of having officers who are generally respectful of citizens' rights (Londregan 2000; Freedom House 1994–2002). As will be observed in chapters four and five, Argentina shows the exact opposite reputation of having a corrupt police that is likely to violate citizens' rights.

Nonetheless, organizations such as AI, Human Rights Watch, CODEPU, and the U.S. Department of State have noted persistent patterns of police brutality in Chile since the reestablishment of democracy (Appendix 1). It is difficult to measure levels of police violence because most of the time citizens do not file complaints, the media is likely to report only unusual cases, and police institutions do not release internal investigations. In Chile, there are three ways by which we can infer levels of police violence: human rights organizations' reports, complaints filed in courts, and qualitative studies.

According to CODEPU, the main human rights group collecting data on police violence in Chile, between 1990 and 2000, there was a very small and declining trend of lawsuits against the police. My own research paints a picture that is quite different from what CODEPU reported (Graph 2.2).[30] According to military court records, the number of cases filed in courts claiming police violence has increased significantly and constantly since 1992. While citizens filed 194 legal complaints before courts in 1990, citizens filed 494 complaints in 1998.[31]

Between March 1990 and December 2000, 3,877 legal complaints were filed in courts in the central part of Chile, that is, every day at least one citizen presented a formal complaint against the police.[32] This probably underestimates the number of cases, since not all citizens have the time, money and willingness to file a complaint against the police.[33] Additionally, only a fraction of the cases presented to a lawyer are actually translated into a formal complaint in court. Lawyers tend to file cases in which the victim can provide enough evidence to prove the case in court.[34] Thus, citizens' allegations against the police are probably higher than the figures given here.

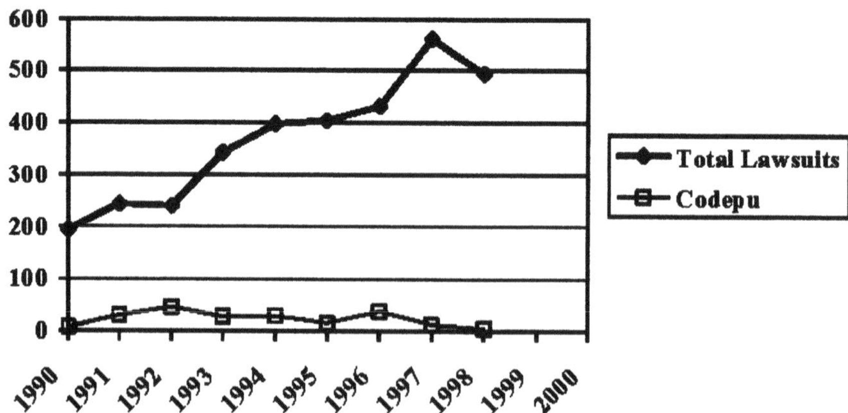

Graph 2.2 Chile: Allegations of Police Violence Filed by Individuals in Courts and CODEPU, 1990–1998

Sources: CODEPU (1999) and Fuentes (2001). Cases filed in Courst in Santiago, IV, V and VI regions.Cases filed in Courts in Santiago, IV, V and VI regions.

An analysis of complainants' socio-demographic characteristics[35] shows that they are mostly males (86 percent), from the lower-middle and lower classes. Only half are employed and 30 percent are students. Ninety-five percent of complainants said police officers beat them using their batons. In 20 percent of the cases they alleged being shot without reason. In 61 percent of the cases, alleged violence occurred in the streets and in 50 percent of the cases, officers took the victims to the hospital.

Other qualitative sources confirm continued police brutality in Chile during the democratic years. A university study suggests that ill-treatment of detainees by the police in the interval between arrest and appearance before a judge or release was fairly common at the beginning of the democratic era (Jiménez 1994). In this study, based on interviews with prisoners in 1992, 22 percent said they had received good treatment, while 71 percent said they had received blows of various kinds, 49 percent said they had received electric shocks; 20 percent said they had been undressed; 6 percent had been hung by their hands and feet; and 5 percent said plastic bags had been placed over their heads (Jiménez 1994:193–206). A more recent study (1998–99) based on interviews with teenagers from Santiago's Center of Detention reveals that 81 percent received "bad treatment" from police officers at the moment of being arrested. Of those who had received bad treatment, 93 percent said they received blows of various kinds, 36 percent said they had been submerged in water containers, and 21 percent said plastic bags had been placed over their heads to produce asphyxiation (Jiménez 2000).[36]

Judges' opinions regarding the police are consistent with previous findings. In the only public survey conducted with 20 of Santiago's 28 criminal judges, 85 percent of the judges think the police physically abuse detainees; 60 percent think that the courts do not control police procedures; and 40 percent think that the police do not follow legal procedures when they make arrests (Jiménez 1994).

A more recent university study makes clear that, despite the re-establishment of democracy, police abuses have not stopped. This research indicates that at least 160 cases of torture have been filed in courts between 1995 and the year 2001.[37]

What are the factors explaining increasing complaints against the police? One plausible explanation is that democracy creates incentives for citizens to take legal action.

While this is partly true, there have been no incentives for citizens to take these actions. For instance, the likelihood of winning a case against the police is close to zero, and neither the government nor advocacy groups have focused on this subject (Fuentes 2001).

This leaves us with two alternative explanations: the deterioration of the socio-economic situation, and the number of arrests made by the police. The first argument states that a deterioration of Chilean socio-economic situations may lead to increasing levels of delinquency and social protest, which may produce more aggressive police reactions. Since there was a smooth decline in unemployment rates between 1991 (7.4) and 1997 (5.3) and a moderate increase in 1998 (7.2 percent), it seems that the levels of unemployment cannot explain the constant increase of allegations since 1993.

Another possibility is that increasing levels of crime increase the likelihood of violent police responses, that is, as delinquents are more likely to use violent methods, and as levels of homicides and violent crimes increase, the police may respond in the same way. But there was a constant decline on the rate of homicides between 1990 and 1998 (from 3.1 to 1.7, respectively), and robbery with violence shows a constant decline between 1991 and 1995 (from 613 to 510 respectively), and an increase after that, reaching levels very similar to those of 1990 (592). Finally, robberies without violence—usually related to crimes against property—also smoothly decline until 1993 (from 146 to 117 between 1990 and 1993), with a constant but not dramatic increase until 1998. Thus, violent crimes in Chile tended to decline during most part of the 1990s. In the case of robberies with violence they tended to increase after 1995, but, by 1998 they had achieved a level similar to that of 1990. The only indicator that is more consistent with increasing levels of police violence is robberies without violence.[38]

Another explanation may be that increased police detentions intensify the likelihood for police officers to use violent methods. However, the overall trend of detentions practiced in Chile by police officers proves to be precisely the opposite: as the police arrested fewer people, allegations of police violence increased. However, if we consider only the number of detainees arrested for public disorder, we observe a more consistent relationship. Thus, as citizens became more willing to protest, the police became more willing to arrest those individuals, increasing the likelihood for using violence. However, since 1996 levels of arrest for public disturbance began to decline, but the number of allegations of police violence continued increasing until 1997.

A final explanation has to do with the political willingness to accept an 'iron fist' approach toward crime and delinquency. As the second part of this chapter will show, political authorities accepted pro-order views regarding the control of public order, providing more support for harsh policies.

Resolution of Cases in Court

Compared to the rest of Latin America, a distinctive feature of the Chilean state is the development of a stable bureaucracy early in the 19th century, and this contributed to the consolidation of a legalistic culture that has persisted until today.[39] By the mid 1990s, however, scholars agreed that having a legalistic culture is not synonymous with the properly functioning judicial system; indeed, several scholars argue that the criminal justice system has important structural problems, including lack of resources, lack of protection of citizens' rights—particularly of the poor—and lack of proper responses to social demands such as public safety and access to justice (Correa and Jiménez 1995; 1997; Vargas 1998b; Duce 1999; Riego 1999).[40]

Inadequate access of the poor to the judicial system is evident when we focus on the abuse of power by police officers. As noted, all illegal acts and crimes committed by police officers are subject to military tribunals, and the evidence indicates that military judges have a clear bias against civilians. For example, from all completed cases in which civilians alleged police violence between 1990 and 1997 (approximately 800), in only four percent of them did military courts sentence officers to prison.[41] Even in these cases, judges tended to sentence officers to the minimum time required by the law.[42] Furthermore, if one considers cases in which *both* civilians and officers alleged violence (approximately 1,900 lawsuits closed between 1990 and 1997), 11.7 percent of such cases ended with a civilian sentenced to prison and only 0.2 percent end with a police officer sentenced to prison (Fuentes 2001).

Public Opinion: Public Safety, Police, and Citizens' Rights

Three dimensions of public opinion are important here: citizens' concern about public safety, the image of the police, and citizens' views regarding the protection of citizens' rights. As a general trend, Chilean public opinion shows a declining concern about delinquency vis-à-vis other social issues such as unemployment, health and poverty. Between 1990 and 1994, individuals clearly saw delinquency as the main problem the government should solve. After 1994, issues of health and poverty became the first two priorities, very closely followed by delinquency. After 1998, unemployment, poverty, and health were considered the first three priorities, followed by delinquency. This trend makes sense given the stable performance of the economy and the relatively low crime rates between 1992 and 1997. As the economy worsened, citizens became more concerned about losing their jobs, increasing poverty, and the availability of health care.

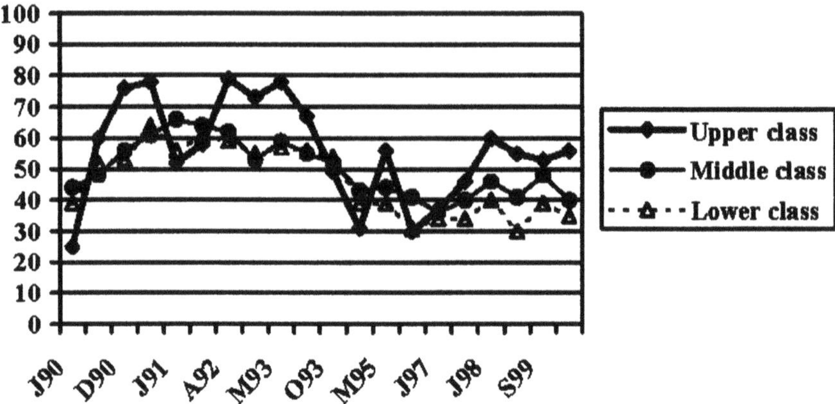

Graph 2.3 Chile: Public Opinion's Concern with Delinquency by Social Class

Source: CEP-ADIMARK 1990–2000. Surveys conducted by CEP-ADIMARK. Random sample representative of adult Chile's population. Probabilistic sample, with 1,505 interviews in each sample.

When we consider citizens' main concerns according to social class (Graph 2.3), we observe that upper-class sectors tend to show a greater concern about delinquency than middle and lower-class sectors. The most significant difference is after 1997, when upper-class sectors defined delinquency as the first priority the government should focus on—an average of 54 percent. Instead, lower classes selected unemployment, health, and poverty as the main priorities followed by delinquency—with an average of 36 percent.

Comparing the public's concern about delinquency with crime rates (Graph 2.4), we observe that, first, between 1991 and 1995 public opinion became less concerned with delinquency, as crime rates decreased in comparison to 1990. Second, since 1997 public opinion became more concerned about delinquency, as robbery with and without violence increased. Finally, concern about delinquency, levels of homicide and robberies with violence are below the level of concern shown in 1990. The only exception is robbery without violence, which is related to crimes against private property.

Regarding the image of the police, the opinion data indicate that citizens maintain high levels of confidence in the police vis-à-vis other public and private institutions. Indeed, since 1996, citizens have shown increasing levels of confidence in the role of the police in solving national problems, while levels of trust in other institutions and social actors such as the Catholic Church, big business, and union leaders have decreased.[43]

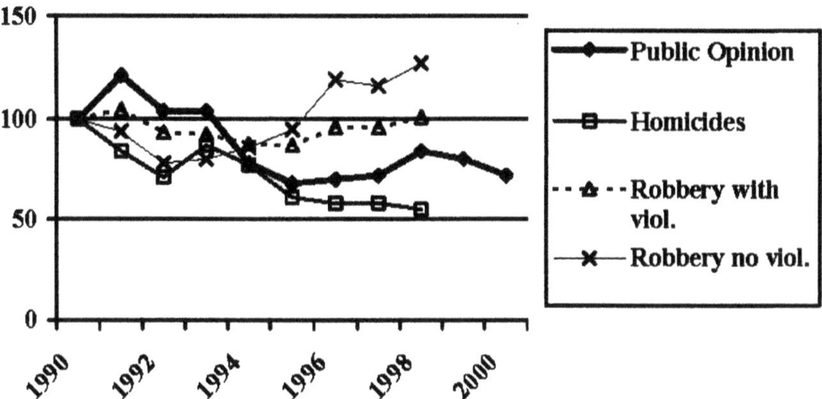

Graph 2.4 Chile: Public Opinion and Levels of Crime Percentage of change (1990 = 100)

Source: Crime statistics in Carabineros and INE, 1999. Survey results in CEP-Adimark 1990–2000

Indeed, the high level of citizens' confidence in the police is a particular feature of Chile in comparison to other countries in the region. Recent surveys on public confidence in institutions show that only in Chile and Panama do respondents have high levels of confidence in the police. This is not the case of Argentina where citizens show low confidence in the police (Table 2.1).

Social class and age are predictors of citizens' perceptions of the police. A survey conducted in 1992 among poor people concludes that these citizens feel that the police provide safety (71.2 percent) and that they "do what they can" (86.5 percent).[44] However, respondents in this survey also perceive that the police are unjust (61 percent), that officers treat people according to their social status (66 percent), that they take bribes (51 percent), and that they beat teenagers (73.1 percent). Moreover, police violence was one of the four most mentioned problems respondents felt the courts should focus on (41.3 percent). Moreover, predictably, those who have been arrested by the police tend to have a more negative opinion of the police than those who have not.

Another survey in 1993[45] shows that while approximately 65 percent of upper and middle class sectors say that the *Carabineros* help them, 52 percent of poor sectors say that the police help, and a significant percentage (36 percent) say that the police do not help them at all. Age is another important predictor. While 68 percent of people older than 35 years report that the police help them, the figure drop to 43 percent among youth aged (18 to 24 years old), and 44 percent think they do not help them at all.

Table 2.1 Latin America: Confidence in Institutions (%) (1997–98)

	Police	Justice	Political Party	Congress	Private Business	Press*
Argentina	17	15	27	25	59	53
Brazil	21	23	10	13	56	43
Bolivia	18	15	16	19	32	65
Chile	55	32	11	35	—	38
Colombia	34	27	11	24	61	56
Costa Rica	36	48	16	30	69	—
Ecuador	24	14	6	15	50	50
Mexico	5	7	9	19	36	41
Panama	46	18	11	15	61	70
Peru	39	21	13	38	—	40
Venezuela	9	9	5	9	72	71
Uruguay	27	41	25	30	—	60

*2001 Survey. Source: CIMA. Iberoamerican Barometer, "Diez años de opinion pública en iberoamérica," 2000. (*www.cimaiberoamerica.com* September, 2002).

Overall, thus, Chileans have a high opinion regarding the police as protectors of public order, but a close look at differences according to class and age show that poor people and young people tend to have a more critical opinion.

Regarding the protection of citizens' rights, most citizens endorse 'tough' policies against crime (87.6 percent), believing that those who disrupt public order should be sent to jail (72.4 percent). When citizens are asked whether delinquents are citizens with rights, the majority agrees (54.1 percent), but a significant minority (44.1 percent) believes delinquents have no rights.

In sum, this analysis shows the following: (a) the uniformed police have maintained their legal autonomy; (b) some legal changes have improved the status of citizens' rights. The police and their allies in Congress have opposed these changes; (c) quantitative and qualitative sources show that police violence is more common than is recognized by public authorities and even by advocacy groups. The targets of this violence are young people and the lower classes; (d) increasing levels of allegations of police violence are not necessarily related to levels of unemployment, the number of arrests practiced by the police, and levels of crime rates; (e) the public shows a decreasing concern about delinquency vis-à-vis other social issues between 1991 and 1996. This is consistent with declining levels of crime rates during the same period; (f) the public, overall, values the role of the

Table 2.2 Chile: Public Opinion and Citizens' Rights in 1997 (percentage)

	Agree or Strongly Agree	Disagree or Strongly Disagree
Wish "Iron Fist" delinquency would end	87.6	12.2
Government should send to jail those who disrupt public order	72.4	25.1
Delinquents are citizens and we need to respect their rights regardless the crime they committed	54.1	44.1

Source: FLACSO-Chile (1997). Survey conducted by FLACSO-Chile in October-November 1997. Representativeand random sample of adult population in Santiago. 967 interviews. The author is not aware of other surveysasking similar questions to provide more consistent evidence regarding this point.

police as protector of public safety. However, the lower classes are more likely to have negative perceptions of the police than the middle and upper classes; (g) finally, the Chilean population is highly divided on whether detainees should have rights.

In this context, human rights advocacy groups have succeeded in influencing the agenda setting and the political debate regarding the status of the political prisoners, and they had played a role in setting the agenda regarding the abolition of the 'arrest on suspicion' clause. Nevertheless, they appear to have no role during the political debate and subsequent policy implementation of the reform. Moreover, issues of the legal autonomy of the police and military justice reform have not been part of the advocacy groups' agenda. More importantly, the evidence shows that while citizens were increasing the number of lawsuits against the police, they were not doing so through human rights organizations. Until 2001, the main human rights organizations were not aware of the increasing level of complaints. Indeed, my research was the first one done in Chile that quantified the number of lawsuits filed in military courts since the re-establishment of democracy and no special permit was required to access such information.[46]

Finally, given the links between domestic and international agencies and transnational human rights organizations, the information that local groups such as CODEPU have provided to organizations such as AI, the U.N., and the U.S. Department of State are only a small fraction of the number of documented allegations in reality.

EXPLAINING THE LACK OF ACCOUNTABILITY

Despite an increasing level of civilian complaints against the police, neither the government nor advocacy groups seem to address this issue in a pro-active way. To understand why, we need to analyze the way structural as well as individual-level factors favor some social groups over others. In Chile, access to the political system and levels of police corporateness favor a cohesive pro-order coalition. Furthermore, the pro-order coalition has taken advantage of the opportunities provided by the context, making it harder for advocacy groups to openly criticize the police—that is, given the way the topic has been framed, governmental authorities have opted not to criticize or even question police performance. As a result, we observe the contradictory outcome of a center-leftist government—that supposedly defends human rights—rejecting international reports that reveal persistent patterns of police violence in Chile.

Pro-Order vs. Civil Rights Coalitions

In Chile, the pro-order coalition includes the police, right-wing parties, and some representatives of the Christian Democratic Party (PDC) in Congress.[47] The primary concern of this coalition is the maintenance of public order. These actors seek to provide the police with broadly defined legal tools to preempt social disorder, terrorism, and crime. These sectors do not reject the existence of individual rights per se, but they emphasize that such rights should be related to the circumstances and that authorities often must restrict citizens' rights and widen police powers in order to maintain social peace.

The police itself has a privileged position to advance pro-order views because it has permanent institutional resources to pursue the objectives of the police as an institution,[48] and it provides an important collective good—'public security'—that is highly valued by all citizens.

The close relationship between police institutions and right-wing parties during the military regime has helped the former gain access to key politicians since democracy was re-established in 1990. As an example of this relationship, the former director of the police, Rodolfo Stange (1986–1993), decided to join one of the two main right-wing parties (*Renovación Nacional*—RN), and won a seat in the Senate in 1994. Additionally, the former president and deputy of RN, Alberto Espina, is a professor at the Police Academy, and another former director of the police, Fernando Cordero (1994–1998), was appointed as institutional senator in 1998, increasing the opportunities for the police to lobby fellow senators on behalf of the police in the Senate.[49]

By maintaining contacts with key political players within the right-wing opposition and the government,[50] the police have formed a cohesive alliance that successfully responds to civilians' attempts to reduce police powers at key political junctures. As will be shown in the next section, this became clear after the abolition of the 'arrest on suspicion' clause that was highly resisted by the police.

The civil rights coalition is composed of lawyers, human rights organizations, politicians generally identified with the center and left, and some civilian government officials, particularly in the ministries of Justice and Foreign Affairs.[51] The main goal of this coalition is to improve the legal as well as actual status of citizens' rights.

At the time of the transition to democracy, the human rights movement consisted of a broad range of voluntary, academic, and professional human rights organizations (Table 2.3), most of them linked to each other in a dense network of collaboration and reciprocity (Ropp and Sikkink 1999).[52]

During the military regime the Catholic Church was particularly important in providing financial, institutional, and moral support to the victims of human rights violations through its Vicariate of Solidarity, created in 1976.[53] However, during the transition, the Catholic Church closed the Vicariate of Solidarity, on the assumption that the new democratic authorities would take care of the human rights problem in the future.

new dilemmas for these groups. Many of the organizations were sympathetic toward the new center-left government but, at the same time, they wanted their demands to be addressed. Additionally, these organizations were aware of the institutional constraints the new government faced, particularly in terms of the high level of military and police autonomy. Thus, the transition to democracy in Chile raised an important strategic question for these organizations: what was the best way to achieve their goals? By the end of 1989, two options were well-defined: influencing the government from within, and influencing the government from outside.

From a strategic point of view, the transition to democracy created Leaders of those groups that were closer to the governing *Concertación* coalition assumed positions in the new administration, with the explicit intention of lobbying authorities from within. Activists from the Vicariate of Solidarity and ChCHRs were politically connected to the PDC and PS, and several of them actively participated, first, in the development of the new government's electoral platform, and then in the implementation of the platform once the transition to democracy took place.[54] Particularly relevant was the decision of the Catholic Church to dissolve the Vicariate of Solidarity and the ChCHR's decision to dissolve a network of more than

Table 2.3 Chile: Human Rights Organizations in 1990 and 2000

Organization	Type of Org. 1990	Type ofOrg. 2000
Vicariate of Solidarity	Vol./Prof./Pol.	—
Chilean Commission for Human Rights	Vol./Pol./Prof.	Pol.
Committee for the Defense of the Rights of the People (CODEPU)	Vol./Pol./Prof.	Vol./Prof./Pol.
National Commission for the Rights of Young People (CODEJU)	Vol./Pol	Vol./Prof./Pol.
Social Help Foundation of the Christian Churches (FASIC)	Pol./Prof	Prof.
Service for Peace and Justice—Chile (SERPAJ)	Prof.	Prof.
Chilean Chapter of the Ombudsman	Pol.	Pol.
Relatives		
Association of Relatives of the Detained-Disappeared	Vol.	Vol.
Youth Comm. of Children of Pol. Prisoners and the Disappeared	Vol.	Vol.
Association of Relatives of Chileans Executed for Political Reasons	Vol.	Vol.
Association of Relatives of Political Prisoners	Vol.	Vol.
Committee for the Return of Exiles	Pol.	—
National Commission Against Torture	Vol.	—
Movement Against Torture "Sebastián Acevedo"	Vol.	—
Ass. of Relatives of Relegated and Formerly-Relegated Persons	Vol.	—
FUNAS	—	Vol.
Academic/Professional Institutions		
Human Rights Program. Academy of Christian Humanism	Prof.	—
Chilean Association for Peace Research	Prof	—
Quercum. Center for Development and Social Studies	Prof.	—
Lawyers' Group for Political Prisoners	Prof.	—

Association of Lawyers pro-Human Rights in Chile	Prof	—
Found. for the Protection of Minors Affected by states of emergency	Prof.	—
International Organizations Based on Chile		
Amnesty International, Chilean Section	Vol.	Vol.
CEJIL-Chile	—	Prof.
Promotion Projects		
Derechos Chile	—	Prof.
Organization of the Defense of the people (ODEP)	—	Prof./Pol.

Sources: Hutchison 1989; Wiseberg et al. 1990: 187–220; and www.derechoschile.cl
Vol.= Voluntary; Prof. = Professional; Pol. = Political.

5,000 volunteers nationwide.[55] As the principal leaders of both organizations were assuming new positions within the state bureaucracy, it was impossible for them to maintain the same level of grassroots activities as before. From being an organization characterized by a dense network of grass roots organizations, the ChCHR transformed itself into a bureaucratic entity with few people, fewer resources, and a lower level of interaction with social organizations.

Insiders have had a difficult time trying to influence the government agenda on human rights. First, *insiders* confronted a trade-off between their loyalty to the new government and their loyalty to the human rights cause. Second, *insiders* in the early 1990s faced a government that was trying to balance the stability of the country with the human rights agenda: the more the government pushed the human rights agenda, the more political instability the government had to confront, given the strong reaction of the right-wing opposition and the military. In practical terms, the *insiders* lost contact with old social networks and they were unable to address emerging social conflicts within the state.

Outside groups, and particularly CODEJU and CODEPU, adopted a more critical approach, distinguishing themselves from the government. Politically, CODEPU was closer to the leftist sectors that did not form part of the new government (the Communist party, for instance) and most *outsiders* faced the dilemma of whether to concentrate their scarce human and material resources in addressing the human rights agenda related to the past, or to incorporate a broader definition of human rights and to also focus on current social problems such as police violence, the environment, and social and economic demands.[56] Early in the transition, CODEPU decided to concentrate most of their resources to address the problem of impunity for past human rights violations. Given this, in 2002, twelve years after the transition, only one CODEPU lawyer deals with allegations of police violence and that no campaign has been made to promote citizens' rights or to promote CODEPU's work.

Political Opportunity Structure Favoring Pro-order Coalition

The mode of the transition, access to the political system, and levels of police corporateness define the political opportunity structure for social actors. In Chile, all three features have favored the pro-order coalition over the civil rights coalition. This section explains how.

The transition to democracy in Chile allowed police and military institutions to maintain high levels of autonomy. As was discussed earlier in this chapter, the President cannot remove the director of the police or any officer without consulting the National Security Council, in which the armed forces and the police have 50 percent of the votes. Additionally, the police are ruled by an Organic Constitutional Law that minimizes civilian interference in the internal administration of the police. Finally, crimes committed by officers in active service are prosecuted exclusively by military courts. The police have taken advantage of the 'culture of secrecy' allowed by the fact that no institution within the state or outside the state has the legal capacity to assess whether the information provided by the police is correct. Moreover, since any judgment depends on a military court, it tends to favor police officers and give the Director of the Police the discretion whether to accept any requests for information made by the government.[57]

For instance, when the U.N. Commission on Human Rights requests information from the Chilean government regarding an allegation of police violence, the most common government response is that the police have initiated internal investigations, that the police have made an internal investigation and the allegations are unfounded, or that the case is under court review. The Ministry of Foreign Affairs usually requests a police report on the status of a given case,[58] but as the government has no legal tools to monitor internal investigations, the police simply do not provide information to either the government or international organizations. [59]

The same thing happens with allegations made by domestic state and non-state organizations. For example, from a total of 43 letters sent by the Ministry of Justice to the *Carabineros,*[60] the police responded to 86 percent of them. From this universe, in 49 percent of the cases the police defended officers' behavior, in 20 percent the police responded that an investigation was taking place, and in 19 percent the police announced that an administrative sanction had been applied because some clerical error was made by the police at the moment of the arrest. In no case did the police specify the sanctions applied or recognize that an act of violence had taken place.[61] The *Carabineros* know that administrative letters will not have further effects because, first, other state and non-state institutions cannot review their decisions and, second, these state institutions send letters to the police when the Ministry of Justice has not been able to collect all the information to make a compelling case before a judge. As the police cannot be monitored in their administrative decisions, letters are formal bureaucratic responses.[62]

Additionally, the mode of the transition influenced the salience of the human rights legacy, which in turn has affected coalitions' agendas. A 1979 military regime decree granted amnesty to those who committed criminal actions between 1973 and 1978 or who covered up or were accomplices in such activities,[63] and the new democratic authorities decided not to challenge the inherited legal framework, limiting their goals to achieving truth and justice "to the extent it was possible." Political authorities aimed to search for those responsible for crimes committed during the military regime to the extent that this would not harm the stability of the transition process (Garretón 1996; Moulián 1997). Given this context, human rights groups focused on pressuring the government on what authorities were not willing to do: solving the situation of political prisoners and searching for truth and justice for human rights violations committed between 1973 and 1990. Indeed, most of the groups' material as well as human resources dealt with the legal resolution of human rights violations committed during the military regime, freeing political prisoners, establishing pecuniary reparation for the victims, and—later on—denouncing those who were torturers during the military regime. [64]

Not only has the institutional and political context of the transition favored the pro-order coalition by maintaining police immunity, access to the political system has also favored them. First, right-wing sectors have strong ties with the police and the military since those sectors supported and actively participated of the military regime. Thus, it is not surprising that since the re-establishment of democracy, right-wing sectors have supported police's claims to promote a punitive approach to crime, recommending policies such as increasing resources for the police to cope with delinquency, improving efficiency in the use of such resources by reducing police bureaucracies and placing more officers on the streets, improving the relationship between the police and the community to prevent crimes, and providing a judicial system that promptly punishes those who have broken the law (Dávila 2000).

Second, right-wing sectors have been institutionally favored by the 1980 Constitution and other laws which remained after the transition. For instance, a 1980 Constitutional clause established nine senators appointed by the National Security Council for eight years. Four of these nine senators must be former commanders-in-chief, ex-deputy-commanders-in-chief, and former directors of the national police. Appointed senators represent 16 percent of the Senate. With a right-wing majority in the Senate and an informal representative of the Police in the Senate,[65] the pro-order coalition holds a veto over governmental decisions.

Third, right-wing sectors have managed to gain popular support since the re-establishment of democracy, maintaining their electoral majority in the Senate and obtaining approximately forty five percent of the seats in the Chamber.

Sectors defending pro-order views have privileged access to the media as well. In Chile, two powerful conglomerates linked to right-wing parties own approximately seventy percent of the distribution of all newspapers of national circulation.[66] Particularly relevant is the role of the Edwards family, which controls three newspapers, including *El Mercurio,* the most influential newspaper in Chile. In the early 1990s, and after one of Agustín Edwards' sons was kidnapped by delinquents, *El Mercurio* made the issue of crime and delinquency a key issue of its editorial agenda (Ramos and Guzmán 2000).

At the same time, as discussed further below, while media ownership is biased against the civil rights coalition, this cannot be considered an insurmountable structural obstacle as there is some room for civil rights to influence the media. And, there are some pro-government media.[67]

The third contextual dimension favoring the pro-order coalition is the existence of a corporate police in Chile. The *Carabineros* was created in 1927 and is constitutionally defined as a military institution. Today, more than 30 thousand police officers have access to institutional benefits such as an institutional health care, housing, summer camps, and social security. Police officers are socialized into a military lifestyle that includes a four-year initial training, full-time dedication to the profession, and a well-established set of rules defining promotions, discipline, and several aspects of the social lifestyle in and outside the institution (Aguila and Maldonado 1996; Caro 1999).

The corporate nature of the police helps the pro-order coalition in at least two ways. First, when faced with cases of police violence, top-ranking officers have tight control over internal affairs, providing the information they want to the media and even to the government. In all the cases picked up by the media between 1990 and 2000, the *Carabineros* Public Relations Office provided a standard response when allegations of police violence were made public. If the case achieved public notoriety, the institution promptly announced that the officers involved had been suspended until an investigation was concluded. Second, police corporateness also affects the responses of police officers because they are rarely willing to independently provide information to the media. A case-by-case analysis of 10 years of press reports on the topic reveals that in only one case was a confidential internal document criticizing police procedures made public.[68] Indeed, police officers have no incentives to independently talk with the media or government authorities if they witness or participate in an incident, because to do so would be considered a betrayal to the institution, resulting in serious social costs to the officer and his family. Indeed, the only sociological study that has been published on the police reveals a strong sense of isolation from society and a strong sense of 'loyalty' toward the institution among officers (Caro 1999).[69] Finally, the institution offers legal support to officers involved in cases of police violence, reducing the risk of being sentenced. Thus, explicit threats and institutional loyalty may inhibit police officers from expressing their opinions to external actors.

Coalitions in Action

Legal prerogatives inherited from the past, access to the political system, and police corporateness are important but not determining conditions for maintaining the status quo. Another important part of the story is how groups take advantage of the opportunities provided by a given context. While the pro-order coalition has been very effective in dominating the policy process in Chile, the civil rights coalition has missed opportunities to act. The following paragraphs will explain why this is the case. I argue that leadership, social networks, and actors' ability to obtain resources are crucial factors in explaining both the success of the pro-order coalition and the failure of the civil rights coalition.

Soon after democracy was re-established in Chile, conservative sectors led by the Edwards group created *Paz Ciudadana,* an influential think-tank that has come to dominate the debate on public safety since 1993. As discussed, by 1991 public opinion considered delinquency the main social problem the government should focus on; however, what apparently motivated Agustín Edwards to create this foundation was the fact that delinquents kidnapped his son that year, requesting a significant reward. After this experience, Edwards decided to create this think-tank to produce comparative studies on crime, to propose preventive policies, and to influence decision makers on these issues. Edwards established a directory with prominent leaders, primarily but not exclusively right-wing representatives.[70]

Paz Ciudadana's work has been developed by a team of young professionals who have both the money and the motivation to make this institution a leading center in Chile. They developed two main projects: first, *Paz Ciudadana* signed an agreement with the government and the *Carabineros* to centralize national crime statistics in Chile. Second, they developed a program to measure public opinion on delinquency, and created an "indicator of citizens' fear" to measure the public's perception on crime. More recently, they have produced comparative studies regarding crime prevention in several urban centers in the world, and the team has also gained first-hand experience on crime prevention in the United States and Europe.[71] Cumulative statistics on crime and public opinion surveys have guaranteed *Paz Ciudadana* enormous visibility in the media on a regular basis.

Soon, *Paz Ciudadana* became a reference point for pro-order views. The main approach of this think-tank emphasizes the need to improve police efficiency, to improve the prison system, to increase penalties, and to establish a plan to control and focus scarce resources in needed areas.[72] The privileged access to the most influential Chilean newspaper has provided extraordinary dissemination of *Paz Ciudadana*'s ideas.

An important aspect of *Paz Ciudadana*'s strategy has been to not only underline the lack of a crime prevention policy by governing coalition, but also to offer policy alternatives. This became evident in 1998 when the government and *Paz Ciudadana* signed an agreement to create an indicator of crime victimization, to support the *Carabineros'* administrative reforms, and to help municipalities to implement public safety reforms.[73] In 2000, *Paz Ciudadana* signed a new agreement with the government to monitor the implementation of the reforms of the Penal Code in Chile.[74]

By 1994, the discourse on public safety was dominated by a very effective pro-order coalition that emphasized the need to strengthen the police in the "war" against crime. Thus, *Paz Ciudadana* took advantage of turning point in the public opinion concern on delinquency (1991–1993), maintaining the issue as a crucial priority, even though public concern and crime rates tended decline until at least 1997 as was shown in Graph 2.4.

The 2000 and 2002 reforms on police powers are good examples of the coordinated work developed by this coalition. The police strongly rejected the 1998 elimination of the "arrest on suspicion" clause. Former director of the police (1994–1998), Fernando Cordero, suggested that: "after the elimination of the arrest on suspicion clause, *Carabineros* did not have any tools to combat crime and this is why crime rates increased abruptly."[75] This argument is clearly misleading, because the police dramatically reduced "detentions on suspicion" already in 1993. Thus, we should expect increasing levels of crime since 1994 and not since 1998, as the *Carabineros* suggested. The only significant increase since 1996 was of non-violent robberies.

In 1999, however, the police took advantage of a bill the executive was sending to Congress regarding improving police efficiency,[76] and successfully lobbied the Ministry of Interior to incorporate a modification of the Penal Code in order to allow detentions to verify identity.[77] The clause established that the police could arrest individuals who are suspected of having committed a crime or a minor offense and who do not carry their official ID. Police officers could take them into custody for four hours until the police could confirm their identities. Individuals could be released before the end of the four-hour waiting period if they voluntarily agreed to have a picture taken or give their fingerprints. If police officers could not verify individuals' identity within four hours, citizens had to be released. The executive sent this proposal to Congress along with a package of reforms seeking to make police work more *efficient* by reducing the number of police officers doing administrative tasks.[78]

With presidential elections scheduled at the end of 1999, the debate in Congress accelerated in the month prior. Congressional representatives wanted to show their commitment to the "hot" topic of public safety, and this reform created a high consensus among politicians, particularly concerning the need to free officers from administrative tasks, putting them to work on the streets.

The pro-order coalition strongly supported the executive proposal. They framed the proposal as a question of efficiency. Several representatives argued that allowing for detentions to check identities would partially solve the serious problems caused by the elimination of the 'arrest on suspicion' clause.[79] Additionally, *Paz Ciudadana* provided important documentation regarding the need to transfer human resources to operational tasks.

Congressional representatives from the civil rights coalition raised three concerns during the debate: first, they argued that new provisions increased the discretionary power of the police by allowing them to determine when individuals were considered 'suspects.' Second, they argued that the establishment of databases of photos and finger-prints would violate essential individual rights, particularly when these people would not even be charged with any crime. Finally, the proposed bill, according to those who opposed it, was ambiguous because it did not define individuals' legal status when police officers took them into custody.[80]

Only two of the concerns made it into the final bill. First, Congress agreed that no picture had to be taken (even though the fingerprint procedure remained). Second, police officers were allowed to ask for an ID only when individuals were suspected of committing crimes, and this excluded minor offenses. However, it was still a matter of police discretion to decide the type of crime individuals may have committed. Additionally, Congress approved the idea that police officers could take into custody people who they suspected might have some information about a crime but who failed to demonstrate their identity. Finally, the approved law did not define the legal status of a person who is transferred to the police station to verify his/her identity. Thus, individuals who failed to prove their identity are not officially detained—and therefore, no *Miranda* rights had to be read—but they are not free to go.

What is interesting in this Congressional debate is the complete absence of human rights advocacy groups either in Congress or in the press. Indeed, between the time the arrest on suspicion clause was eliminated (July 1998) and the time the new law was approved (August 2000), few activists questioned the pro-order coalition's attempt to reform the penal code, and on those few occasions when this actually happened, the pro-order coalition promptly responded to the challenge. For example, when in January 1999 CODEJU complained that the police continued practicing arrests on suspicion, and less than a week later a group of right-wing mayors responded by supporting the re-establishment of the "arrest on suspicion" clause because of the increasing levels of crimes in shantytowns. Three months later, the police released to the press a document that they had sent to the government criticizing the abolition of the 'arrest on suspicion' clause and requesting more powers. The document states that "there is a sentiment of frustration in the community because police officers cannot do anything when suspects are on the streets. Delinquents feel they can act with impunity because the police cannot arrest suspects." [81]

The lack of participation of advocacy groups during the Congressional debate is not surprising because they have not developed the expertise and skills to produce technical documents to be discussed in Congress and they were focused on past human rights problems.[82] Representatives generally invite recognized experts from universities and government agencies to comment on a given bill.[83]

While the pro-order coalition has been pro-active, the civil rights coalition has had problems articulating a police reform agenda and responding to the pro-order strategies. This section provides evidence of missed opportunities for action and explains the internal factors that have allowed for sporadic, fragmented, and (at best) reactive strategies.

In terms of legal debates, with the exception of the Penal Code reform (which will be discussed in chapter three), advocacy groups have not pressured congressional representatives on bills such as the abolition of the "arrest on suspicion" clause or the two bills that partially reestablished police powers in 2000 and 2001. Advocacy groups recognize their weakness in terms of lack of expertise and resources to participate in the political debate.[84] But, even if advocacy groups lack the necessary expertise, we should still expect them to pressure the government when cases of police violence are denounced. This has not always been the case. As was observed earlier, advocacy networks are not collecting information regarding police abuses and they are not taking advantage of the opportunities provided by the context to frame the issue of police violence as a relevant social problem. The following three cases illustrate the latter point.

The U.N. Report on Torture. After receiving reports of increasing levels of police violence in Chile, the U.N. Special Rapporteur on Torture, Nigel Rodley, decided to visit Chile in August 1995 to gather first-hand information from government and non-government organizations. Human rights activists inside and outside the government considered this visit an opportunity to address important issues such as police violence in a democracy, the lack of mechanisms of accountability, and the wide discretion of military courts.[85] Rodley met with representatives of several human rights groups, including CODEPU and the ChCHR. However, the government restricted the public impact of Rodley's visit.[86] Indeed, the Ministry of Foreign Affairs provided a short press release stating that Rodley's visit "responded to an invitation of the Chilean government" and that his activities "were part of his work as Special Rapporteur on human rights considering allegations of torture received all over the world."[87] Preempting a potential conflict with the *Carabineros,* Chilean authorities framed the visit as the government's initiative when, in fact, it was due to Rodley's interest in investigating increasing allegations of police violence. Moreover, this visit was framed as part of a global tour when, in fact, it was a visit to Chile specifically.

One year later, the Special Rapporteur made public a report asserting that although torture is not practiced either systematically or as a result of government policy in Chile, "the cases currently occurring are sufficiently numerous and serious for the authorities to continue looking into the problem and for the State's rejection of torture to be reflected in the adoption of specific measures" (United Nations 1996). The government adopted a defensive position, suggesting that "several cases in the report had not been verified" and that the report actually underscored the government's efforts to protect human rights.[88]

What is interesting is the lack of reactions by left-wing politicians and human rights organizations. Activists did not take advantage either of the Rodley's visit or of the result of his report to publicize the issue and point out government contradictions. Lawyers linked to human rights groups and who were working on cases of police brutality at the government-linked Corporation of Judicial Assistance were surprised that nobody mentioned to Rodley the existence of such a division.[89] Even though Rodley's report made explicit suggestions regarding necessary institutional and legal changes to diminish police brutality, no human rights group developed suggestions about how to demand a government commitment to such reforms.

Furthermore, those sectors defending pro-order views within the government were much more effective in reducing the impact of the U.N. report. For example, journalists from the National TV channel *Informe Especial*[90] produced a special documentary called "Torture in Democracy," addressing the main conclusions of the report and interviewing individuals who had suffered police violence in recent years. This one-hour documentary was suppressed by the channel's director for three consecutive years, arguing that the program could affect the Chilean police's public image and its relationship with the government.[91] Although no government intervention in this decision has been proven, probable pressure by the government "is consistent with the government's frequent statements in defense of *Carabineros* when the police have been criticized for brutality. If the TV stations were genuinely autonomous and its role was to inform the public, it would not likely be concerned about the effect its program would have on the government's relation with the uniformed police" (Brett 1998: 128).

Police violence against indigenous communities. Several indigenous organizations have recently denounced abusive police practices in a long-standing conflict over land in the south of Chile. The allegations made by one of the indigenous leaders were supported and publicized by the leftist deputy Guido Girardi in December 1999.[92] Less than a month later, new allegations of police violence in another region of the South were made public by three other deputies.[93] In October 2000, the Director of Amnesty International, Pierre Sané, visited Chile to address the continuance of police violence against the indigenous population.[94] Two months later, the press released an internal report by the *Carabineros* that recognized several improper actions taken by the police against the indigenous population, including offensive and arrogant treatment, the disproportionate use of force, indiscriminate use of weapons, and lack of knowledge of the "self-defense" concept—on several occasions police officers shot indigenous people when the latter were running away.[95]

Despite the increasing public attention that this conflict had achieved by the end of the year 2000, no advocacy group in Santiago coordinated a campaign demanding a change in police practices, for instance, or suggesting institutional changes to improve accountability over police procedures. These cases received public attention because of deputies who wanted to solve a specific case.[96]

As the indigenous population began to use more violent methods of protest, right-wing representatives framed the conflict as a 'national security' issue, requesting the use of the anti-terrorist law to cope with the protests.[97] Thus, right-wing politicians reframed the debate, shifting the discussion from the problem over land and police procedures toward whether the indigenous groups were terrorists or not.

"Torture in Democracy" Report. A new opportunity for action came in August 2002, when the weekly magazine *Qué Pasa*[98] published a special report on its cover called "Torture in Democracy." The article reported on an ongoing research project by the *Universidad Diego Portales* showing that police brutality is still common in Chile, and it suggested that, despite the arrival of democracy, there are structural barriers for the full establishment of a mentality of individual rights, including weak civil society, the maintenance of an inquisitorial judicial system where the notion of individual rights is unknown, and practices of violence that are embedded among the police.[99] One week later, the same magazine published a new report on practices of violence in Chilean jails and police stations. The report ends with a quote from an officer from the Investigative Police who stated that "when delinquents are arrested, we have a limited time framework to work with them. We need to find out methods to make them talk, to make them provide information . . . otherwise, we need to apply more coercion, and if we need to threaten him with a weapon, we do it; if we need to scream at him, we do it." Another officer stated that "the 'iron fist' policy is not a crime. If you do not impose yourself to the delinquent, then your boss punishes you." [100] Despite this open recognition of police violence, no political sector or social group reacted.

An analysis of political and social reactions toward media reports on police violence confirms the low levels of responsiveness by sectors supportive of civil rights (Table 2.4). Through an analysis of 52 cases reported by the press, three patterns can be observed. First, in half of the cases the police preempt criticism by suggesting that internal actions have been or will be taken. Second, with the exception of a single case reported in 1998 and the allegations of police violence against communist party leaders in 2001, pro-civil rights leaders and activists tend to react case-by-case (59 percent). The

Table 2.4 Chile: Responses toward Allegation of Police Violence Documented by the Press. Responses from the Police and Civil Rights Coalition 1994–May 2002[101]

Total cases 52	Police reactions	percent
Press Release	25	48
—Rejection of allegations	2	8
—Internal review announced	9	36
—Officer dismissal announced	6	24
No reaction reported	26	50
Internal information released	1	2
	Civil Rights Coalition	**percent**
Active Reaction	31	59
—Denouncing abuse	21	67
—Lawyer announcing lawsuit	10	32
—Request of internal investigation	1	3
—Request legal change/ Procedures	1	3
No reaction reported	21	40
	(of 31 cases)	**percent**
Social and political Actors		
—Deputies (Center-left)	12	38.7
—Human Rights NGOs	12	38.7
—CAJ-Lawyers (Ministry of Justice)	5	16.1
—Others	6	19.3

most common pattern is that a congressional deputy denounces a case—usually related to his or her district—and asks the police to pursue an internal investigation.

A third pattern is that lawyers—generally from the Corporation of Legal Assistance—announce lawsuits against the police. As human rights groups do not frame police violence as an "institutional problem," neither politicians nor policymakers close to these views have incentives to demand or even support reforms.

EXPLAINING THE LACK OF RESPONSIVENESS

Within a political opportunity structure clearly unfavorable to the civil rights coalition, and in part due to the incentives generated by it, pro-civil rights advocacy groups were poorly coordinated in responding to issues of police violence. In particular, as presented in chapter one, three factors turn out to be crucial in further understanding why they missed several opportunities which even this unfavorable context presented them: their internal composition, the nature of their leadership, and their inability to obtain additional resources (particularly due to poor grant-seeking skills).

In Chile, human rights groups emerged during the 1970s and 1980s to protect citizens from the Pinochet regime (1973–1990). As was stated earlier, by the end of the 1980s, these organizations had developed extensive social networks. However, between 1989 and 1992 the human rights groups decided to discontinue voluntary organizations, maintaining only professional non-governmental organizations to legally and psychologically protect human rights victims from the military regime. Moreover, several of these professionals assumed governmental positions within the new democratic government, weakening the ability of non-governmental organizations to extend their work. In addition, most human rights organizations are formed by middle class professionals (lawyers, social workers) who are mainly working on cases related to past human rights violations. Since victims of police violence tend to be lower-middle class and lower-class (Fuentes 2001), the human rights groups' early decisions to disconnect themselves from their social bases has had an important impact on the quality of information they obtained. This fact explains why citizens channel their complaints individually or through state lawyers, but not through advocacy groups.[102] This also explains why a high percentage of allegations reported in the press (40 percent) are motivated by individual complaints rather than by the active intervention of human rights groups.[103]

This leads to a second issue: lack of leadership. The main human rights organizations (CODEPU, the ChCHRs, FASIC, and CODEJU) are generally led by professionals who voluntarily give part of their free time to the promotion of human rights.[104] In several cases, these professionals are lawyers who split their time between litigating in court, teaching in a university, and participating in human rights groups.

Moreover, the division between *insiders* and *outsiders* has inhibited collaborative work among these groups. Indeed, human rights groups in Chile have experienced several tensions during the transition to democracy between *insiders,* who decided to promote a human rights agenda within the government, and *outsiders,* who took a more critical view of government policies on human rights issues. With few exceptions, lawyers and activists outside and inside the government do not share information, cases, and strategies to deal with issues of human rights, despite their common interest in improving the status of citizens' rights. Moreover, conflicts among human rights groups on how to solve past human rights violations have increased tensions among them.[105] As a general trend, lawyers deal with their specific cases, without sharing ideas and strategies with their colleagues.[106] This reduces the ability of the group to create a unified front within the human rights movement and to generate a coherent agenda regarding past and present violations of human rights.

These disputes have also affected the way advocacy groups have framed human rights issues. Most if not all human rights organizations have concentrated on a very important but narrow segment of human rights issues—the legacy from the Pinochet period—and excluded other issues such as police violence. As was stated before, the political context of the transition encouraged human rights organizations to frame human rights problems as the need to achieve truth and justice for crimes committed during the military regime. Emerging conflicts such as police violence against the indigenous population were, at best, considered part of a new agenda of citizens' rights, but they were rarely considered as part of a comprehensive "human rights" agenda.[107] Only in 1994–95 did CODEPU and other organizations begin to consider other issues such as indigenous rights, police violence against the poor, and discrimination against immigrants as part of their main concerns. This is in stark contrast to the case of Argentina discussed in chapter four, where certain NGO leaders contributed to the re-definition of police violence as a human rights concern.

Finally, the lack of resources has also affected human rights groups. Since 1990, international agencies, particularly from Europe, have decided not continued to provide funding to advocacy groups in Chile, weakening their ability to develop new programs. However, other local institutions have received international support from the Ford Foundation to develop programs regarding judicial reform, human rights, and public interest advocacy. Thus international resources are still available, but advocacy groups lack the expertise and skills to obtain such resources. Those who have obtained resources are generally associated with more institutionalized organizations such as universities and research centers.

A recent example demonstrates this point. In recent years, a network of politicians, lawyers, and social scientists linked to human rights organizations and leftist political parties created a new think-tank called *Corporación Justicia y Ciudadanía* [Corporation Justice and Citizenship] to provide an alternative view to *Paz Ciudadana* on issues of public safety and judicial reform. Even though representatives of this new think-tank have had meetings with public authorities, as yet they have not been able to obtain funds to initiate research and policy-oriented programs given their lack of resources and grant-seeking skills in requesting international support.[108]

Another example showing the lack of responsiveness by human rights organizations in Chile is an experiment I decided to run between August and December 2001 (Appendix 2). The test involved an e-mail message sent to more than 100 key social and political and social actors in Chile and abroad, explaining the results of a new study that demonstrates increasing levels of police violence in Chile.[109] The e-mail provided a summary of the main results of the study and a link to a website with the whole document. The e-mail was sent three times, coinciding with key junctures in which police procedures were being questioned by political and social leaders because of their inefficiency, and because relevant cases of police violence were being reported in the press.

Given the findings of my field research, I expected to observe low levels of responsiveness from human rights organizations in Chile, government officials, Congressional representatives, and the media. Since the topic of police violence has consistently been denied by public authorities, we should not expect to observe major reactions from incumbents. Moreover, as human rights organizations are focused on the "legacy," we should not expect human rights groups to use this information to pressure the government or the police. On the other hand, I expected to observe high levels of responsiveness from the uniformed police (given its public relations system) and international actors (given their expertise and leadership on the subject worldwide).

The results of this experiment confirmed my expectations. First, international actors tended to respond more than local human rights organizations. In two cases (Amnesty International and US Department of State), they not only responded to my e-mail but also requested additional information. In both cases, it was clear that they had taken the time to read and critically analyze the document.[110] Moreover, Human Rights Watch was also interested in obtaining the document.

A second expected outcome was the low response level from human rights organizations in Chile. The only response came from CODEPU, which did not ask about the content itself, but about a way to obtain a printed copy to save in the Documentation Center. While international actors saw this document as a source to make a statement, local actors tended not to respond, or responded passively.[111]

The media, the government and representatives in Congress all had low levels of responsiveness. What is interesting is that the only state authority that actually responded to my e-mail—even though only in formal terms—was the *Carabineros*. This fact confirms my expectations regarding the "efficiency" of the *Carabineros*' public relations system in responding to external criticism that involves adopting a proactive position in the form of a promise to study the subject in detail.

Overall, the civil rights coalition has faced a strong collective action problem due to ideological differences as well as differences of opinion and priorities among organizations that are concerned about human rights, the lack of social networks to connect different social actors, and the lack of expertise in obtaining resources. This has led to reactive and case-by-case responses.

SUMMARY

This chapter shows that the political opportunity structure does not favor the civil rights coalition; indeed it favors the pro-order coalition. The mode of the transition, access to the political system and police corporateness increase the opportunities for the pro-order coalition to impose their views at both the public and political levels, and they also reduce the ability of the civil rights coalition to address issues related to reform of military courts, police reform, and accountability.

And, second, beyond these structural and institutional conditions, there are also a series of other internal factors such as the type of leadership, networks, and strategies and resources used by the civil rights and pro-order coalitions, which allow us to understand why pro-order views prevailed during the 1990s. On the one hand, groups holding pro-order views were able to take advantage of certain opportunities in the early 1990s, articulating a coherent and consistent platform for action. They took advantage of the public's concern regarding delinquency in the early 1990s, the specific kidnapping of an important figure, and public opinion that valued "tough" measures against crime. On the other hand, groups holding civil rights views had a hard time adapting themselves to a new post-authoritarian environment. They have not taken advantage of several opportunities in which the police have violated citizens' rights. Moreover, the civil rights coalition has not been able to articulate an alternative discourse to the pro-order coalition, even though empirical evidence suggest that there is some room for maneuver. In other words, while the political opportunity structure was negative and consistent with a fairly negative outcome for civil rights views, some internal characteristics of advocacy groups made them to miss some opportunities for action.

In this context, the constant governmental rejection of international reports suggesting continuing patterns of police abuse in Chile should not be surprising. As local advocacy groups have not gathered information on the issue and convinced allies on the political level that police violence is a social problem in Chile, incumbents tend to favor pro-order views. These views see abuses as exceptional and, when abuses take place, most believe that the Chilean legal system will redress them. This chapter suggests that while these views are dominant, they are inaccurate.

Chapter Three

Explaining an "Unexpected" Legal Reform in Chile

Chapter two argues that police violence is not considered a relevant issue among politicians and policymakers in Chile mainly because contextual and individual-level factors have favored the establishment of a cohesive pro-order coalition that has dominated the debate on crime and delinquency. Moreover, compared to Argentina, the civil rights coalition has shown less coordination in articulating their demands, and human rights groups have focused on the legacy of the military regime.

Given this context, the approval of the bill eliminating the "arrest on suspicion" clause in 1998 seems unexpected. In other words, we should not expect the approval of a pro-civil rights norm in a context in which the pro-order coalition dominate the discourse on crime and in which the political opportunity structure is unfavorable to civil rights groups. In this chapter, I argue that the elimination of the arrest on suspicion is less unexpected than we may think because, even though the outcome implied reforming the status quo, the new law clearly favored pro-order views. Facing a scenario in which all actors agreed on restricting police powers, the 1998 policy outcome incorporated most—if not all—concerns of the police. Thus, the elimination of the "arrest on suspicion" clause and its replacement by a "verification of identity" clause was the second best choice for the pro-order coalition—being the status quo the ideal choice for pro-order groups.

Given this context, three factors explain why this reform occurred: first, the existence of a network of professionals who actively lobbied the opposition and the government, offering policy alternatives on the modernization of the judicial system; second, the existence of pro-active policymakers who embraced and pushed for this judicial reform; third, the way these professionals and policymakers framed the debate. With the exception of one police incident that took place in January 1998, the overall discussion on the restriction of police powers focused on the modernization of the judicial system rather than on police officers' misconduct. Thus, no social pressure from "below" was needed to restrict police powers.

POLICY EXPERTS AND JUDICIAL REFORM

During the military regime, a group of lawyers and researchers tied to the Christian Democratic Party, the non-governmental Corporation for the Promotion of University Studies (CPU) developed several proposals concerning the modernization of the judicial system.[1] Supported by USAID, CPU conducted training program for judges and administrators in the years 1988–1989. The initial success of this project gave the CPU access to new resources, which led to the development of a more comprehensive research and training program with the judiciary.[2] CPU established an important relationship with the National Association of Judges and, beginning in 1990, began a new set of training programs, judicial assistance, and research on the criminal system nationwide. Even though this program did not attempt to transform the judiciary, CPU's professionalism helped it gain legitimacy among more conservative officials in the judiciary (Vargas 1998b; Urzúa 2000).

On a parallel track, the *Universidad Diego Portales* law school created a research program to analyze problems of the criminal system and to propose structural reforms. In 1992 and 1993, these lawyers published important studies demonstrating the inefficiency of the Chilean penal system.[3]

In 1993, the CPU, the *Universidad Diego Portales,* and several other actors including lawyers, judges, law professors, representatives of professional associations, and policymakers created a Forum for the improvement of the criminal system.[4] They met every fifteen days to discuss several aspects of a potential reform. In 1994, the conservative think tank *Paz Ciudadana* joined the Forum to promote changes in the judicial system. The incorporation of *Paz Ciudadana* allowed this Forum to gain the support of the right-wing opposition. Moreover, the incorporation of *Paz Ciudadana* allowed the Forum to address the relationship between the reform of the judicial system and the reduction of crime rates. Finally, given the close links between *Paz Ciudadana* and the most important Chilean newspaper (*El Mercurio*), the debates regarding the judicial reform soon became part of the mainstream media.[5]

The Forum included an executive directorate with representatives of CPU and *Paz Ciudadana,* plus a technical commission which was chaired by a representative of *Universidad Diego Portales.* Between 1993 and 1994, this team met with key governmental authorities to lobby and promote the main aspects of their proposed reforms.[6] Inspired by the works of Maier, Binder and their colleagues in Argentina (Duce 1999), the *Forum* proposed a major reform to the penal code in order to abolish the traditional inquisitorial system in which the judge assumed prosecutorial functions. The proposal included the establishment of a prosecutor's office to be in charge of the investigative part of the trial, and the creation of an oral trial based on adversarial hearings in which both parties have the right to produce their own evidence and contradict the evidence presented by the other side. In this new system, the judge would still maintain the right to question witnesses. As empirical studies revealed serious violations of individual rights under the inquisitorial system as it functioned in Chile (Correa 1993; Jiménez, 1994), the reform was framed in the context of the protection of citizens' rights such as the right to have a fair trail based upon cross-examination of physical evidence.

After the inauguration of the second democratic government in March 1994, the Forum lobbied the new Minister of Justice, Soledad Alvear. She supported the proposal for three reasons: first, it provided a solution to increasing pressures exerted by right wing sectors regarding the lack of a government policy to deal with delinquency; second, it provided a set of policies compatible with the government platform; and third, it was supported by diverse and important sectors of the political spectrum (Vargas 1998b: 113). At the end of 1994, the Ministry of Justice officially added two Ministry officials into the Forum's executive commission, and other Ministry official experts to the Forum's technical commission. To demonstrate government commitment to this reform, the Forum was invited to move its headquarters to the Ministry of Justice. Six month later, in June 1995, the Ministry sent proposed legislation to Congress; it was approved in 1998.[7]

Transforming the Penal Code procedure also implied redesigning the relationship between the police and prosecutors. The *Universidad Diego Portales*' empirical studies demonstrated a serious lack of due process in police procedures. For example, an analysis of court files revealed that in 92 percent of the cases, police reports included "spontaneous" testimonies by detainees. From this 92 percent, in 81 percent of the cases individuals admitted having committed the crime, and 68 percent of these police reports based their conclusions exclusively on these "spontaneous" testimonies and not on physical evidence. Moreover, in most convictions (96 percent), judges used police reports as proof to reach the verdict.[8] In other words, while police reports were mostly created on the basis of interrogations, judges' decisions strongly relied upon these reports, increasing the chance of abuse of power.

By 1996, most congressional representatives agreed on the need for a substantial modernization of the legal system. The debate in Congress was not about the principles driving the reform, which most actors supported, but about the power that specific actors such as prosecutors and the police would have in the new system.[9]

THE "ARREST ON SUSPICION" CLAUSE: POLICY DEBATE

The debate on police powers in the Chilean Congress illustrates the differences between the civil rights and the pro-order coalitions. The original 1993 bill was introduced in Congress by representatives closely linked to human rights advocacy groups.[10] The proposal sought the establishment of an equivalent of the *Miranda* rights that should be read by the police to detainees at the moment of the arrival to the police station. Additionally, the bill sought the elimination of certain legal justifications for detaining individuals such as "wearing unusual costumes," "being in unusual or suspicious places," "loafing," and "begging." The proposal was still conservative because it allowed the police to detain individuals who fail to authenticate their identity. This proposal was never discussed in Congress mainly because the Aylwin government felt it did not have the majority in the Senate to restrict police powers.[11]

After the second democratic government sent the penal code reform bill to Congress in 1995, policymakers in the executive branch became interested in reforming police powers to make such powers consistent with the proposed penal code project. In May 1996, the Ministry of Justice proposed a new bill, eliminating the "arrest on suspicion" clause. According to the government, the goal was to reform detention procedures of the police: "to make them consistent with those reforms proposed in the penal code procedure bill."[12]

The government also proposed that "torture" be made a crime, that individuals held incommunicado be allowed to contact their relatives or a lawyer at the moment of the arrest, and that judges ask individuals whether law enforcement officials told them their rights. If officers failed to do so, police reports must be invalidated as reliable proof during the trial. This proposal also specifically rejected the establishment of a "verification of identity detention" clause, arguing that it was unconstitutional to detain people who do not carry their ID simply because the Constitution does not mandate that individuals carry their IDs.[13] In other words, the government's bill went beyond the original proposal, adopting a more progressive position than the most pro-civil rights deputies in Congress.

In May 1996, however, the Chamber's Commission of Constitution and Legislation modified the Executive proposal, suggesting a "verification of identity detention" clause, allowing the police to arrest individuals who could not authenticate their identity into custody for a period of four hours. This proposal was rejected by the Chamber at the end of 1996, which accepted the government proposal.

As the debate entered the Senate, the pro-order coalition had more opportunities to influence the outcome. In March 1997, the Constitution and Legislation Commission of the Senate approved the establishment of the "verification of identity detention" clause, allowing the police to keep people under custody for four hours. Testifying before this commission, the police suggested that imposing a time framework for detentions was not realistic. Additionally, the police rejected the idea of reading detainees' rights twice. The police suggested that reading individuals' rights in the police station was enough.[14] In September 1997, the Senate approved establishing the "verification of identity" detention, established no time restriction for such detentions, and agreed that police officers should read detainees' rights only in the police station. Moreover, the Senate restricted the right of individuals held incommunicado to contact their relatives or lawyers. They mandated that police officers should be in charge of contacting detainees' relatives.[15]

Thus by December 1997, both houses of Congress agreed on (a) approving the incorporation of "torture" as a crime; (b) the abolition of the "arrest on suspicion" clause; (c) the establishment of the *Miranda* bill of rights; and (d) the suppression of the police report as valid evidence if the police did not explain their rights to detainees. The more conservative Senate and the more pro-civil rights Chamber of Deputies disagreed on whether the police could detain individuals to authenticate identity, whether *Miranda* rights should be read once or twice, and whether individuals held incommunicado should contact their relatives directly or through a law enforcement officer.

These discrepancies were to be resolved by a mixed commission in Congress. An incident that occurred in January 1998 had a partial effect on speeding this process. On January 15 the press reported the case of a taxi driver, Raúl Palma, who died as a result of police torture. Doctors found clear evidence that Palma had been subject to mistreatment and torture at a police station. On January 18, two days after the medical report proved the use of torture by the police against Palma, the executive branched asked Congress include the proposed bill in the extraordinary congressional period, giving it urgent status.[16]

The civil rights coalition reacted in two ways. First, congressional representatives demanded quick approval of the pending bill in Congress. Second, human rights organizations and their allies within the state bureaucracy (i.e., the Corporation of Legal Assistance) announced that mistreatment by the police was more common than generally reported by the media; and over a period of two weeks, human rights groups denounced more than fifty cases of police violence occurred during 1997.

At the executive branch level there was inter-ministerial tension. Authorities of the Ministry of Interior rejected claims of police violence, arguing that torture does not exist in a democratic regime, that cases denouncing the police were the exception rather than the rule, and that the police had taken all legal steps to punish those responsible in the Palma case. But the Ministry of Justice announced that the government was requesting that the consideration of the bill in Congress be accelerated. After this announcement politicians stopped complaining about the police's illegitimate use of force.

In February 1998, Congress created a jointed commission to solve the two houses' differences of opinion. This commission achieved consensus in April 1998,[17] eliminating the "arrest on suspicion" clause, but the Senate vote regarding the "verification of identity" detention prevailed; that is, now police officers could arrest individuals who failed to authenticate their identity. In these cases, the police should provide all means possible to facilitate individuals' self-identification. Moreover, the Senate vote regarding the time framework for such detentions also prevailed: individuals could be held in custody for an unlimited period of time. Additionally, the Senate vote regarding incommunicado detentions also prevailed: individuals could only contact their relatives or a lawyer through a law enforcement officer. Finally, the Chamber's position regarding the need for officers to inform individuals' rights twice prevailed (Table 3.1). The bill was promulgated in July 1998, incorporating most of the initial Senate version.

The decision-making process reveals three interesting features. First, the passage of the legislation was framed by pro-civil rights sectors in the Ministry of Justice as part of a broader debate regarding the modernization of the judicial system. The pro-order coalition supported the reform because it believed Chile required modernization of the judicial system, and the new provisions provided an adequate equilibrium between individuals' guarantees and police powers.[18] In this sense, police abuses were not part of the policy debate. The Palma incident in January 1998 contributed to speeding up an ongoing debate, but it did not alter the content of the reform.

A second element is related to the existence of a group of professionals who offered technical recommendations to policymakers. These lawyers were part of an elite group of professionals closely linked to government officials and, later on, to leaders of the opposition (Duce 1999). As the issue

Table 3.1 Chile: Debate on the Abolition of the Detention for Suspicion

	Credible cause Detention	Torture as crime	Verification of Identity Detention	*Miranda* Rights	Incommunicado Rights
93 Motion	✓		✓	Read twice	
96 Gov. amendment	✓	✓		Read twice	✓
96 Chamber Commission	✓	✓	✓ (4 hours)	Read twice	✓
96 Chamber of Deputies	✓	✓		Read twice	✓
03.97 Senate Commission	✓	✓	✓ (3 hours)	Read once	
09.97 Senate	✓	✓	(Unlimited)	Read once	✓
04. 98 Mixed Commission	✓	✓	✓ (Unlimited)	Read twice	(✓)
07.98 Outcome	✓	✓	✓ (Unlimited)	Read twice	(✓)

( ) Blank: no proposal suggested.
(v) Partial improvement of individual rights.

of police violence was not part of the government agenda, and as traditional human rights groups were not pressuring the government on this particular issue, these professionals did not have incentives to contact human rights advocacy groups. Finally, another important element was the existence of proactive policymakers in the Ministry of Justice proposing innovative policy initiatives to Congress. These policymakers recognized the need for the modernization of the judicial system and assumed a strong pro-civil rights stand.

The final draft that passed and became law did not reflect the wishes of the Ministry of Justice; rather it favored the position of the pro-order Senate. Now, police officers could hold individuals who do not carry their IDs without any restrictions. Human rights advocacy groups did not react to the new bill once it was promulgated in July, 1998. A close look at the newspapers in that period shows no reactions from human rights groups or pro-civil rights politicians regarding questionable points of the new law. The press framed the new law as the establishment of *Miranda* rights and the abolition of the "arrest on suspicion" clause.[19] No word was mentioned about the establishment of a new and arguably unconstitutional "verification of identity detention" clause.

SUMMARY

The analysis of the political debate of this bill and the actual policy outcome confirm the central aspects of my theoretical framework. First, the pro-order coalition took advantage of its position of power in the Senate, minimizing the impact of the reform. Facing a context in which most political actors were willing to reform police powers, they chose a second best alternative: the approval of the "verification of identity" clause. Second, the civil rights coalition had problems in articulating their demands and objectives. While groups outside the state tried to denounce continuous police abuses—particularly in January, 1998—policymakers at the Ministry of Justice sped up the approval of a conservative reform to respond to increasing allegations. In this context, human rights advocacy groups played a minimal role during the political debate and policy implementation of this reform. As was observed in chapter two, these groups' internal characteristics (focus on the legacy, disconnected from social bases, and without grant-seeking skills to generate resources) explain their lack of attention to contemporary problems of human rights violations in Chile.

However, the approval of the *Miranda* rights for detainees is still an important outcome that deserves some recognition. The analysis of this case reveals that the role of "policy experts" and their strategies may be more relevant than originally expected. Because pro-civil rights professionals framed the restriction of police powers as the need to modernize the judicial system and this framing received the support of pro-order sectors, advancing the reform was easier than originally expected.

Chapter Four

Argentina: Strong Advocacy Groups, Fluctuating Influence

On September 17, 1999, three men entered a bank in *Villa Ramallo,* in Buenos Aires province, with the intention of robbing it. While they were inside the bank, close to two hundred police officers surrounded the building and demanded the men surrender unarmed. Instead, they took seven hostages and waited for nine hours, until they decided to leave the bank with three of the hostages—the manager of the bank, his wife, and another banker.

At this point, TV channels and radios were reporting live from *Villa Ramallo,* providing all the details of the tense situation. Once the robbers and their hostages left the bank in a car, the police followed them closely. Even though the police had clear orders to protect the lives of the innocent people, at some point the police started shooting at the car. Seventy bullets were found in the car and no police officer was wounded. Only two people survived the assault: the banker's wife and one of the delinquents. However, the latter died the next day under police custody. The official report stated that he committed suicide.

The subsequent judicial investigation has determined that some police officers were linked to the people who planned the robbery. Moreover, the same evidence shows that passengers were taken from the car and killed while defenseless (Cecchi 2000). During 20 hours, millions of people witnessed on TV the lack of coordination within the provincial police and, probably more importantly, the tendency of officers to use what is called an "easy trigger" (*gatillo fácil*) to deal with delinquents. This case was one more in a series of sometimes incredible stories of abuse of power by the provincial police. Thus, it is not surprising that the public's confidence in the police in Buenos Aires is very low.

Since the province was holding elections for governor the next month, this incident had some impact on candidates' proposals regarding public safety and police reform. Indeed, the center-left coalition's candidate—Graciela Fernández Meijide—strongly emphasized the need to reform the police and end practices of police violence in Argentina. She argued that this tragedy "may be the result of my contender's early declarations about the police."[1] Indeed, several weeks before, the Peronist candidate, Carlos Ruckauf, had supported an 'iron fist' approach toward delinquency by stating that "we need to shoot delinquents," and "kill them" to solve the problems of delinquency in the province.[2] In October 1999, Ruckauf was elected provincial governor, and he initiated a set of reforms that allowed the police to reestablish some powers lost during the 1990s.

This chapter explains the story of partial success of the civil rights coalition in promoting individuals rights until 1999, when the trend was reversed with the rise of a cohesive pro-order coalition in Buenos Aires province after the October elections. In contrast to Chile, the Argentine political opportunity structure has provided more opportunities for advocacy groups to influence the policy process, in part because the nature of the transition favored the development of activism related to current and past human rights violations, and also because advocacy networks faced a favorable political context by the mid- 1990s. Additionally, low levels of police corporateness stimulated conflicts inside the police, which has allowed advocacy groups to take advantage of such divisions to demand further reforms. The internal characteristics of human rights advocacy networks played an important role as well. By the mid-1990s, advocacy groups became focal points, setting the agenda and generating policy reforms. As the government delayed making changes, human rights groups searched for allies domestically and abroad, increasing international pressure to stop police brutality and to transform a legal framework that allowed it.

This pressure has not been enough to implement policies and change police behavior, however; a strong pro-order and anti-reformist coalition has used legal and illegal strategies to maintain the status quo.[3] The first part of this chapter provides a background on police prerogatives, legal changes during the 1990s, police practices, and public perception of the police in the Buenos Aires province of Argentina. The second part explains the contextual and individual-level factors that have led to fluctuating or oscillating influence of advocacy groups regarding the enhancement of citizens' rights.

BACKGROUND: INSTITUTIONS, LEGAL CHANGES, PRACTICES, AND PUBLIC PERCEPTION

Police Legal Prerogatives

Argentina is a federal country with a decentralized police organized at the provincial level. The federal (i.e., national) police force is responsible for public safety in the Capital (with a population of approximately 3 million), and it conducts federal criminal investigations nationwide. The provincial police are in charge of public safety in the surrounding area of Buenos Aires Province (14 million population).[4]

Three political authorities intervene in monitoring police institutions: (a) the national government that is directly in charge of the federal police, (b) the government of the City of Buenos Aires that achieved autonomy in 1996, but has no authority over the federal police,[5] and (c) the provincial government that is in charge of the Buenos Aires provincial police (BAPP). This chapter will mainly focus on the BAPP, given the series of transformations undertaken in this police department since the re-establishment of democracy in 1983.

An important difference between Chile and Argentina is the civilian legal control over police affairs. While in Chile the President appoints the head of the police for a fixed term of four years, during which he cannot be removed without the approval of the National Security Council, in Argentina promotions and removals depend directly on governors.

From an institutional point of view, the BAPP is a militarized institution with approximately 48 thousand officers and a centralized command. As in many Latin American police institutions, the BAPP is organized on the basis of a military system with a hierarchical structure of officers, sub-officers, and the troops (Gobierno de la Provincia, 2001). Even though civilians have legal control over public safety planning and command, until the mid 1990s the police forces managed their own internal affairs, including decision-making and policing strategies (Saín 2001; Abregú et al. 1998). With the exception of the 1997–1999 period, civilian authorities have appointed police officers in top-ranking positions within the force. As Argentina has an inquisitorial system, the police are in charge of maintaining public order and criminal investigation.[6]

In the BAPP, internal mechanisms of accountability protect top-ranking officers from their subordinates. For example, the statement of a superior officer is enough to prove a subordinate's misbehavior. A subordinate cannot lodge an official complaint against an officer unless the latter has committed a serious offense or one that directly affects the individual complainant (Gobierno de la Provincia, 2001: art.172 and 248).

From a legal point of view, both Chile and Argentina allow for the arrest of individuals on simply the basis of suspicion. As was stated in chapter three, the 1901 Chilean Penal code established the 'detention on suspicion' clause that was not eliminated until 1998. In Argentina, the 1868 and 1888 Penal Codes gave the federal police the power to practice detentions on suspicion. In 1944, authorities increased police powers by allowing officers to arrest individuals who fail to prove their identity. Additionally, authorities promulgated police edicts [*edictos*] authorizing security forces to arrest individuals on the basis of minor offenses such as public disorder, "scandals," loafing, begging, and prostitution (Blando 1995). Following the same path, in 1970 the Buenos Aires province established in 1970 a code of misdemeanors [*Código de Faltas*] permitting the arrest of individuals on the basis of anyone of more than fifty minor offenses.

By the re-establishment of democracy in 1983, Argentina's police forces enjoyed high discretionary powers to arrest and hold citizens without external interference. They could arrest, interrogate, and detain suspected offenders for up to 30 days without bringing them before a judge. Police could carry out preventive detentions simply for ID verification or to check whether a 'suspect' had a police record.

Legal Changes in the Buenos Aires Province

From a legal standpoint, Argentina has faced three significant waves of reforms (Table 4.1). The first wave came at the federal level between 1991 and 1996 and involved an important recognition of citizens' legal rights through the abolition of the 'verification of records' detentions (1991),[7] the reform of the penal code (1991) and the approval of a new Constitution (1994).

By the mid-1980s, government authorities and the legal community agreed on the unsustainability of the inquisitorial system established in 1888.[8] As in many Latin American countries, the system was based on a written procedure with no jury and in which the judge held both investigative and jurisdictional powers.[9] The ambitious reform proposed by the centrist Alfonsín government (1983–1989) did not achieve congressional support, given the opposition of the Peronist party, but President Menem (1989–1999) proposed a more moderate reform that was approved by Congress in 1991. The new Federal Penal Code established a division between the investigative part of the trial, to be in charge of a prosecutor, and the ruling aspect of it, to be in charge of a judge.[10] Menem's Minister of Justice, León Arslanián, played an important role during the congressional debate on this reform and, later on, during the reform of the BAPP.

Table 4.1 Argentina: Main Reforms at the Federal level and Buenos Aires Province

Federal Level	Reforms	Provincial Level	Reforms
1983–89 Alfonsín UCR	84-Military Penal Code	1983–87 UCR Armendáriz	
1989–94 Menem PJ	91–National Law of Interior Safety 91–Abolition verification of records detention 91-Penal Code procedure 94-Constitution	1987–91 PJ Cafiero 1991–95 PJ Duhalde	
1995–1999 Menem PJ tion	98-Code of Civility (City) 99-Decree on detention	1995–99 PJ Duhalde	96-Intervention of the police decree 97-Penal Code Procedure 97-2nd interven- 98-Public Safety Law 98-Police Organization Law
2000–2001 De la Rúa UCR-Frepaso		2000—2001 PJ Ruckauf	00-Penal Code reform on police powers 00-Reorganization police

UCR: Unión Cívica Radical (centrist party)
PJ: Peronist party (populist party)
Frepaso: Leftist coalition.
Bold indicates rules restricting citizens' rights

These new regulations restricted police powers to detain individuals at the federal (national) level. Now, police could detain a suspect for up to 10 hours without an arrest warrant, if they had a "well-founded belief" that he or she had committed, or was about to commit a crime, or if individuals were unable to identify themselves. Moreover, police needed to orally warn individuals before using a weapon. Police could only question people to determine their identity once they had read them their rights and guarantees.[11] Even though the first wave of reforms did not have a legal effect on the Buenos Aires province, the debate set the agenda for further reforms at the federal level in different provinces of Argentina (Blando 1995; Struensee and Maier 2000).

The second wave of reforms mainly concerned Buenos Aires province (1997–1999). It included two substantial reforms: first, at the end of 1996, the provincial legislature approved new penal procedures similar to what the federal government had approved, establishing a public prosecutor and a new *judicial police* in charge of the investigative part of the trial. This reform should have been implemented in March 1, 1998, but budget problems delayed its implementation until the end of September, 1998.

Second, increasing allegations of police misbehavior made by advocacy groups, along with growing evidence of BAPP's engagement in illicit activities, provoked a serious institutional crisis. In December 1996, Peronist governor Eduardo Duhalde decided to intervene with the police. Originally, this reform attempted to transform the structure of the police, to rationalize human resources, to dismiss corrupt officers, and to improve the public image of the police (Gobierno de la Provincia, 2001: Law 11,880).

These changes were highly resisted by a coalition of police officers and representatives of the Peronist party who pressured Duhalde to reduce the reforms (Saín 2001; Dutil and Ragendorfer 1997). Nevertheless, new allegations of police violence and the electoral setback of the governing Peronist party in the Buenos Aires legislature in April 1997 forced Duhalde to promulgate a second decree of intervention in December 1997 (Decree 4508/97).

Duhalde explicitly recognized the need for a major transformation of the police by suggesting that "civilian authorities must intervene because we believe there is a corporatist spirit that is impeding structural reforms."[12] Two prestigious lawyers—Alberto Binder and León Arslanián (the former Minister of Justice)—designed the main guidelines of this reform. Binder and Arslanián's original plan was to create a new model of safety: "this crisis has structural roots in all segments of the system. This crisis is not about the police in particular, but about the whole model of public safety and criminal investigation" (Arslanián and Binder 1998). As a result of this process, the Buenos Aires legislature approved a new law of public safety (Law 12,154, July 1998), a new law regulating the internal organization of the police (Law

12,155, July 1998), and a new law creating the Secretary of Justice and Public Safety (Law 12,090 August 8, 1998).

These reforms sought to divide the police into three forces: a judicial investigative police, a road police, and a preventive police in charge of public safety. The reform de-centralized the police into several districts [*departamentos*] and included the creation of citizens' forums in coordination with police departments. Additional legal changes incorporated and recognized international treaties related to human rights.

Regarding detention rights, the reforms included the right to remain silent, the right to make a call, and the right to have a lawyer. Additionally, police officers were required to read detainees their rights. However, police officers could still practice 'verification of records' detentions.

The third wave (1999–2001) partially reversed these reforms at the federal and provincial level. In a context of electoral campaigns and increasing criminal violence, the federal government promulgated a decree (No 150/1999) instructing the police to prevent conduct that "without constituting misdemeanors, nor infractions in the Code of Misdemeanors, should be avoided." This decree was interpreted to allow the police to detain suspicious individuals. At the provincial level and after the election of Peronist Carlos Ruckauf as the new governor, the Buenos Aires Provincial legislature approved a similar reform allowing police to interrogate detainees and witnesses during the arrest but before they arrive at the police station. The legislature also allowed police officers to make "preventive" searches of personal packages, cars, and private property. In the year 2001, the legislature was debating a bill proposed by the governor, allowing the police to shoot suspects without having to alert suspects of their presence.

Additional changes restricted the impact of the 1997–98 reforms. First, the new provincial government re-centralized the top-ranking positions in the police. Second, the BAPP continued performing investigative tasks for the judiciary. Third, the governor promulgated a decree allowing evidence from police officers' interrogation of detainees to be used in court. Finally, the governor re-hired hundreds of officers who had previously been dismissed because of their abusive and corrupt behavior.[13]

Police Practices

Although Argentina made important legal reforms on the protection of individual rights during the 1990s, the actual record of police practices shows the difficulties in implementing such rights. Since the reestablishment of democracy in 1983, several international and independent national sources have denounced serious violations of human rights by police forces, focusing on two related illegitimate practices: officers' illegal practices in order to obtain private benefits by using their position of power—that is, corruption—and, practices of violence against the population.

By the mid-1990s several press sources and specialists revealed the existence of a complex network of illegal businesses, led by police officers and political brokers in different districts of Buenos Aires province (for examples, see Appendix 3). This network included profiting from prostitution and illegal gambling, trafficking of stolen-cars, kidnapping, trafficking of police reports, and drug trafficking. This network could be considered a "ladder of illegality" that goes from street-level police officers and districts' political brokers to top-ranking officers, politicians and businessmen (Oliveira and Tiscornia 1997; Dutil and Ragendorfer 1997; Saín 2001).[14]

Some salient cases revealed by the press were BAPP officers' involvement in the 1994 bomb attack against the Buenos Aires Jewish Cultural Center (AMIA), causing 87 deaths, and the kidnapping and murder of the journalist José Luis Cabezas, who was investigating the links between the BAPP and organized crime as well as the activities of a controversial businessman.[15] In part, these junctures led the governor at the time, Eduardo Duhalde, to dismiss more than 1,200 officers involved in illegal activities between 1997 and 1998.

Additionally, both international and local advocacy groups have revealed that the police forces have been involved in unlawful practices such as 'easy trigger' [*gatillo fácil*],[16] torture, arbitrary arrests, disappearances in police custody, harassment of or attacks on witnesses to these crimes, and fabrication of evidence of shoot-outs (e.g. planting of a gun on the victim's body).[17]

Advocacy groups have systematically reported cases of police violence since at least 1985. However, one of the main problems in assessing trends in human rights violations in Argentina is the lack of a centralized agency collecting civilians' complaints against the police.[18] In this sense, probably the best existing indicator of police behavior is trends of civilian deaths by police in the streets. Human rights organizations such as the Center for Legal and Social Studies (CELS) and the Coordination against Institutional Repression (CORREPI) have followed all cases reported by the press since 1993, providing extremely valuable data.

We need to keep in mind some important methodological considerations regarding available data, however. First, advocacy groups have collected information on civilian deaths in confrontations with the police using newspapers sources, which may not constitute the universe of incidents. However, when CELS's researchers have had the opportunity to compare their figures against official sources provided by the police, they tend to be similar.[19] Second, CELS—which is one of the main organizations collecting this information—does not discriminate between police officers acting in self-defense and police officers abusing power. Despite these methodological considerations, this is an important starting point in considering levels of police violence in Argentina.

Considering Buenos Aires Capital and the province together (Graph 4.1), the first significant trend is the constant decline of civilian deaths by police officers between 1986 (306 deaths) and 1991 (83 deaths). Then, we observe a relatively constant increase until the year 1999 (274 deaths). Second, civilian deaths in Buenos Aires province represent approximately 74 percent of the total.[20] Reduction of civilian deaths between 1986 and 1991 does not necessarily mean lower levels of police abuse, per se. Indeed, international and local reports suggest that more than 700 allegations of ill-treatment and torture were made in Argentina between 1989 and 1991 (Americas Watch and CELS: 1991).

What are the factors explaining CELS's trends of decline (until 1992) and partial increase after that year? First, it seems that the cycle of inflation and organized labor protests do not explain trends in civilian deaths. to growing use of deathly methods of coercion by the police. This may be due to the nature of social conflicts that Argentina faced in 1990 and 1991. In

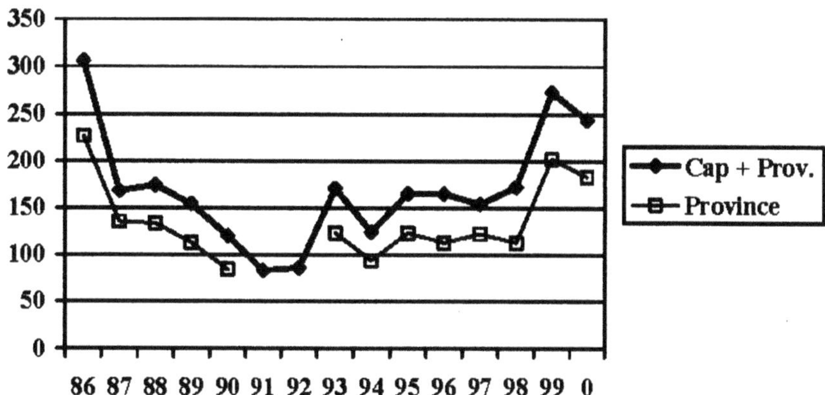

Graph 4.1 Argentina: Civilian Killings in Buenos Aires Captial and Province

Sources: Americas Watch and CELS (1991); CELS and Facultad (1994–95); CELS (1996–97, 1998b, 1999–2001)
Cap + Prov.: Capital plus Province

those years protests were mostly led by unions supportive of the governing Peronist party, which may have led to less repressive methods by the police.

Why, then, did the police begin to use deadly methods more frequently during the 1990s? Two socio-economic indicators may explain this increase: unemployment and crime rates. First, Argentina experienced an important transformation of its economy during the 1990s, causing higher levels of unemployment. From having an average of 5.5 percent unemployment between 1983 and 1990, Argentina achieved a historical record of 22 percent unemployment by 2002. In this sense, the Menem administrations (1990–1994 and 1995–1999) had to deal with a new 'threat;' jobless citizens protesting against the economic model being implemented in Argentina. We could plausibly assume that the police reacted in a more violent way against unorganized sectors of society that were protesting in the streets.

Moreover, the deterioration of socio-economic indicators such as levels of inequality, employment, and job stability probably had a clear impact on crime rates during the 1990s. Indeed, a second important transformation was the constant increase in all types of crimes including homicides, and crimes against property and individuals.[21] Thus, the Buenos Aires metropolitan area became more violent than it used to be. This can also be observed when we compare civilian and police deaths in confrontations during the 1993–2001 period. While CELS registered 23 police officers and 123 civilians' death in confrontations in 1993, by the year 2000 such figures were 64 and 183 respectively.

While changes in social conditions created a more conflictive environment, another important factor explaining the increase in police violence during the 1990s is the political decision made by federal and provincial authorities to allow the police themselves to define the best strategies to deal with social protest and crime. This is evident in several government actions. First, as soon as Menem came to power in 1989, police forces pressured the government through strikes and public displays of discontent, for higher salaries and greater autonomy in conducting their affairs. Responding to this pressure, the highest representatives of the Peronist party–President Menem and Buenos Aires province governor Duhalde—partially improved the economic conditions of the police.[22] More importantly, Duhalde established an agreement with the police guaranteeing that the government would not intervene in various illegal activities of the police (Dutil and Ragendorfer 1997; Saín 2001).

Additionally, both Peronist leaders supported an 'iron fist' policy with regard to public safety. This became evident when President Menem and Governor Duhalde explicitly supported two Chiefs of Police, Luis Patti and Pedro Klodczyk, officers who were questioned by human rights organizations due to the accusation that they engaged in torture of dissidents during the military regime (Americas Watch and CELS 1991; CELS and Facultad 1995). Governor Duhalde took some steps such as the dismissal of 2,400 officers who were under judicial scrutiny due to illegal activities between 1991 and 1996.[23] However, Duhalde focused on improving police institutions' material resources and supporting an 'iron fist' approach toward crime and social protests. For instance, responding to criticisms coming from CELS on the disproportion between civilian and police deaths, the Secretary of Security of Buenos Aires province, Eduardo Pettiagini, argued that "this is a sign of police professionalism."[24] Responding to criticisms of police corruption, Governor Duhalde justified it by suggesting that "it is logical to find delinquents among police officers because there are delinquents in all activities including journalism, politics, law, and even in the priesthood." [25]

Resolution of Cases in Court

As in many other Latin American countries, Argentina's judicial system shows high levels of inefficiency and a lack of modernization. Trials tend to be slow, a significant percentage of individuals are in jail without trial, and judges tend to avoid prosecuting police officers (Correa and Jiménez 1997; CELS and Human Rights Watch 1998; Garrido, Guariglia, and Palmieri, 1997).[26] For instance, a government report indicates that of 81 cases alleging police brutality—in which 47 presented documented injuries—no case ended with a sentence for the police officer involved between 1992 and 1995.[27] Of the 456 cases reported by CORREPI between 1989 and 1998, in only 7 percent of the cases was a sentence obtained.

An important distinction between Chile and Argentina is that in Argentina police violence is a matter handled by civilian courts. As the federal court (since 1994) and the provincial court (since 1998) have reformed their penal systems allowing oral and public trials, in those exceptional cases where trials get to an oral stage, police officers are exposed to public scrutiny. This was the case in the six-year investigation into the torture and murder of university student Miguel Angel Bru, where the constant pressure exerted by advocacy groups exposing several irregularities committed by the investigative judge was crucial for the prosecution of the officers responsible of his death. In a more recent case in 1999, the quick intervention of a prosecutor, who promptly collected proofs in the case of the police torture and murder of Héctor Galván, led to the prosecution of one officer (CELS 2000).

Public Opinion: Public Safety, Police, and Citizens' Rights

As in Chile, three dimensions of public opinion are relevant: citizens' concern about public safety, the image of the police, and citizens' views regarding the protection of citizens' rights. Regarding the first sphere, between 1986 and 2000 Argentine citizens show a relatively low concern on delinquency. Between 1986 and 1994, the main concern was low salaries and an increasing concern about corruption. Since 1995 and given important transformations of the Argentine economy, the central concern was by far unemployment. Citizens' concern about delinquency became more important by the end of the decade of the 1990s.

By 2000, respondents were concerned about corruption as much as delinquency (Graph 4.2). Another survey conducted in 1998 reveals that while 37 percent of respondents considered unemployment as the main problem the government should focus on, 17.7 percent mentioned delinquency and 12 percent mentioned corruption (CEUNM, 1998). While in Chile and Argentina the problem of unemployment became the main citizens' concern, the main difference between the two countries is the significantly lower priority that citizens in Argentina gave to the problem of delinquency. This seems contradictory because Argentina—and particularly the Buenos Aires province, shows higher levels of crime than Chile. However, this makes sense given the deep impact of the transformation of the economy in Argentina, which had a deep impact on the Argentine population. Indeed, for the first time in the Twenty Century, this country has experienced unemployment rates greater than 10 percent.

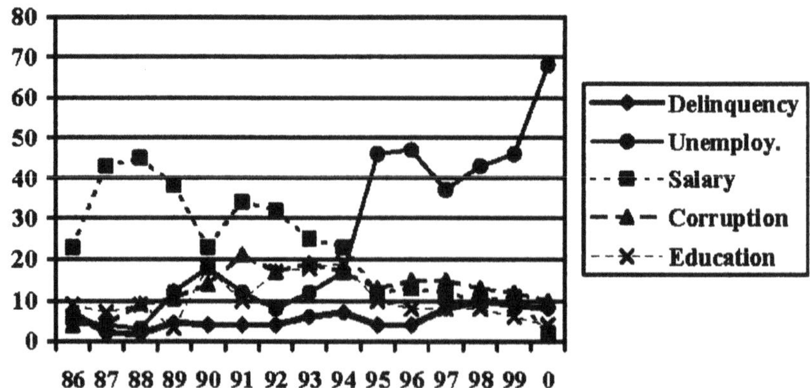

Graph 4.2 Argentina: Main Concerns of Public Opinion 1986–2000[28]

What is the main problem the government should focus on?

In relation to the image of the police, citizens in the province show a relatively constant pattern of distrust for the police. Surveys in the early 1990s demonstrate that—on average—only 24 percent in the province have a positive image of the provincial police (Table 4.2). As an average, more than 60 percent of respondents had a regular or negative image of the police.

In 1996 and in a context of growing public exposure of police scandals, citizens perceived abuses as a structural problem. For instance, 57 percent of respondents in the Capital and the Province believed that police abuses were an institutional characteristic of the police and only 34 percent considered them as due just to individual carelessness.[29] By the year 2000, 80 percent of respondents in the Buenos Aires province had a regular or negative image of the police. Only 16 percent had a positive image (Catterberg 2000).[30] Moreover, surveys conducted by the Argentine Ministry of Justice by the end of the 1990s confirm previous trends. When citizens are asked to evaluate police work, more than 50 percent of respondents in the province said that "they don't do a good job" (Table 4.3).

Thus, one of the main differences between public opinion in Chile and Argentina is the higher level of confidence toward the police in Chile

Table 4.2 Argentina: Public Opinion Perception on the Police, 1990–1993[31]

	March 1990		March/May 1991		March/May 1992		March/May 1993	
	FP	BAPP	FP	BAPP	FP	BAPP	FP	BAPP
Positive	30		27.6	25	16.6	12	32	35.2
Regular	35.8		34.1	38.8	32.9	28.6	31.3	29.2
Negative	30		37.1	33.6	46.2	56.7	30	32.8

FP: Federal Police; BAPP: Buenos Aires Province police

Table 4.3 Argentina: Evaluation of Police Work 1998–2000[32]

	Buenos Aires Capital and Province					
	1998		1999		2000	
	FP	BAPP	FP	BAPP	FP	BAPP
They do a good job	31.4	26.6	36.1	35	36.7	32.5
They don't do a good job	52.0	58.2	49.4	51.9	45.6	51.3
Don't Answer	16.6	15.2	14.4	13.1	17.7	16.2

FP: Federal Police; BAPP: Buenos Aires Province police.

and lower confidence in Argentina. However, in both countries citizens are highly divided regarding the trade-off between citizens' rights and public safety. Surveys conducted in Buenos Aires province in 1998 and 2000 show that, despite the fact that citizens tend to have a negative perception of the police, almost half are in favor of giving the police more powers to fight crime.[33]

Citizens who are from the lower class (49.3 percent) and Peronists (49.7 percent) are more likely to support increasing powers to the police. The middle and upper classes (56.9 percent) and the center-left (60 percent) are less likely to support increasing powers. This is consistent with other surveys that show that people from the lower class, with lower levels of education, and citizens who support the Peronists, have a better opinion of the police than people from the middle and upper classes, with higher levels of education, and who are center-left.[34]

In sum, this analysis shows the following: (a) there was an important legal recognition of citizens' rights in Argentina during the 1990s. However, there was an important reversal by the year 2000. Monitoring and lobbying activities by human rights organizations did not stop policymakers from increasing police powers; (b) available data allow us to infer increasing levels of police repression during the 1990s. This is correlated with growing rates of crime and an overall deterioration in the level of employment; (c) Public opinion in the province of Buenos Aires tends to exhibit mixed opinions of the police. On the one hand, citizens distrust the police but, on the other hand, nearly half are willing to give up certain rights to fight delinquency.

As will be demonstrated in the next section, human rights advocacy groups have played a key role in setting the agenda and influencing the political system to promote police reforms. These groups have constantly monitored police institutions and they have developed policy alternatives, becoming focal points for the civil rights coalition. However, these efforts have not translated into institutional change and the ultimate reduction of police violence. I argue that this is due to the actions of a well-coordinated pro-order coalition and its use of both legal and illegal methods to maintain the status quo.

EXPLAINING ADVOCACY GROUPS' FLUCTUATING INFLUENCE

When compared to Chile, certain socio-political features of the context and specific human rights groups' internal characteristics have given Argentine groups more opportunities to access the political system and to influence it. The balance of power among political parties, media pluralism, the structure of the police (particularly in the Province), and specific internal characteristics of human rights groups have created conditions conducive to action.

As human rights views gained recognition by policymakers, the pro-order coalition faced strong incentives to organize in order to maintain the status quo—to block reforms during the policy implementation stage. As a result, human rights groups and their allies have been able to influence problem definition and political debate, but they have been unable to influence the implementation of crucial reforms. This section explains, first, the structure of the coalitions and, second, the mechanisms by which specific contextual conditions restrict or allowed action, and the strategies both coalitions have used to achieve their objectives.

Coalitions' Composition

The pro-order coalition includes a cohesive alliance between police officers and certain sectors of the Peronist party involved in illegal activities in Buenos Aires province. It also includes policymakers—particularly in the Ministry of Interior—and members of Congress who support "tough" measures against crime. As legal reforms threaten their interests, they rely upon both legal and illegal strategies to maintain the status quo. Probably the most common legal strategy has been to delay the implementation of certain policies that attempted to break down the existing provincial structure of power. Moreover, this coalition has taken advantage of citizens' concerns about public safety, gaining their support in the 1999 electoral campaign. This has allowed the pro-order coalition to apply "tough" policies against crime and to dismantle police reforms approved in 1997.

The civil rights coalition includes human rights advocacy groups, some lawyers, member of Congress from the centrist UCR and leftist FREPASO, and policymakers from the Federal government, particularly from the Ministry of Justice and the Ministry of Foreign Affairs. Human rights advocacy groups have played a key role in the civil rights coalition.

The comparison between Argentina and Chile in terms of human rights organizations reveals a higher rate of survival of old groups and emergence of new groups in Argentina. First, in Argentina 80 percent of voluntary organizations that were active at the moment of the transition were still functioning by 2002 (Table 4.4). In Chile, only 50 percent of the organizations that were active at the moment of the transition were functioning by 2002. Second, in Argentina 8 new human rights groups

Table 4.4 Argentina: Human rights Organizations 1983–2001

Organization	Type of Org. 1983	Type of Org. 2001
Relatives		
Abuelas de Plaza de Mayo	Vol.	Vol.
Asociación Madres de Plaza de Mayo	Vol.	Vol.
Familiares de Desaparecidos y Detenidos por razones políticas	Vol.	Vol.
Hijos (1995)	—	Vol.
Other Organizations		
Asamblea Permanente de Derechos Humanos (1975)	Vol.	Vol./Pol.
SERPAJ (1974)Vol.Vol./Prof.		
Asamblea Permanente de derechos humanos-La Plata (1979)	Vol.	Vol.
Liga Argentina por los derechos humanos	Vol.	—
Movimiento ecuménico por los derechos humanos	Vol.	—
Memoria Abierta (1999)	—	Vol.
Memoria Activa (1994)	—	Vol.
Movimiento Social Teresa Rodríguez (1997)		Vol.
Voluntary organizations concerning police violence		
CORREPI (1992)	—	Vol.
COFAVI (1992)	—	Vol./Pol.
Professional/Academic		
CELS	Prof./Pol/Vol.	Pol/Prof.
Centro de profesionales por los derechos humanos (1997)	—	Pol/Prof.
Equipo Argentino de Antropología Forense (1984)	—	Prof.
International Organizations Based on Argentina		
CEJIL—Argentina	—	Pol./Prof.
Amnesty International	Vol.	Vol.

Source: Personal Interviews in Argentina and web search.
Vol.= Voluntary
Prof. = Professional
Pol.=Political.[35]

emerged after the transition. In Chile only 2 organizations of human rights emerged after the transition.

In Argentina, there are both "historic" and "new" organizations.[36] Historic organizations were created during the military regime and were active on a local and international level. These organizations include *Madres de Plaza de Mayo* [Mothers of Plaza de Mayo], *Abuelas de Plaza de Mayo* [Grandmothers of Plaza de Mayo], and the Center for Legal and Social Studies (CELS), among other organizations. The new organizations were created after the transition to democracy and include groups that are concerned about the legacy of the military regime such as *Hijos* [victims' children] and groups that are focused on current abuses such as the Coordination against Institutional Repression (CORREPI). As will be observed below, CELS and CORREPI have played key roles in setting the agenda and influencing the political debate regarding police reform inBuenos Aires Province in the 1990s.

Political Opportunity Structure

Argentina's political context offers more opportunities for the civil rights coalition to influence the political system than in Chile. However, greater openness does not necessarily translate into more favorable outcomes. This section explains how the mode of the transition, access to the political system, and police corporateness have affected both coalitions.

Argentina's transition to democracy was characterized by the collapse of the military regime after Argentina's defeat in the Malvinas war against Great Britain. This was followed by a rapid process of democratization with high levels of social mobilization that ended with the election of the centrist president Raúl Alfonsín in 1983 (Karl and Schmitter 1991; Waisman 1999). While in Chile the transition to democracy implied a limited pact between the military regime and the opposition, in Argentina the armed forces and the police could not impose rules on the new authorities. The discrediting of the armed forces provided more opportunities for new civilian authorities to bring the military and the police under civilian control and to prosecute military officers involved in human rights abuses (Karl and Schmitter 1991; Skaar 1994).

One of the first steps of the democratic authorities was to reform the Code of Military Justice in 1984, transferring prosecutions of the military for regular crimes to civilian courts. Additionally, Argentina's military regime did not impose restrictions on future authorities' ability to either dismiss or promote police officers, as happened in Chile. Indeed, in Argentina the most common tool to control the police has been the dismissal of police officers involved in corruption scandals (Abregú, Palmieri and Tiscornia 1998). Moreover,

Argentina has also enacted some reforms regarding civilian oversight capabilities over police institutions such as the reform of the Code of the Military Justice in 1984, the establishment of an Undersecretary of Human Rights in 1987, the creation of a National Public Safety Council and a national ombudsman in 1994, and the establishment of a legislative commission to oversee police reforms in Buenos Aires province in 1998. However, often these new legal tools are poorly implemented (Abregú, Palmieri and Tiscornia 1998).

From a political point of view, civilian authorities of the new democratic regime faced more freedom to prosecute military and police officers involved in past human rights violations. While in Chile the issue of justice was left to the decision of the Supreme Court, in Argentina the first democratic government took some steps to prosecute nine generals as well as to indict another 400 officers between 1985 and 1987 (Skaar 1994). From the beginning of the transition in Chile, advocacy groups had to spend most of their resources trying to solve cases in courts, while in Argentina at least until 1987 advocacy groups used their resources to pressure the government in order to expand trials to lower-ranking officers. As the government opened a window of opportunity for the prosecution of military and police officers involved in human rights violations, advocacy groups promptly collected information regarding those responsible for such crimes, individualizing and making campaigns against those who continued in active service. This process helped some advocacy groups to frame human rights as a present-day problem and not as a "legacy" problem as occurred in Chile.

Concerning the access to the political system, the presence of a strong center-left coalition favorable to civil rights views should increase the opportunities for advocacy groups to influence the political system. This was the case in Argentina at the Capital level, where the city council [*Legislatura de la Ciudad*] enacted several measures to enhance citizens' rights in 1996–98, and at the provincial level, where the Buenos Aires provincial legislature passed important pro-civil rights legislation in 1997–98. In both cases, a strong coalition of center-left parties (UCR and FREPASO) approved legislation restricting police powers. As will be observed in the next section for the case of the Province, and in chapter four for the Capital, human rights advocacy groups played a key role in setting the agenda and influencing the political debate in both cases.

Moreover, internal divisions within the governing Peronist party during the 1990s also favored the civil rights coalition, particularly between 1997 and 1998. While the Ministry of Foreign Affairs and the Ministry of Justice adopted a pro-civil rights strategy, the Ministry of Interior and the Presidency generally supported pro-order points of view.[37]

Another facilitating condition for advocacy groups' influence is the presence of a relatively pluralist media in Argentina. Particularly after the military regime, Argentina's mass media developed a culture of investigative independent journalism. Media pluralism allows social groups to express their views and 'make the case' regarding the need to reform the police. Newspapers such as *Página 12* and *Clarín* and certain TV journalists have taken a critical stand on issues concerning police violence and corruption. Moreover, journalists have published many articles and even books extensively documenting cases of police brutality and corruption.[38] The fact that Horacio Verbitsky—a prestigious journalist of *Página 12*—is also part of the CELS board of directors has helped transmit pro-civil rights views to the public.[39] The threat that journalists pose to pro-order sectors is revealed by the murder of journalist José Luis Cabezas in 1997, who was investigating police corruption.

While the previous two factors—balance of power and media pluralism—have favored advocacy groups, the fact that governors at the provincial level and the President at the national level have veto powers have to some extent counter-balanced the impact of pro-civil rights views. This is true in most reforms that included restricting police powers.

Finally, regarding police corporateness, the main concern here is how the degree of corporateness affects the ability of pro-civil rights groups to influence the policymaking process. As was mentioned in chapter one, information regarding cases of corruption is controlled in more corporate institutions by top-ranking officers who want to protect the reputation of the institution and themselves. Relatively well-developed mechanisms of internal administration allow top-ranking officers to preempt eventual scandals by dismissing officers or by monitoring investigations. Moreover, strong mechanisms of internal socialization and the actual cost of losing membership keep officers from exposing the institution to external actors. This is the case in Chile (chapter two) and in Argentina's federal police (chapter five) where the police maintain high control over internal affairs.

Lower levels of corporateness imply poor levels of training and education, a lower sense of identity, and less effective internal administrative procedures. The BAPP is a good example of this. While in Chile, candidates must complete secondary education, in Argentina 64 percent of police officers have only completed primary education.[40] Poor training became evident in Buenos Aires province after civilian authorities decided to restructure the police in 1997: studies demonstrated serious problems such as inadequate health and physical conditions of police officers, absence of basic training with weapons, and lack of instruction regarding police legal procedures.[41]

Additionally, the absence of a strong sense of institutional identity means that top-ranking officers have less incentive to protect members than they would in a more corporate environment. If the position of the *comisarios* (chief of police stations) depends on who is ruling (mayor, governor, president), then this officer is more likely to respond to such political leaders rather than to the high command of the police. Indeed, *comisarios* of the BAPP many times respond to interests that do not necessarily follow the traditional chain of command. For instance, while internal rules state that police officers must rotate after one year in their position, some *comisarios* have maintained enough political connections in certain territories to keep their position for five or even seven years (Oliveira and Tiscornia 1998: 165). Thus, because police officers are linked to particularistic interests, a change in the balance of power in the political system may affect certain interests, creating rivalries and disputes among police officers that are exposed publicly.[42] This creates divisions between those who attempt to protect the institution from "bad apples" and those who prefer to maintain the status quo. If these disputes are made public, advocacy groups can take advantage of them and pressure the government to enact reforms.

This was the case of Governor Duhalde when he decided to dismiss approximately 300 top-ranking officers in 1997. This political decision generated an intense dispute within the police. A group of officers publicly criticized Duhalde, holding him responsible for the internal crisis in the police force. They argued that many of the fired officers had not been subject to judicial prosecution, hence, to due process. Moreover, they argued that several corrupt officers remained in service. This group demanded higher salaries, an investigation to determine illegal acts committed by those who were dismissed by the government, and the creation of a police union (Dutil and Ragendorfer 1997). Since these internal conflicts reached the public, advocacy groups and particularly CELS and political parties took advantage of the dispute to demand further reforms (CELS 1997; 1998).

Low degrees of corporateness also imply that top-ranking officers have less control over their subordinates. In corporate environments we should expect two situations: (a) if there is a case of corruption, it generally implies a chain of command that controls certain illegal actions, and (b) if an individual officer is involved in illegal behavior, the police should promptly react to 'clean' the public image of the institution. In less corporate environments we should expect to observe more cases of top and lower-ranking officers' illegal behavior—particularly corruption—given the lack of mechanisms of internal control, and weak institutional mechanisms to respond to external accusations. In contrast, as chapter two illustrates, in Chile the police had developed effective mechanisms of public relations to respond to external accusations—regardless of whether justice was achieved in those cases. In addition, the comparison between the federal police and the BAPP illustrates this point. As will be argued in chapter five, the federal police enjoy relatively higher levels of corporateness. Officers receive more training, internal administrative procedures are more developed, and there is a stronger sense of institutional identity than in the BAPP.

Appendix 3 considers a sample of cases of corruption denounced by the press between July 1998 and June 2001.[43] The data systematized shows two trends: first, higher levels of illegal activities committed by top and lower ranking officers in the BAPP; second, the federal police show a more pro-active role in defending police officers, announcing internal investigations, and responding to criticisms. The BAPP is more passive in this regard. In this case, activists, prosecutors, and journalists are those who denounce the BAPP, and in no case do the police take the initiative to criticize internal irregularities or to inform the public regarding internal investigations.

In an environment of low police corporateness, inexperienced and untrained officers on the streets and internal disputes that become a matter of public scrutiny are more likely, and lower internal control over subordinates' behavior. In this context, advocacy groups have more opportunities to obtain relevant information, making the case for police reform even more strongly. In fact, advocacy groups in Argentina recognize the institutional difficulties in setting the agenda for more substantial reforms of the federal police, given its more corporate nature.[44]

Coalitions in Action

As in Chile, the political opportunity structure in Argentina does not completely determine political outcomes. An important factor influencing the fluctuating trends of reforms and reversals in Argentina is related to the way the civil rights coalition and the pro-order coalition have dealt with the issues of police reforms and citizens' rights. The following paragraphs explain how strategies and issues of leadership and social networks have affected both coalitions.

In contrast to Chile, the civil rights coalition in Argentina has successfully influenced agenda setting and political debate, however it has been less influential in terms of policy implementation where the pro-order coalition is entrenched in key institutions. On the other hand, the pro-order coalition has taken advantage of certain junctures to resist changes by blocking policy implementation, and even reestablishing police powers.

Chapter two illustrated how Chilean politicians who are supportive of civil rights views chose to individually (and not collectively) respond to allegations of police violence, given the lack of an organized civil society demanding accountability over the police. In Chile, the most significant reform regarding the enhancement of citizens' rights was due to the existence of a network of lawyers who were committed to reforming the judicial system (see chapter three).

In contrast, in Argentina human rights groups became focal point for the civil rights coalition. Human rights advocacy groups have used six strategies to influence the policy process and gain allies within the political system. These strategies are: collecting information, establishing allies with policy "experts," organizing social mobilizations, searching for international allies, providing international institutions with information, and developing media campaigns.

An essential task for human rights—along with providing support to the victims of police violence—is to collect information regarding police abuses. An accurate and permanent compilation of cases of police brutality allows them to gain credibility domestically and abroad. In Argentina, CORREPI and CELS have considered this as a vital objective of their work. CORREPI was created in 1987 by a group lawyers and human rights activists to help victims of police violence in Argentina. They created a nationwide voluntary network of grassroots organizations to provide both legal and social support to victims of police violence. By 1997, this network included representatives of thirty-five organizations and approximately 700 activists.[45] CORREPI have systematized cases of police brutality since 1989 nationwide thanks to this network of grassroots organizations

The story of CELS is particularly telling. This center was created in 1978 as an advocacy and legal advice organization for the victims of human rights violations. By 1989–91, its faced a serious internal crisis regarding its objectives and goals in a democratic context. In 1991, one of the founders of CELS, Emilio Miñones, outlined the Center's main problems and challenges. He recognized the need to widen CELS' orientation, incorporating a new approach to human rights. Thus, under the lead of a new generation, in 1993 CELS initiated new programs including, along with the traditional work on the legacy, issues such as police violence, social and economic rights, freedom of expression, indigenous rights, immigration, and international law. [46]

For each topic, the center has organized teams of professionals who collect data on the subjects, build databases, and propose policy reforms. Regarding the case under scrutiny in this study, CELS created a database on cases of police violence reported by the press. CELS's annual reports include information on trends in police violence, qualitative analysis of police practices, and profiles of the victims. Moreover, after a set of legal reforms was passed in Congress in 1997, CELS monitored these legal changes, providing several policy suggestions in its annual reports. More recently, CELS has created an online monitoring system of police violence work that is sponsored by the Federal Direction of Criminal Policy and the Secretary of Justice and Security of the City of Buenos Aires.

By documenting cases of police violence and monitoring police practices, CELS has contributed to agenda setting for police reform in Argentina. By 1996, pro-reformist politicians, policymakers, and journalists were using this data to justify the need for urgent reforms.[47] Moreover, CELS has had some success in monitoring public authorities. For instance, in 1994 a CELS report on police violence was quoted by the annual report on human rights published by the U.S. Department of State. This allowed politicians and human rights activists to join forces and pressure for a change in government policies. As a result of this pressure, the Buenos Aires Province Secretary of Public Safety, Eduardo Pettigiani, resigned (CELS and Facultad 1994: 21). In 1996, CELS filed a lawsuit requesting police information on detentions and civilian and police deaths, opening a debate regarding public transparency and accountability.[48] In 1995 CELS, along with other organizations, successfully pressured the government to dismiss Buenos Aires Province Secretary of Public Safety Alberto Patti, who had been involved in human rights violations during the military regime.[49] Finally, given CELS's allegations, in 2000 authorities from the Federal Council for the Protection of Children requested CELS's help in designing a new policy to prevent torture against children by the police.[50]

Other strategy refers to the establishment of links between activists and policy experts. In 1986, Alfonsín's government supported the proposal of the influential lawyer Julio Maier that sought a major reform of federal penal code procedures. Two years later, a network of penal lawyers—led by Maier and other Latin American lawyers—established in Brazil the Iberoamerican Institute of Penal Law, developing a "Model Penal Code for Latin America." Soon, several countries in Latin America began to follow this model, transforming the traditional inquisitorial system.[51] These pro-civil rights lawyers—including Julio Maier, Raúl Zaffaroni, León Arslanián, and Alberto Binder—occupied important government positions and provided policy proposals to transform either the judicial system or police institutions. These lawyers maintained close contacts with human rights organizations and pro-civil rights political parties.[52] CELS have particularly incorporated pro-civil rights experts in their activities through the organization of seminars and academic events to reach political and social actors regarding police institutional reforms.

Additionally, social mobilizations are also considered as relevant strategies for agenda setting and monitoring authorities. CORREPI is probably one of the most effective grassroots social organizations denouncing police violence in Argentina. The death of seventeen-year-old Walter Bulacio on April 19, 1991, constituted a landmark case for human rights activists.[53] Every April 19th, CORREPI along with several other social organizations organizes a social protest in Buenos Aires demanding justice and the end of police violence in Argentina. Thousands of people representing a wide range of social organizations have marched in the streets of Buenos Aires demanding justice and police reform. In addition, CORREPI generally organizes protests after some particularly shocking act of police violence has occurred. Most demonstrations are reported by the press, thanks again to the personal contacts between CORREPI's leaders and journalists.

Another strategy frequently used by Argentine human rights groups is to search for allies abroad. CORREPI, for example, has managed to put information online through the establishment of an alliance with a Spanish human rights network, and it has implemented an e-mail listserv to inform about activities and to promote campaigns.[54] CELS has established an extensive network of international alliances to pressure the government from abroad.[55] For instance, CELS co-published a document on police violence with Americas Watch in 1991. By the mid-1990s, CELS had established a key alliance with CEJIL (Center for Justice and International Law) based in Washington, D.C., to co-sponsor lawsuits before the Inter-American Court of Justice. The Center has also prepared an alternative report for the U.N. Commission of Human Rights (CELS 2001). Finally, CELS has constantly provided information to embassies and international organizations (U.N. Commission on Human Rights, Amnesty International) to maintain pressure on public authorities.

Finally, both CORREPI and CELS have developed a communicational strategy to widen their impact. CORREPI's activities are frequently reported in the press thanks to a well-established relationship between these lawyers and some journalists.[56] CELS's communicational strategy to influence the policy process has become more sophisticated since the mid-1990s. First, they hired a professional journalist who understands newspapers' needs for information, anticipating public debates by providing relevant information before or during the discussion of a policy initiative. This expertise has allowed CELS to become a focal point for policymakers and local and international actors.

In terms of leadership, both CORREPI and CELS have been led by relatively young professionals (lawyers) highly committed to human rights and who have had the ability to keep these organizations alive. Contrary to other human rights organizations in Latin America, CORREPI evolved as a grassroots network without having a bureaucratic structure. CORREPI's horizontal organization has allowed it to reach lower-class sectors particularly in the Buenos Aires metropolitan area. CORREPI's leaders—a group of lawyers and representatives of social organizations—have been willing to share their experiences and activities with other grassroots organizations, creating a dynamic web of relationships nationwide. As of 2001, CORREPI was not interested in receiving funding from international donors because of its anti-capitalist ideology.

A turning point for CELS was when the directors re-shaped the institution's principal orientation in 1993–94, attracting a new generation of researchers, widening the scope of interests, and developing important grant-seeking skills. By 2002, CELS received financial support from 13 agencies and had an annual budget of approximately $ 840,000. The old generation of directors allowed a new generation of professionals to expand CELS's work toward a wider concept of human rights.

Another sign of leadership in these two organizations is the way they have overcome ideological differences. While CORREPI rejects a dialogue with public authorities, CELS attempts to influence the policy process. However, this difference has not inhibited the two organizations from sharing experiences and information, and helping each other at critical junctures. One example is their collaboration to bring Walter Bulacio's case before the Inter-American Court of Justice. While CORREPI documented the case, CELS has provided its international expertise and international links to pressure the Argentine government to solve this case.[57]

Influencing Policy Reforms

The reform of the BAPP is an example of an initial well-coordinated effort by the civil rights coalition to influence the policy process and enact several reforms restricting police powers. As was stated, by 1995 several human rights organizations had documented extensive violations of human rights committed by the BAPP (Americas Watch and CELS 1991; CELS and Facultad 1994–1995; CELS 1996). Press reports documented practices of "easy trigger," corruption, and clandestine businesses controlled by police officers.[58] On December 19, 1996, the Governor of the Province, Eduardo Duhalde, declared the provincial police to be in a "state of emergency" to allow him to reform the structure of the police, reassign material and human resources, and dismiss officers involved in crimes and illegal activities.

Social pressure increased after the assassination of José Luis Cabezas in January 1997. Cabezas was a photographer who was investigating the links between the police and a specific businessman in Buenos Aires province (Sdrech 1997). Lawyers, specialists on police issues from different parties, deputies of the national and provincial Congress, and human rights groups developed a set of proposals to reform the police.[59] The *Alianza* coalition between FREPASO and the UCR incorporated these demands within their electoral platforms, making police reform a crucial issue during the 1997 provincial legislative electoral campaign. In April 1997, CELS organized a seminar on democratic control over the police, inviting key political actors, representatives of police institutions, and human rights organizations. In this event, representatives of FREPASO, UCR and the Peronist party discussed several proposals to reform the police.[60]

Anti-reform sectors were also active, however. They are dominated by high and lower-ranking officers of the police, provincial government officials, the heads of several *intendencias* (districts) within the province, and 'brokers' within the Peronist party who controlled a network of illegal businesses including drugs, prostitution, traffic of stolen cars, and gambling (Dutil and Ragendorfer 1997).[61] As the potential changes threatened their profits and interests, they managed to postpone Duhalde's reforms until after the October elections (Saín 2001), but the electoral triumph of the *Alianza* at the provincial level made it more difficult for Duhalde to delay these changes any longer. In December 1997 Duhalde promulgated a new decree, taking over the provincial police (Decree 4508/97), and appointing Peronist lawyer León Arslanián as Minister of Justice and Security. Arslanián had previously participated in the reform of the penal code at the federal level, and now executed important changes such as the dismissal of more than 1,200 officers involved in illegal practices, the decentralization of the police command structure, the appointment of civilians to key high-ranking positions within the police, the creation of citizen review boards to monitor police practices, and the creation of internal mechanisms to control police practices. The center-left *Alianza,* human rights organizations, as well as professional organizations supported these initiatives, and by July 1998, three major bills related to the changes were approved in the provincial legislature.

The provincial government also created the Institute of Criminal Policy and Public Safety. This was a multiparty initiative in which representatives of the three major political parties (Peronist, UCR, and FREPASO) and human rights organizations—particularly CELS—were represented.

This Institute was conceived as a center to produce empirical studies and policy initiatives to support the governor's reforms.

Resisting Change, Reversing Policies

The reform discussed above was strongly resisted by a cohesive alliance between some sectors of the police, political brokers in several districts, some *intendentes* [the equivalent to mayors], and important representatives of the Peronist party. They used illegal, institutional, and electoral strategies to block and reverse some of the policies the government was seeking to implement. The following paragraphs explain the mechanisms used by these actors to maintain the status quo.

Soon after the government announced the transformation of the police, the press reported threats by "anonymous sources" toward those who were promoting police reforms. In December 1997—one week after the governor's announcement of a second intervention—a group of officers organized in the so-called Police Movement (MOPOL) held a meeting to study measures of pressure against the government. They threatened to produce chaos in the public safety system by not reacting to judicial or citizens' requests. As a representative of MOPOL stated: "the best strategy is to do nothing and, if there are problems, this will increase insecurity, and therefore they [the government] will feel more pressure to stop reforms."[62] In March 1998, a police officer who was investigating police agencies received telephone threats.[63] The same month, two legislators who were working on the legislation to reform the police received new threats from 'the big family of the Buenos Aires police.'[64]

Another way to resist the reform was by not implementing policies already approved. *Intendentes* who had a close relationship with anti-reform officers resisted the implementation of certain policies. Moreover, *intendentes* lobbied the governor to maintain in place certain chiefs of police stations whose positions were threatened. For instance, former policymakers who worked during the reform period recognize that they received hundreds of calls from *intendentes* and judges requesting they not dismiss certain police officers.[65] Moreover, they manipulated certain appointments. For instance, a press note suggests that the police and *intendentes* were manipulating the election of the representatives of civil society into a Citizens' Board of Safety in charge of monitoring policy implementation.[66]

But probably the most effective way to undermine the reform was not the use of illegal methods but the promotion of an 'iron fist' electoral discourse during the 1999 gubernatorial electoral campaign. Until July 1999, Peronist governor Eduardo Duhalde and his pro-active Secretary of Justice

Arslanián strongly supported the need to reform the police. However, candidate Carlos Ruckauf—a Peronist as well—was one of the most important representatives of the pro-order coalition. Ruckauf was leading the public opinion polls and, on August 3, 1999, he re-framed the electoral debate by suggesting that: "I will not have compassion with delinquents. We need to shoot delinquents; we need to fight them without contemplation."[67] Two days later he insisted on the point, arguing that "we need to shoot in the heads those who commit crimes. I want to see these assassins killed."[68] Within a few days, Ruckauf outlined his programmatic goals by suggesting the need to approve tougher rules against delinquency, to appoint police officers in top-ranking positions related to public safety, to keep criminals in jail, and to increase the number of police officers in the streets.[69]

The evident inconsistency between Arslanián's program and Ruckauf's proposals created a serious division within the Peronist party. Arslanián resigned one day after Ruckauf's declarations, arguing that he was not willing to change his plan and that a political conflict within the party would not help the country.[70] In the following two months, governor Duhalde chose to reverse some of the ongoing changes, given the increasing public support for Ruckauf's tough proposals. For instance, Duhalde reincorporated 1,000 officers previously dismissed for violent or corrupt behavior.[71] Additionally, Duhalde appointed several *comisarios* who had links with corrupt police officers.[72]

But the main changes came after Ruckauf won the election in October 1999. His first decision was to appoint former military officer, Aldo Rico, as Secretary of Security. In the 1980s, Rico had led a military uprising against the democratic government and he had a clear hard line approach to delinquency.[73] Moreover, Ruckauf re-incorporated most of the officers dismissed by the previous administration and appointed police officers in key positions that had been previously occupied by civilians. Additionally, Ruckauf sent two bills to the legislature to re-centralize the police, increase police powers, and allow officers to detain suspects on the streets. These reforms were approved by the legislature in February 2000, albeit after long negotiations between the governing party and the *Alianza*, given its majority in the legislature. Additionally, the government unsuccessfully attempted to restrict television's live transmission of robberies in the city.

The civil rights coalition attempted to stop some of these changes. In the legislature, the *Alianza* approved some of the government's proposals such as reducing the ability of prisoners to be released before the end of their sentences, and allowing the police to interrogate suspects at the moment of their arrest. Given the *Alianza*'s distrust toward police procedures, however, it rejected one proposal to create a photo database of suspects, and another to allow police interrogation of detainees to be used as evidence during a trial.[74] Given the *Alianza*'s majority in the legislature, Ruckauf agreed to the conditions. However, two weeks later Ruckauf unilaterally broke the agreement, promulgating a decree that allowed police interrogation to be used as evidence during a trial.[75]

Human rights advocacy networks also attempted to reduce the impact of these counter-reforms. CELS tried to demonstrate through the press that shooting delinquents was a common practice in Buenos Aires province before Ruckauf, but that this method had not produced good results.[76] The Leftist FREPASO and some human rights organizations publicly accused Ruckauf's Secretary of Public Safety of past corruption which forced Ruckauf to ask his Secretary to resign twenty-five days after he was appointed.[77]

Despite all these efforts, the new government was able to impose several pro-order reforms, including the centralization of the police high command and the approval of rules increasing police powers. The new Chief of Police, Amadeo D'Angelo, summarized the new orientation in a few words: "we will close down shantytowns so that delinquents will not get out. If they leave, we will arrest them."[78]

SUMMARY

In sum, while advocacy networks have become focal points for the coordinated actions of those who promote civil rights in Argentina, as of 2001 they have failed to shape police practices. Police officers have continued to use repressive tactics such as "easy trigger" to deal with social protests, crime, and delinquency. These strategies have been supported by a pro-order coalition that has used illegal, legal, and electoral methods to maintain the status quo.

In Argentina, while a well-placed network has been an important factor in blocking reform attempts by the provincial government, it was not the only factor. More important was the electoral triumph of a governor who was a promoter of the pro-order approach, which allowed for a reversal of an ongoing process of reform. Thus, a favorable political opportunity, effective strategies, and constant local and international monitoring have not led to a change in legal rights or police practices. What matters in this case is the comparative analysis of the two coalitions in competition and how they have been able, on the one hand, to frame a problem, gaining the support of a critical mass of people who were willing to protect citizens' rights from police abuses (in the mid 1990s) and, on the other hand, to give up rights in exchange for increasing police powers (after 1999).

Chapter Five

Dealing with a Corporate Police Force in Argentina

In Argentina, contextual conditions—the nature of the transition, access to the political system, and levels of police corporateness—have created more opportunities than in Chile for the civil rights coalition to influence the political system. Moreover, early decisions made by advocacy groups' leaders allowed them to frame human rights as an ongoing problem. This partly explains why advocacy groups became relevant during the 1990s and why policymakers initiated important reforms at the provincial level in Buenos Aires.

However, a skeptical reader may argue that higher levels of advocacy groups' influence in Argentina can be explained by higher levels of police violence in Buenos Aires. In other words, as police violence became a relevant topic, advocacy groups increased monitoring activities, which in turn activated the consolidation of a cohesive civil rights coalition that demanded policy reforms. In contrast, the Chilean case may suggest that the lower levels of police violence made policymakers and NGOs less concerned about the subject. Following this argument, police violence produces grievances, which in turn lead to social protests by organized sectors of society. Given protest, politicians may become more receptive to initiating reforms.

In chapter two, I argue that police violence in Chile is higher than it has been generally recognized, and therefore in Chile grievances are not in fact leading to increased social organization and policy change. However, a skeptical reader may still argue that levels of police violence are significantly greater in Buenos Aires Province than in Chile.

In order to respond to this issue and to control for some variables such as access to the political system, the nature of the transition, and internal characteristics of human rights groups, this chapter introduces the case of Argentine advocacy groups monitoring the Federal Police in the Federal District of Buenos Aires (generally called the "Capital Federal" or "Capital"), the Argentine equivalent of Washington D.C. If we accept that politicians will be more receptive to initiating reform when faced with high levels of police violence and social pressures, we should expect advocacy networks to be relatively successful in influencing policy change in the Capital because levels of police violence are relatively high, advocacy groups are well-organized, and crucial political conditions have favored the civil rights coalition.

However, the analysis of this case demonstrates that despite the previous favorable conditions, advocacy groups have faced enormous obstacles in trying to transform the Federal Police. I argue that this is due to the combination of facing a highly corporate police institution and the way the pro-order coalition has responded to attempts of reform.

BUENOS AIRES CAPITAL: POLICE LEGAL POWERS AND PRACTICES

The Capital has 3 million inhabitants and it is the only area of the country in which the local government of the city has no control over the police force in its territory.[1] The Federal Police patrol the city but is under the direct supervision of the national (federal) government.

The Federal Police is a militarized institution with 48,000 officers, 10,000 of whom work in the Capital. The Federal Police have a hierarchical structure with low levels of transparency regarding internal mechanisms of accountability (Oliveira and Tiscornia 1998). According to Network International, a U.S. based company specializing in police reforms, Argentina's Federal Police "is a professional force, well-trained and commanded." The main problems they note are that the Federal Police have focused on maintaining social order rather than fighting crime (Comisión de Seguridad Interior 1998: 18). This means, for instance, that the police are more prepared to deal with social protests rather than to conduct regular patrols to prevent crime in the city.

The Federal Police have historically had two legal mechanisms to detain individuals: the "verification of identity detention" clause and police edicts [*edictos*] (Table 5.1).

The "verification of identity detention" clause was established in Argentina in the 1868 and 1888 penal codes. Later on, de facto regimes (1944, 1958, and 1980) institutionalized this rule, which allows the police to arrest individuals without judicial order to authenticate their identity and records. As of 1991, the police could detain individuals who did not carry

Table 5.1 Argentina: Federal Police Powers and Their Reform

	Verification of Identity Detention	Police Edicts
Legal background (Blando 1995)	1868 Penal Code 1888 Penal Code 1944 Decree 33,265 1958 Federal Police Organic law 1980 Decree 9551	1944 Decree 33,265 1947 law 13,030 1956 law 17.186 1958 Federal Police Organic law 1958 Law 14,467
Definition	Police power to detain individuals without ID or people who are engaged in "suspicious" activities or behavior	Police power to detain individuals who commit minor offenses and behavior such as prostitution, begging, loafing, public distrubance.
Police power	Detainees could be held 24 hours under police custody	The police evaluate the evidence, formulate accusations, and decide charges
Reform	1991 Restriction of Verification of Records Detention to 10 hours	1998 Restriction of Police Edicts

their IDs for up to 24 hours. Estimates indicate that on average, 40,000 people are detained in Buenos Aires using this clause every year (Garrido, Guariglia, and Palmieri 1997; Martínez, Palmieri, and Pita 1998).

Police edicts are legal devices to prevent disturbance of public order, including more than fifty misbehaviors such as "scandals," "begging," "gambling," "use of forbidden weapons," "carnivals," "disturbance of public order," "drinking on the streets," "prostitution," and "loafing." Until 1998, the Federal Police could detain individuals, collect evidence regarding the detention, and dictate sentences on these cases. In essence, the Federal Police adopted judicial powers without guaranteeing minimal conditions of due process. For example, individuals did not have a right to a lawyer, and they only had 24 hours to appeal a sentence. The Federal Supreme Court had declared that these police procedures were not unconstitutional because the judiciary should exert control over police decisions through the appeals process. However, a minimal fraction of police sentences were actually appealed due to the short time period in which to appeal the sentence, the absence of a legal advisor, and extensive bureaucratic procedures.[2]

In terms of police practices, Buenos Aires province seems to show a worse record than the Capital in the absolute number of both civilian and police deaths in confrontations (Table 5.2).

However, on per capita basis, the record is quite similar. Each year between 1993 and 2000, one in every 100,000 people died in a confrontation with the police in the Capital, while one in every 97,000 people died in the province. Moreover, in both the Capital and the province the proportion of officer deaths in relation to the total force are similar (1 every 1,200). This means that civilians and police officers are equally likely to be shot in the Capital and in the province.

From another point of view, while in the Province the number of civilian deaths in confrontations with the police represents 11 percent of the total homicides, in the Capital it represents 30 percent for the period 1994–1999. Thus, even though the Capital shows a lower record of homicides and of the absolute number of civilians who died in confrontations with the police than in the province, these civilian deaths were comparatively more significant in the Capital than in the province.[3]

Regarding police corruption, several sources have charged institutional involvement of the Federal Police in corruption including prostitution, illegal gambling, and trafficking of stolen cars (Oliveira and Tiscornia

Table 5.2 Argentina: Civilian and Police Death in Buenos Aires Province and Capital

Year	Buenos Aires Capital Federal Police		Buenos Aires Provice Povincial Police	
	Civil	Police	Civilian	Police
1993	48	7	123	23
1994	30	6	94	9
1995	42	1	123	29
1996	52	10	113	44
1997	32	6	122	39
1998	59	9	113	42
1999	71	10	202	66
2000	61	13	183	64
Total	395	62	1073	316
Average per year	49	8	134	40

Source: CELS and Facultad (1994–95) CELS (1996–97, 1998b, 1999–2001)

1997; 1998). The maintenance of a network of illegal businesses has been explained by the weakness of other state agencies to control police corruption, the involvement of political actors in this network, the profitability of these illegal activities, and the specific internal structure of the Federal Police (Oliveira and Tiscornia 1998; see also Abregú, Palmieri and Tiscornia 1998). Moreover, by 1999, the main political parties in Argentina agreed that "the Federal Police are conducted independently from civilian rule and there is no external control over police corruption."[4]

Despite the evidence of police corruption at the federal level, a comparison between what the media report on the federal and provincial police shows that there are substantially fewer cases reported involving the Federal Police (Appendix 3). These cases in which the provincial police are involved tend to include mostly but not exclusively lower-ranking officers. In contrast, the press reports only few cases lower-ranking officers of the Federal Police involved in illegal activities and, when the press has reported some case, it generally considers a network of lower and top-ranking officers. Moreover, the Federal Police have a more efficient public relations system that promptly responds to allegations of police abuse and corruption.

The public images of the federal and provincial police are not substantially different. Surveys conducted between 1990 and 1993 suggest that more than 60 percent of respondents have a regular or negative image of both police institutions. Moreover, changes in citizens' perception tend to go together in both cases (see Table 4.2, chapter four).

In 1996, and in a context of greater exposure of the police to criticism, 50 percent of the respondents in Buenos Aires Capital had a negative perception of the Federal Police and only 18 percent of the population had a positive perception.[5] Nevertheless, when citizens are asked about ranking levels of safety in their location, while 70 percent of respondents in Buenos Aires Province considered that public safety was "bad" or "very bad," only 39 percent of those in Buenos Aires Capital did so. Additionally, while 27 percent of respondents of the province fear the police, only 8 percent of respondents in the Capital do so. Paradoxically, citizens are more willing to give the police more legal powers in the province (44 percent) than in the Capital (32 percent).[6]

By the end of the 1990s, the Buenos Aires Capital and province observed increasing levels of insecurity due to raising levels of crime and increasing allegations of police corruption. In this context, when citizens were asked to evaluate the police, the majority of respondents in both areas thought that they were not doing a good job (see Table 4.3, chapter four), individuals in the province being more critical than in the Capital. The image of both police institutions was particularly negative in 1998. Indeed, 1998 was a critical juncture in both areas due to three factors: the increasing exposure of police cases of corruption—particularly in the province, the discussion of legal initiatives to reform the police, and the existence of a pro-active civil rights coalition pushing for reforms in both areas.

EXPLAINING THE INSTITUTIONAL STATUS QUO AND LEGAL CHANGES CONCERNING DETENTIONS

Even though the Federal Police observe a record of violence similar to that of the BAPP, few attempts have been made to transform this institution along the lines of what was attempted with the BAPP. As was mentioned, in the province civilian authorities attempted to intervene the police between 1997 and 1999, dismissing thousand of officers, and re-structuring the internal organization of the police. In the case of the Federal Police, the first democratic government (1984–1989) did not attempt to transform the institutional structure of the police mainly because it focused on the relationship with the armed forces and past human rights violations, and it needed the police to control increasing levels of social protests during the 1980s (Lauzán 2000).

The second democratic government (1989–1999) did not attempt to reform the structure of the police either. The only changes that decade were prompted by partially successful congressional attempts to restrict police powers regarding detention rights. In both cases, federal authorities responded by attempting to restrict the impact of such reforms. Thus, even in cases in which advocacy groups have achieved some success, federal (national) authorities have managed to partially reverse such transformations. The following section suggests that the lack of major reforms is due to the corporate nature of the Federal Police, and the use of veto powers by key political actors supportive of law & order views at the federal level.

Federal Police and External Influences

Two institutional characteristics of the Federal Police have made it more difficult for advocacy groups to influence policy outcomes: the top-down control the Federal Police has over the behavior of police officers, and the public relations system of the Federal Police that preempts criticisms by re-framing controversial issues related to public safety.

Regarding top-down controls, Argentina's Federal Police has a militarized and hierarchical organization in which top-ranking officers maintain tight internal control over lower-ranking officers. This system does not allow lower-ranking officers to denounce illegal acts committed by their superiors. It allows superiors to control potential internal dissidents (Abregú, Palmieri and Tiscornia 1998). In 1998, the Federal Police organized an internal system of accountability by which high-level officials of a given police station is in charge of controlling "even the private life of lower-ranking officers."[7] According to the Head of the Police, most cases of corruption are solved by chiefs of police stations. However, if a given case achieves public impact, the Department of Internal Affairs intervenes to determine legal or administrative responsibilities (Comisión de Seguridad Interior 1998).

In 1996, when the police were exposed to several cases of corruption, the high command decided to increase the oversight powers of the Department of Internal Affairs (Comisión de Seguridad Interior, 1998). Moreover, the Federal Police have punished some of its officers in cases of corruption by applying administrative sanctions. Between 1995 and 1997, 1,356 officers were dismissed for minor offenses, administrative transgressions, and clerical errors, all involving corruption (Comisión de Seguridad Interior, 1998).

High degrees of police corporateness may reduce police corruption and police violence given the existence of internal top-down controls over police officers. However, if top-ranking officers are involved in cases of corruption, or if they support tough measures against delinquents, two patterns are likely to emerge: first, the high command is likely to protect officers from judicial investigations. For example, in several cases against the police, the Federal Police have assisted officers with their legal defense, have not provided evidence requested by judicial authorities, and have threatened victims of police violence to stop officers' prosecution.[8]

A second pattern is the involvement of the chain of command in cases of corruption. In this regard, in March 1999 the press reported the existence of a network of Federal Police officers in 12 of the 52 police stations of the Capital who were illegally charging for the protection of citizens' small businesses as well as controlling prostitution in the Capital.[9] The police officer who denounced this illegal network received death threats and was the victim of three failed attacks against his life.[10] In 2000, the press released an internal document of the Federal Police in which the head of the police recognized having used its intelligence service to spy on political parties. According to the police, internal norms allowed security forces to interfere in domestic affairs, despite the fact that the Constitution and the Interior Safety Law explicitly forbid such intelligence operations.[11] Finally, in 2001, a federal court reported the involvement of top and lower-ranking officers in the adulteration of evidence in more than fifty-five criminal cases.

A second institutional element is the existence of a pro-active police public relations system that responds to criticisms by re-framing the debate on public safety at crucial junctures. A comparison between the Federal Police and the BAPP show that the Federal Police is more likely to constantly respond to external criticisms by stating that "internal investigations" have been executed, even though these mechanisms are not transparent and civilian authorities have no control over such investigations (see Appendix 3 and Abregú, Palmieri, and Tiscornia 1998).

As regard re-framing, at crucial junctures such as the approval of a reform restricting police powers, the Federal Police have alerted the public to increasing levels of delinquency and of the potential damage a restriction on police powers may have on public safety. In some cases, the Federal Police have emphasized the number of officers who have died maintaining public order.[12]

In this sense, the Federal Police have used their institutional resources to maintain the status quo to protect their officers. According to human rights groups, it has been more difficult to reform the Federal Police than the provincial police precisely because the Federal Police spends institutional resources in lobbying policymakers and the public on the need to preserve the status quo, and because they protect their officers from public exposure and control the flow of information regarding police affairs.[13]

Coalitions in Action

If the degree of institutional organization to respond to external pressures is one component in reducing the ability of outsiders to reform the police, the existence of a cohesive pro-order coalition is a second. The following paragraphs analyze two instances in which social groups have pressured to restrict police powers. In both cases, a pro-active pro-order coalition has managed to partially reverse such reforms.

Verification of Identity Detention Clause. As was stated earlier, until 1991 the Federal Police had the power to hold for 24 hours individuals who failed to authenticate their identity in custody. Since the reestablishment of democracy, advocacy groups have claimed that this legal tool has allowed the police to indiscriminately detain innocents (Americas Watch and CELS 1991; CELS 1997). Moreover, advocacy groups claimed that this norm was unconstitutional because—as in Chile—the Constitution does not require individuals to carry their IDs. In 1989, a group of pro-civil rights deputies led by Simón Lázara[14] proposed the elimination of this detention practice. One year later, another group of deputies led by Lorenzo Cortese proposed to restrict the detention to 4 hours.[15]

During the congressional debate, the executive and the Federal Police argued that this clause was an essential tool to cope with delinquents, and that reducing the time framework from 24 hours to 10 or even 4 hours would seriously undermine their work. After listening to representatives of the government and the Federal Police, in August 1990 the Commission for Penal Legislation approved the restriction of police powers to detain individuals without an ID to 10 hours.

As the Congress was debating this bill, a serious incident sped up the approval of the reform. On April 19, 1991, seventeen-year old Walter Bulacio was arrested along with 62 other teenagers outside of a Buenos Aires stadium after being caught by the Federal Police trying to enter a rock concert. Twelve hours later, Bulacio was transferred to a hospital with serious bruises in his head, face, and body, where he died eight days later. According to other detainees, the police brutally beat Bulacio and did not provide water, food, or access to bathroom facilities to the detainees. Moreover, the police contacted neither the teenagers' parents nor a juvenile judge.

Political and social actors particularly criticized the police procedure in this case because the penal code explicitly specifies that officers must report when minors are arrested to both to their parents and to a juvenile judge. Moreover, during the criminal investigation judicial authorities found out about the existence of an institutional and secret instruction (Memorandum 40) by which the high-command of the Federal Police instructed chiefs of police stations to use "their discretion on whether to contact the juvenile judge when a police officer arrests individuals under 18 years old." This formal written internal instruction explicitly violated the federal penal code.[16]

Human rights groups strongly reacted against the police, demanding justice and the derogation of the "verification of identity detention" clause. CORREPI's lawyers assumed the defense for Bulacio's relatives, calling for several public mobilizations in the Capital.[17] In Congress, several deputies requested that the debate on a reform bill be accelerated.[18] On May 29, 1991, one month after Bulacio's death, Congress approved the bill restricting police powers (Law 23,950), allowing the Federal Police to arrest individuals only when officers have clear evidence that an individual has committed or is willing to commit a crime and when individuals cannot authenticate their identity. Citizens in custody have the right to call a relative or their attorney and the right not to be held in prison with convicted detainees. The police can hold them in the police station up to 10 hours.

The Federal Police and the federal executive did not like the bill. One month later, President Menem vetoed this congressional initiative with the Presidential Decree number 1,203/91, justifying his position with the same arguments that the police had used before Congress: (a) that the Federal Police would not have enough time to verify citizens' identity, (b) that the lack of human resources would make it impossible for the Federal Police to implement the reform, and (c) that provincial police forces continued to have the power to detain individuals for up to 24 hours. On July 3, 1991, the Chamber of Deputies overwhelmingly rejected the presidential veto, 144 against 4 votes. One month later, on August 14, 1991 the Senate also rejected the presidential veto in a unanimous vote.

But an analysis of the implementation shows that the Federal Police have not put into practice several aspects of the new legislation. In general the Federal Police respect the ten-hour time restriction for citizens held in custody. However, the police have continued arresting individuals on a discretionary basis. For example, police testimonies reveal that officers have usually practiced massive detentions to demonstrate that they are in control of public order in some conflictive neighborhoods. Moreover, in several instances officers have arrested and interrogated citizens who actually have their IDs (Garrido, Guariglia, and Palmieri 1997; CELS and Facultad 1995; CELS 1997). From a random sample of 2,156 detentions in 1995, one study found that only 7 cases individuals had a pending judicial order for their arrest (Martínez, Palmieri, and Pita 1998).

Police Edicts of the Buenos Aires Capital. While the "Verification of Identity Detention" clause allows the police to arrest suspects, police edicts permit the police to arrest and prosecute individuals who commit a wide range of minor offenses. Between 1992 and 1996 more than 500,000 people were detained in Buenos Aires under these edicts; generally they were related to drinking on the streets and social disturbance (CELS and Human Rights Watch 1998).

After the death of Walter Bulacio in 1991, every year thousands of people have marched in the streets of Buenos Aires demanding justice and the elimination of Federal Police edicts.[19] As part of the human rights groups' strategies, CELS has conducted specific empirical as well as legal research into the effects of these edicts (CELS 1996; Tiscornia 1998). The increasing levels of police arrests during the 1990s[20] and several cases of police brutality against teenagers brought human rights organizations, lawyers, and civil rights associations together to campaign against these edicts.

The year 1996 opened a "window" favorable to civil rights activists, because the City of Buenos Aires (the Federal Capital) achieved political autonomy from the national government. Most representatives in the city council (*Consejo Deliberante*) supported the elimination of police edicts. However, the mayor and the federal government were more receptive to the views of the Federal Police. In 1996, the Federal Police effectively influenced the city government to postpone the debate on the derogation of the edicts.[21]

Once the Federal Police realized that a vast majority in the legislature as well as public opinion supported the derogation of police edicts, they re-framed the debate, asserting that the elimination of the edicts would increase crime in the city (Chillier 1998).

In July 1998, the Buenos Aires city council approved a new urban code abolishing Federal Police edicts. The new code addressed the main concerns of human rights organizations, establishing guarantees for citizens at the moment of arrest. The author of the bill worked closely with human rights organizations and pro-civil rights lawyers.[22]

The pro-order coalition did not accept this outcome. Soon after the city council approved the code, the Federal Police implemented a new plan called "urban spiral" to cope with an alleged increase in the level of violent crime. Within a few weeks, the police put four hundred officers on the streets and "saturated" some areas of the city with police officers. According to the General Director of Operations of the police "the new Urban Code does not provide the tools to prevent crime, and the only way to do it is by putting more police officers on the streets."[23] In the first thirty-two hours of the plan, the police arrested more than three hundred people. The federal executive supported this new aggressive policy, arguing that the lack of police powers had forced the Federal Police to preempt an increase in crime.[24] He also held several meetings with public authorities at the federal level to pressure them to re-establish some of the lost powers, particularly regarding the issue of prostitution.[25] As the new Urban Code did not penalize prostitution on the streets, the Federal Police, the federal government, and some citizens' organizations complained about the potential increase of delinquency and moral scandals as a result of this new measure.[26] The association of transvestites and prostitutes and some legislators of the City argued that the Federal Police was behind the citizen organizations' protests simply because the new rules ended the practices of extortion that the Federal Police maintained against prostitutes.[27] Indeed, a judicial investigation revealed that before prostitution was forbidden on the streets, the Federal Police used to charge prostitutes to allow them to work in some streets of Buenos Aires.[28]

At the beginning of 1999 and in a context of a presidential election year, the federal government took a strong stance against crime. The major of the city, Fernando the La Rúa, was the most likely presidential candidate of the center-left *Alianza,* and the Peronist party at the national level criticized the way de la Rúa had handled crime in the City. On January 24, the Peronist federal government linked the increase of delinquency in Buenos Aires with the increase of illegal immigrants and with the "weak" laws of the City of Buenos Aires.[29] On February 25, Peronist President Menem openly criticized the Capital's Urban Code, arguing the code was a "mess" and that he was studying the possibility of reestablishing police edicts through a presidential decree.[30] Finally, on March 3, the federal government promulgated a presidential decree, reestablishing police powers to arrest individuals under the suspicion that they may infringe on the law (Decree 150/1999). This decree re-established the power of the police to arrest citizens "who disrupt or affect social peace," and "those who behave suspiciously in public spaces." Even though the national Congress has the power to repeal presidential decrees, the center-left majority in Congress did not want to contest a strong commitment with "tough" policies on crime. Obviously, Fernando de la Rúa did not want to be portrayed as weak on the issue of crime either, and two days later he proposed the reform of the Urban Code to forbid prostitution in the city.[31] The city council approved this reform after several hours of debate. The most prominent politicians of the *Alianza* lobbied the legislature in order to obtain a favorable vote, arguing that the *Alianza* needed to show a sign of "toughness" on the issue of delinquency in the context of the presidential campaign.[32]

In sum, human rights activists played a crucial role by framing the topic and by influencing policymakers in the Buenos Aires city council. This influence was countered by the pro-order coalition which first shifted the debate toward an alleged crime wave as a result of the restriction on police powers, and then, shifted the debate to one of public morality.

SUMMARY

This chapter explains the difficulties advocacy groups have faced in the city of Buenos Aires with dealing with the reform of the Federal Police. The analysis of this case allows us to confirm the relevance of police corporateness and of the political context in which such reform attempts have taken place. Regarding the former, the story of the Federal Police demonstrates that it is more difficult for advocacy groups to set an agenda of reforms when faced with a highly corporate police institution, even in a case with a bad reputation in terms of corruption, and the common use of "easy trigger" to contain crime. The Federal Police exerts more control over what lower-ranking officers do and they use their institutional resources to respond to challenges coming from the civil rights coalition in a more coordinated way. Regarding the political context, advocacy groups have faced an environment in which the pro-order coalition has used institutional and political tools to preempt reforms, including bureaucratic blockage in the case of the restriction of the "verification of identity" clause, and "anti-crime" strategies and veto powers in the case of the derogation of police edicts.

Chapter Six

Contesting the Iron Fist

When a journalist asked Argentina's former Secretary of Justice and Safety, León Arslanián, whether proposing "iron fist" measures would deliver more votes in an election, Arslanián did not hesitate to respond "yes, I believe so."[1] Arslanián led one of the most comprehensive attempts to reform a police force in contemporary Latin America. His attempt failed because of the strong institutional and political resistance from a powerful pro-order coalition, as well as a simple electoral factor: proposing "tough" punitive measures against delinquency is a strategy that many politicians are likely to use because many citizens are likely to applaud. This seems to be the case in many Latin American countries[2] and, indeed, in democracies everywhere. Indeed, the French National Assembly adopted a sweeping anti-crime law in early February 2004, giving prosecutors and the police new power to fight organized crime, including the extension from two to four days the period in which suspects can be detained and questioned without charges against them.[3]

The main argument developed here is that what explains resistance to change in police practices and institutions is a structure of incentives favoring those who want to maintain the status quo. First, citizens want to be safe from police abuse as much as they want to be safe from delinquency and, therefore, on this highly divisive issue, constituencies can be mobilized in two directions. They can be mobilized to promote police reforms if violence against citizens is detected and to increase powers if the perception of crime is rising. Second, governments are likely to rely on increasing police powers to control public safety, even in cases in which the record of security forces show that police practices are contributing to increased levels of violence. Third, those who defend pro-order views enjoy comparative advantages over those who defend pro-civil rights views in terms of institutional resources, access to policymakers, and available strategies. As "public safety" is highly valued by policymakers, the police and their allies in the political system have more room to maneuver over what policies are likely to be implemented.

Even in political systems that are more favorable to human rights advocacy groups, and even when a "window of opportunity" to gain allies and influence the policy process presents itself to these groups, the possibilities for successful reform are likely to be counter-balanced by a generally well-organized pro-order coalition. My work suggests that advocacy groups may effectively impact agenda setting in some critical junctures but that their impact on policy implementation and police practices are likely to be, at best, transitory. In sum, the task of the enhancement of individual rights is extremely difficult given a structure of incentives that favors those who aim to preserve the status quo.

This volume began by examining the conditions under which human rights advocacy groups are likely to influence the policy process. It has focused on macro-level factors as well as on micro-level internal characteristics of advocacy groups. In this account, institutional conditions have been conceptualized as antecedent (contextual) causes, whereas actors' actions have been assumed to be the proximate causes of policy outcomes (Scharpf 2000). However, I argue that analyzing the contextual and groups' internal characteristics is not enough. We need to observe nature of the policy issue at stake and the characteristics of the policy actors involved, assuming that on highly divisive issues, actors are likely to engage in some degree of coordination to promote their demands. Indeed, in the cases under scrutiny, one can clearly observe the establishment of two coalitions (civil rights and pro-order) both attempting to influence the policy process. Second, these two coalitions have structural differences, which make it more or less likely for them to succeed. We can understand policy shifts and reversals by considering the comparative power and strategies of both those who challenge the political system and those who protect the status quo.

THINKING ABOUT FACILITATING CONDITIONS

In recent decades, the literature has addressed the importance of the conditions that allow some groups to succeed and others to fail—when and under which conditions policy change is more likely to occur, and the mechanisms explaining such changes.[4] The examination of legal reforms either to increase or restrict police powers in Chile and Argentina shows that conditions such as increasing levels of crime and the public concern on delinquency alone cannot explain policy reforms.

As one may expect, rising levels of crime seems to be a facilitating condition for government to promote higher police powers. However, our cases suggest that this is not a sufficient condition. For example, high levels of crime were present in Argentina (1997–1998) and to some extent in Chile (1998) and, yet, police powers were restricted. In this sense, increasing police power is also associated with the existence of a well-organized pro-order coalition that is willing to use different resources and strategies to either resist change or promote reforms favorable to them.

Regarding public opinion, two elements must be considered: citizens' perception on the police and citizen's perception on crime. Here, again, we find contradictory evidence. For instance, in Chile police powers were restricted in 1998 in a context in which the police had a good public image. In Argentina, on the other hand, police powers were increased in 1999, despite citizens' negative opinion on the police work. Finally, in Argentina police powers were restricted in 1997–98, precisely when the public was increasingly concerned about levels of crime in the city and province.

As citizens are concerned about both public safety and the protection of individual rights, policy change seems to be related to the way social groups take advantage of a "window of opportunity" provided by a changing environment. For example, a well-organized civil rights coalition in Argentina took advantage of critical cases of police violence, a crucial change in the balance of power favorable to the center-left to request for reforms in 1997. This "window of opportunity" allowed the civil rights coalition to gain allies within the state and the general public, initiating important structural reforms in the province. But in 1999, an efficient pro-order coalition was able to take advantage of the growing public concern on delinquency, dominating the 1999 provincial and presidential elections. The civil-rights coalition was not able to convince citizens that police violence and crime were somehow related, despite other critical cases against the police were denounce by the press. Thus, rather than observing crime and public opinion trends alone, we need to observe who are the main actors responding to such conditions, and how these actors articulate their responses.

Within this context, I have examined the specific influence of human rights advocacy groups within a broader political context. This study shows that human rights advocacy groups in Chile have clearly been less influential than in Argentina in terms of agenda setting, political debate in Congress, and policy implementation. In Chile, human rights groups influenced agenda setting regarding the "detention on suspicion" clause at the beginning of the 1990s. However, after 1993 they had no influence in the political debate and policy implementation of the counter-reform that followed. In contrast, Argentina's advocacy groups have done a better job in terms of agenda setting. Their constant monitoring activities have allowed

Table 6.1 Determining Factors In Chile and Argentina

		Chile	Buenos Aires Federal Capital	Buenos Aires Province
Political Opportunity Structure	Mode of Transition	Pact	Reform	
	Access to political system	Favors Pro-order	Favor Civil-rights coalition	
	Police corporateness	High	High	Low
Resource Mobilization	Leadership	Weak	Strong	
	Social Networks	Weak	Strong	
	Ability to obtain resources	Weak	Strong	
Advocacy Groups' Influence	Agenda Setting	Fluctuating	High	High
	Political Debate	No	Fluctuating	Fluctuating
	Policy Implementation	No	No	No

them to make police violence a crucial topic in Argentina and to become a credible and legitimate source of information. Politicians generally request advocacy groups' advice on issues of police violence and police institutional reforms. However, this influence has not been translated into an actual reduction of levels of police violence through the 1990s.

The first question to be asked is what contextual or structural factors explain the differential impact of advocacy groups in Chile and Argentina in terms of agenda setting. This study demonstrates that both macro and micro-level factors explain the outcomes. Three macro-level factors are constraining social actors: the nature of the transition, access to the political system, and police corporateness (Table 6.1). The differing nature of the transition in the two countries differentially influenced advocacy groups' establishment of priorities during the transition. Concretely, the transition byreform in Argentina imposed fewer institutional obstacles for human rights groups to address the issue of the legacy of human rights violations. Moreover, the particular way in which Argentine authorities handled the resolution of human rights violations committed during the military regime opened a window of opportunity for advocacy groups to identify those officers involved in violations of human rights who remind in service in democratic times. In Chile, the transition by pact forced activists to overcome enormous institutional and political obstacles before trying to address other more current social problems.

Second, the different access to the political system that advocacy groups have had in Chile and Argentina affects policy responses. In Chile the pro-order coalition has more opportunities to influence the policy process due to a favorable balance of power in the Senate and the control of the media. The favorable balance of power is due to the existence of appointed senators, which allow the police to maintain a privileged position in influencing the policymaking process. Additionally, conservative sectors exert control over the media, reducing the space for pro-civil-rights views in the press. Human rights advocacy groups have had some ability to influence the policy process through the establishment of alliances with the executive (the Ministry of Justice) and representatives in the Chamber in Congress. However, these two access points have not been enough to obtain favorable policy outcomes. Right-wing sectors in the Senate have blocked legal attempts to restrict police powers.

Argentina's political system has been more open to advocacy groups, given its balance of power favorable to center-left parties in the Capital and province, at least from 1995 to 1999—precisely the period in which most pro-civil rights laws were enacted. Moreover, advocacy groups have had more access to the media than in Chile, given greater levels of pluralism in terms of ownership. While media pluralism and a favorable balance of power in Congress allow for civil rights views to gain visibility, the pro-order coalition has also taken advantage of access to the media and supportive executives at the federal and provincial levels.

Two important qualifications are necessary. A first is related to media pluralism. My original—intuitive—hypothesis was that the greater media pluralism, the more opportunities for advocacy groups to gain visibility. However, the examination of the Chilean case shows that, despite a highly concentrated media, the issue of police violence has still been widely reported by newspapers and TV channels. Further studies are necessary to analyze the specific impact of media ownership on agenda setting and framing, something that is beyond the scope of this study. For instance, it would be important to study the role of editors and owners—how they filter certain information and the way they depict cases of police abuse.

This volume recognizes the importance of veto points blocking certain initiatives and the close relationship between veto points and the balance of power. The case of Argentina illustrates this relationship in a puzzling way. In 1991, President Menem attempted to block a restriction of police power by vetoing a congressional initiative. However, Congress overrode this presidential veto, approving the final reform. Interestingly, the governing Peronist party controlled both chambers at that time, but the overwhelming majority of Congress favored a restriction of police powers. In 1999, President Menem promulgated a decree to overcome a restriction of police powers approved by the Buenos Aires City Council. However, this time a National Congress that was controlled by the center-left *Alianza* did not override the presidential veto, given the context of an electoral campaign and the "tough on crime" agenda.[5] In other words, the use of veto powers is not only related to the distribution of power among political actors but to the specific political context in which this power is used.

A third contextual factor influencing groups' success is the level of police corporateness. The comparison between Chile and the Buenos Aires Provincial Police (BAPP) shows that advocacy groups have been more successful in raising the issue of police violence where police corporateness is low. However, one may fairly argue that higher levels of police violence in the Buenos Aires province explain this outcome. Chapter five introduces the case of a more corporate federal police in the Buenos Aires Capital. This permit us to control for alternative explanations such as the nature of the transition, access to the political system, levels of police violence, and advocacy groups' strength. This case study demonstrates that greater police corporateness reduces advocacy groups' ability to influence the policy process. Highly corporate police institutions are more likely to spend their institutional resources preempting eventual criticism (due to top-down internal controls) and re-framing the debate on public safety (due to a well-organized public relations system). Less-corporate police institutions are more vulnerable to external monitoring activities, given the power struggles within the police that are difficult to control.

However, advocacy networks' influence over agenda setting does not imply that police reforms are easy when faced with less corporate environments. My research suggests distinguishing between the influence over agenda setting and policy implementation. While advocacy groups have more possibilities to influence agenda setting in a less corporate environment, once police reforms have been recognized as a social and political necessity, the actual implementation of reforms seems to depend on other factors including the relationship between political leaders and the police, officers' internal leadership, and levels of police organization. Other studies suggest that some degree of institutional corporateness is necessary to implement reforms.[6]

The context may define the rule of the game in which social actors interact, but actors have some agency to influence the policy process. This agency is defined by actors' leadership, the establishment of social networks, and actors' ability to access new resources to keep organizations functioning. Soon after the transition, in Argentina policy entrepreneurs realized the importance of framing human rights as a present problem.

Moreover, activists in Argentina kept important social networks intact and in many cases they developed grant-seeking skills in order to finance their activities.[7] Moreover, these groups overcome ideological differences by co-operating with each other. In contrast, soon after the transition in Chile, leaders of human rights organizations deactivated social networks and many of them decided to influence government policies from within, closing down several organizations. The lack of funding and a clear decision to concentrate on the past meant that advocacy groups were less-attentive to issues such as trends in police violence, restriction of police powers, and monitoring the implementation of specific reforms.

COMPETING COALITIONS

An exclusive analysis of contextual conditions and advocacy groups' resource mobilization (leadership, social networks, and ability to obtain resources) and strategies does not explain why they have not been able to produce enduring policy reforms. The fluctuating influence of advocacy groups—particularly in Argentina—compels us to observe more closely the forces preempting change. A close look to six policy issues in Chile and Argentina (Table 6.2) confirms the relevance of analyzing the structure of incentives favoring the pro-order coalition.

As regard police internal reforms,[8] Chile has one of the most autonomous police institutions in Latin America and, yet, few social actors have addressed the need to transform internal mechanisms of accountability. [9] In Argentina, social pressures from a well-organized civil rights coalition during the 1990s did not produce institutional changes in the Federal Police on issues of internal accountability. The major attempt to reform the police was made in the Buenos Aires province, but this was partially reversed after the election of Carlos Ruckauf as governor in October 1999.

The most important legal transformations in the two countries involved the protection of individual rights at the moment of arrest. However, we need to qualify these outcomes. In Chile, the reform was mainly due to the existence of a pro-civil rights network of professionals that framed the reform as part of the modernization of the judicial system. Even though the outcome improved the legal status of citizens at the moment of arrest, it clearly favored the position of the police, establishing a verification of identity detention in Chile. In this case, the influence of pro-order senators and the police was crucial in enacting a law. Moreover, the effective think-tank *Paz Ciudadana*, allied with the pro-order coalition, has dominated the public discourse on crime and safety in Chile during the 1990s, leaving little room for critical views of police practices. In this context,

Table 6.2 Coalitions and Policy Outcomes

	Police Reform* Chile	Police Reform* Federal Police	Police Reform* Province 1997	"Detention" on Suspicion" Chile 1998	"Verification of identity" BA Capital 1991	Police Edicts Capital 1998
Pro-Order Coalition	✓	✓	✓	✓	✓	✓
Policy Network Experts	X	✓	✓	✓	✓	✓
Civil Rights Coalition						
Advocacy Groups	X	✓	✓	X	✓	✓
Policy Outcomes						
Legal Change	No	No	Partial Reversal	Partial Improve ment	Partial Improve-ment	(Partial) Improve-ment

* Police reform = Issues exclusively involving improvement of internal mechanisms of accountability to detect and punish police misbehavior.

issues such as the lack of internal mechanisms of accountability within the police and the need to reform the military justice have not made it into the political debate. Advocacy groups have made no attempt to monitor policy implementation of specific legal changes such as the enactment of the *Miranda* rights.

In the Buenos Aires Capital, partial improvements have been made. The partiality of the reforms is due to changes in the balance of power, bureaucratic blockage, and use of veto powers. In 1991, the National Congress approved a restriction of the still existing "verification of identity" clause. While pro-civil rights groups argued that this clause was unconstitutional, the favorable balance of power to the governing party allowed a restriction of the police power to detain individuals from 24 to 10 hours. However, evidence suggests that the Federal Police have used institutional mechanisms to block the full implementation of this clause.

The elimination of police edicts in Buenos Aires City is probably the most favorable legal outcome for pro-civil rights views. A favorable balance of power for pro-civil rights groups in the city council allowed advocacy groups to gain support for their demands. Moreover, the Buenos Aires mayor did not have the power to stop the enactment of this reform. Thus, even though the mayor did not support the bill approved in March 1998, his only alternative was to propose amendments to the already approved legislation. However, because the Federal Police depend on the federal government, President Menem used his veto power to overcome police restrictions—particularly to detain suspects on the streets. Overall, the elimination of police edicts clearly improved the legal protection of citizens' rights, eliminating the power of the police to detain and prosecute individuals for minor offenses. The government of the city and the federal government successfully lobbied the legislature to partially modify some polemic issues of the new law (i.e. prostitution and detention on suspicion). In 1999, the legislature agreed to forbid prostitution on the streets.

In all cases, we observe a relatively cohesive pro-order coalition of police forces and some policymakers, politicians, and even citizens' organizations attempting to preempt pro-civil rights reforms. The volume shows how security forces are using their institutional resources to gain allies within the political system and influence the policy outcomes. Moreover, these police forces are in control of a valuable public good—public safety—and they are willing to use this asset to gain allies and pressure public authorities.

The civil rights coalition does not enjoy an equivalent institutional support. Since this coalition is likely to have more problems of coordinating collective action (Oxhorn 2001), advocacy networks' influence is more likely under the following conditions:[10]

(a) *When like-minded groups cooperate with each other overcoming ideological and political differences.* Despite the existence of ideological differences among CELS and CORREPI, and several other advocacy groups in Argentina, they have been able to cooperate, organizing a common front at key junctures. This has not been the case in Chile, where human rights groups show similar ideological disagreements but less cooperation. Overcoming ideological differences and solving collective action problems helps advocacy groups gain visibility and strength vis-à-vis competing groups in society.

(b) *When groups gain a positive public reputation.* Being recognized as a serious organization may help groups to access the political system and gain visibility in the media. This has been the case of CELS in Argentina during the 1990s, where a continuous and serious compilation of the different spheres of political, civil, and socio-economic rights has helped them become a credible source of information for different local and international actors.

(c) *When groups offer realistic policy alternatives (links with epistemic community).* Advocacy groups do not only need to denounce what is wrong but also offer policy alternatives to solve the problem. For example, specific alliances between advocacy groups and the epistemic community of lawyers in Argentina have helped the former to offer a broader set of policy proposals.

(d) *When groups gain allies within the state apparatus.* Effective influence requires establishing alliances within the three branches of the state apparatus. The restriction of police powers in detaining individuals in the two countries has required a coordinated effort among pro-civil rights lawyers, policymakers, and politicians.

(e) *When groups are able to mobilize public opinion.* Finally, groups need to influence and mobilize public opinion regarding an issue at stake. This has been the case in Argentina where human rights advocacy groups' influence in agenda setting brought about growing consensus on the need to initiate police reforms during the 1990s.

Coalition Strategies

This book shows that social actors use different strategies to advance their agendas, and that the pro-order coalition has a comparative advantage over the civil rights coalition. The comparative analysis of Chile and Argentina (Table 6.3) suggests the following differences: First, in Argentina and given the extension of police reforms, both coalitions have attempted to use all strategies available to them to influence the policy process. Besides common strategies such as social mobilization and media campaigns, the civil rights coalition in Argentina acted in Congress to repeal the presidential veto in 1991. Strong and permanent links between human rights advocacy groups, policy "experts," and policymakers have helped to solve collective actions problems among these groups. In Chile, less coordination among human rights groups and fewer contacts between advocacy groups, policy "experts," and policymakers have weakened options of influencing the policy process.

In the case of the pro-order coalition, the main difference between the two countries is the use of illegal tactics in the case of Argentina and the strong influence of pro-order think tanks in the case of Chile.

In sum, while the context and the specific internal characteristics of human rights advocacy groups tell us something about the necessary conditions for policy influence, this is not enough. This study has analyzed the availability of institutional and political resources as well as the strategies used by both coalitions—which certainly define the power these groups have within the political system. One of the central inhibitors of policy change in

Table 6.3 Strategies Used by Social Actors

	Pro-order Coalition		Civil Rights Coalition	
	Chile	Argentina	Chile	Argentina
Socio-Political				
Social Mobilization	—	✓	(✓)	✓
Electoral platform	✓	✓	—✓	
Media Campaign	✓	✓	—	✓
Bureaucratic (Policy Process)				
Anti-crime activism	✓	✓	n.a.	n.a.
Police bureaucratic blockage	—	✓	n.a.	n.a.
Veto powers	—	✓	—	✓
Technical policy influence	✓	—	✓	✓
Illegal				
Threats	—	✓	n.a.	n.a.
Coercion	—	✓	n.a.	n.a.
Disruption of service	—	✓	n.a.	n.a.
International				
International networking	✓	—	(✓)	✓
International Institutions	✓	—	(✓)	✓

n.a. Non available strategy
(✓) Strategy used in Chile only in the 1990–1994 period.

this area is the existence of strong and many times cohesive pro-order coalition ready to contest civil rights activists. The comparative analysis of both coalitions' power and strategies reveals that the pro-order coalition has comparative structural as well strategic options to respond to challenges.

Incumbents' Strategic Incentives

This analysis raises another inquiry: why do policymakers choose to support either an increase or a restriction of police powers? A comparative analysis of Chile and Argentina allows us to identify the factors that induce incumbents to support one or another policy.

Six factors influence incumbents' incentives to increase police powers to arrest individuals. Several of these factors are complementary and go together, as the cases of Chile and Argentina show. The first factor is an objective increase in the level of crime in the country. This is generally accompanied with critical cases such as police killed by delinquents or spectacular cases of robberies reported by the press that may create a greater perception of insecurity among citizens. As crime rates increase, public perception on the need to use "tough" measures against delinquency is likely to increase. In this scenario, we are likely to observe a coordinated effort among police institutions to lobby the government to increase police powers and pro-order social and political sectors (think tanks, politicians, policymakers, citizens) suggesting policy reforms. Finally, the increase of social protests against the government can also influence incumbents' support for reforms, as they seek to exert control over specific sectors of the population.

By the end of the 1990s, all these factors were part of Argentina's political and social context. In contrast, the increase of police powers in Chile at the end of the 1990s coincided with a partial increase on levels of crime, an effective pro-order coalition in Congress promoting reforms, and a strong police lobby. The public in Chile was not particularly concerned about delinquency—it was ranked the fifth priority after employment, salaries, health, and poverty.

Other factors may motivate incumbents to restrict police powers. Again, these factors are complementary and they are usually linked to one another. The first factor is public exposure to cases of police violence and corruption. Second, some critical cases of allegations of police torture and killing may trigger incumbents to promote reforms. The public exposure to cases of police violence and corruption may lead to changes in the public's perception of the police and an increase in social mobilization demanding reforms. Another factor is related to an organized civil rights coalition offering policy alternatives. Finally, international actors pressuring governments to reform can be another factor triggering incumbents' incentives to transform the police.

In Argentina, all these factors were present during the 1990s in both the Buenos Aires Capital and the surrounding Province. In the case of Chile, however, the restriction of police powers was mainly due to the influence of a well-coordinated effort of professionals outside and inside the state who framed the reform as part of the modernization of the judicial system. The existence of a critical case helped members of Congress to speed up an ongoing process of reform, but it did not alter the content of the proposal or the outcome.

THEORETICAL IMPLICATIONS

Scholars have increasingly addressed the importance of transnational advocacy networks influencing domestic politics in a progressively interconnected world (Risse-Kappen 1995; Meyer et al. 1997; Clark et al. 1998;

Keck and Sikkink 1998; Dallmayr 1999; Samhat 1999; Forsythe 2000; Guidry, Kennedy, and Mayer 2000; O'Brien et al. 2000; Thome 2000; Khagram, Riker and Sikkink 2002). States are expected to respect individuals' civil and political rights. As international mechanisms of enforcement are weak, transnational advocacy networks become crucial in monitoring different states' activities both locally and internationally. Scholars have suggested that "if a nation-state neglects to adopt world-approved policies, domestic elements will try to carry out or enforce conformity. Where the state has not adopted the appropriate policies, local units [advocacy networks] are likely to call for national action" (Meyer et al. 1997: 161). If the state does not respond to such domestic pressures, advocacy groups are likely to seek allies abroad to pressure from "above," producing a *boomerang effect* (Keck and Sikkink 1998). These advocacy networks are influential by "creating issues, mobilizing new constituencies, altering understandings of interests and identities, and sometimes changing state practices" (Khagram, Riker, and Sikkink 2002: vii).

This volume confirms that these transnational advocacy groups can have an important effect in terms of agenda setting, but they have less impact on policy implementation—particularly concerning changing police practices. Even though international actors have pressured Chilean authorities to control police violence in democratic Chile (1990–2002), the government has either ignored or contested such claims. In democratic Argentina (1983–2002), well-organized advocacy groups have effectively organized international alliances to stop police violence and corruption, but their impact has fluctuated in terms of legal changes, and no major reduction of police violence has taken place.

While the conceptualization of the "boomerang effect" has been mainly applied to authoritarian contexts, this study suggests a more complex relationship between international and domestic forces in a democratic context. First, even though democratic regimes are substantially more open than authoritarian regimes, democratic incumbents can still face incentives to block advocacy networks' influence. Second, in a democratic context both governments and advocacy groups may use international tools to advance their demands. For example, incumbents are likely to use international forums to respond to allegations of human rights, which—to some extent—may diffuse the initial impact of charges made by human rights groups.

As mentioned in chapter one, some scholars have recognized the need to observe the domestic conditions that make advocacy networks' influence more or less likely (Risse-Kappen 1995; Keck and Sikkink 1998). Moreover, other authors have emphasized issues concerning legal and cultural legacies making police forces more likely to violate citizens' rights (Chevigny 1995; Wiarda 2001). The comparative examination of four legal reforms in two Latin American countries suggests that while the existence of a cultural heritage and authoritarian legacies may partially explain police violence, there is an additional mechanism explaining persistent patterns of police violence and shifting policies on legal powers: the nature of the policy issue at stake makes citizens both concerned both police abuses and crime. At the political level, this trade-off tends to create two opposing coalitions—the pro-order and civil rights coalition. Whether police powers are increased or reduced heavily depends on how well organized and how much power those who want to increase police powers and those who want to protect individual rights have.

Moreover, this work suggests new ways to observe the impact of social actors within a national and international setting. For instance, the social movement literature has mainly focused on the questions of why people protest and the conditions under which they succeed or fail. Scholars have developed an important body of literature, providing structural as well as individual-level explanations for success and failure (Rucht 1991; Tarrow 1994; Gamson and Meyer 1996; McAdam 1996).[11] The study of social movements in Latin America has addressed the same questions, focusing on explaining the internal, cultural, institutional, and structural conditions behind a given movement (i.e., Alvarez and Escobar 1992; Foweraker 2001; Baldez 2002).

Responding to McAdam, Tarrow, and Tilly's more recent challenges (2001), this study has attempted to clarify the causal mechanisms explaining how certain independent variables are affecting policy outcomes. However, this inquiry has taken a slightly different approach from the traditional social movements literature. Instead of exclusively studying the internal dynamic of one single social actor, I argue that in highly divisive issues, actors who share ideas and interests are likely to develop some level of coordination to advance their claims. In this sense, my study relies on the premise of the advocacy coalition framework (Sabatier and Jenkins-Smith 1999), capturing the dynamics of a complex social reality in which competing groups of society emerge and compete for influence over time. The cross-national analysis of several instances of policy reform in a twelve to fifteen-year period allowed me to recognize similar dilemmas and common patterns of behavior among social actors in different political contexts.

The debate on the enhancement of individual rights generates a very particular combination of policy interests among politicians, policymakers and the police who are interested on preserving the status quo. If these actors act together, they will enjoy institutional and political resources and strategies, that is, the power to influence the political system in a way that is not frequent in other policy issues where the monopoly and use of force is not at stake.

While the advocacy coalition framework is a very useful analytical device to understand public policy decisions, it certainly presents some limits. First, this framework can be applied only to highly divisive issues (i.e. abortion, police powers, death penalty).[12] Second, this theoretical framework makes a—sometimes—problematic assumption that actors will get together to defend their *beliefs*. My research suggests that it is difficult to determine whether actors are responding to their beliefs or to more concrete material interests. These two issues require further exploration.

Finally, this investigation departs from studies that consider the state a single "black box" affecting policy outcomes. As this study has demonstrated, the state includes agencies that have manifestly different policy interests. In relation to the protection of citizens' rights and police powers, the examination of two countries and four instances in which police powers have been at stake shows that policymakers at the Ministries of Justice and Foreign Affairs are more likely to assume a pro-civil rights approach. In contrast, policymakers who are working more closely with the police at the Ministry of Interior are more likely to adopt pro-order positions. Interagency differences may generate a "window of opportunity" for social actors to influence the policy process.

IS IT POSSIBLE TO CONTEST THE IRON FIST?

This book offers a pessimistic view regarding the ability to advance in the protection of individual rights in newly democratic regimes. Problems of collective action, advocacy groups' lack of expertise, lack of information, the public's concern with crime, institutional veto points, police corporateness, the vested interests of police and politicians, and the existence of well-funded and well-organized pro-order groups are all factors hindering the enhancement of individual rights. This seems to be the case in Chile, Argentina, and several other countries in Latin American and elsewhere (Johnson 1990; Neild 2002; Ziegler and Neild 2002; Davis, D. 2002).

However, the comparative analysis of stories of more or less success allows us to underline potentially successful strategies. First, strategies that may work well in an authoritarian context may not be adequate within a democratic regime. Democratic authorities have a set of legal and political tools to preempt and respond to criticisms domestically and internationally.

In general, democratic authorities have depicted allegations of police violence as the exception rather than the rule. Moreover, authorities are likely to argue that domestic institutional mechanisms will solve eventual allegations of police misbehavior. Advocacy groups—locally and internationally—have continued using a strategy that addresses allegations on a case-by-case basis. The experience of CELS in Argentina demonstrates that while denouncing specific cases is a crucial strategy in order to gain legitimacy, this should be combined with proposing institutional reforms, because institutional mechanisms to deal with police abuses in Latin America are weak, and lacking both transparency and basic principles of fairness.

Second, gathering reliable information locally and disseminating it internationally is a crucial strategy to "make the case" of police violence. Again, the experience of CELS in Argentina shows how advocacy groups can become a relevant focal point for civil rights organizations in Argentina and Latin America due to their innovative approach regarding how to gather information, how to pressure the state to access public information, and how to disseminate information of such cases abroad. Advocacy groups should not exclusively focus on collecting cases of police violence but also on designing methods to monitor police behavior once a reform is (or should be) implemented.

Third, the understanding of the political and institutional context may help advocacy networks to advance their agenda. Especially if these groups face a well-organized pro-order coalition, they should seek to frame the issue of citizens' rights as complementary to and not detrimental to the protection of public safety. Moreover, if the police show high levels of corporateness, then advocacy groups should develop strategies to overcome the obstacles this raises, providing better information and suggesting institutional reforms where they are needed.

Finally, advocacy networks should improve their capacity to monitor legislative debates and develop alliances with policymakers, the epistemic community, and technical experts to generate a more persistent influence over the policy process. Denouncing police abuse alone is not likely to have an effect on the policy process. Social actors need to offer plausible policy alternatives and monitor the implementation of policy outcomes. As crime is likely to be a central concern in developing countries, and as citizens are likely to be supportive of a "tough on crime" approach, the main challenge for local and international advocacy groups today is how to contest the "iron first" discourse in new and innovative ways.

Appendix One

Chile: Government's Reactions Toward International Report

Report	Allegation	Government Reaction	Authority
US Department of State, Feb. 1994	"Police forces were again responsible for human rights abuses in 1993"	In Chile there is an absolute respect for human rights. Excesses are punished.	Undersecretary of Foreign Affairs
Human Rights Watch, May 1994	"Military courts' powers should be restricted"	"The report recognize recent progress made on HRs"	Undersecretary of Foreign Affairs
	"Persistent abuses"	"We do not agree totally with this observation"	Undersecretary of Justice
Amnesty International, July 1994	"Persistent human rights violations"	"These cases have not been proven"	*Carabineros*
Association against torture, Nov 1994	"Torture continues in Chile"	No reaction	
CODEPU, Jan. 1995	"Torture continues in Chile"	"These accusations are false"	*Carabineros*
Amnesty International, July 1995	"Recurring cases of torture committed primarily by Carabineros"	No reaction	
US Department of State, March 1996	"Most serious cases of abuse involve police brutality"	No reaction	

Report	Allegation	Government Reaction	Authority
UN report on torture, April 1996	"Cases are sufficiently numerous and serious for the authorities to continue looking into the problem"	"Cases should be verified" "The report recognizes government's efforts"	Chilean Commision on UN Commision
US Department of State, Jan. 1997	"Some problems remain. The most serious are complaints of torture, brutality and excessive use of force by police"	Report is based on allegations that have note been proven" "The report recognizes government's efforts"	Undersecretary of Interior
UN Report on Torture, March 1997	"Government should accelerate approval of bills to protect citizens' rights" "Concern regarding torture"	Press distorts human rights reports. The report was positive" "The government is trying to reform the judicial system to improve citizens' rights"	Minister of Foreign Affairs
US Department of State, Jan 1998	"Continuing allegations of police brutality"	"The government respects HRs" "In cases of abuse, officers are under judicial scrutiny" "In the U.S., immigrants are submitted to mistreatment as well"	Minister of Interior
US Department of State, Feb 2000	"Although the govt. respect citizens' rights, problems remained in some areas. The police committed a number of HRs abuses"	"Alleged cases are not investigated enough"	HRs Division, Ministry of Foreign Affairs
Amnesty International, Oct 2000	We still receive denounces of police violence"	No reaction	

US Department of State, Feb 2001	Police abuse, the main problem of HRs in Chile"	It is unacceptable that other state make comments about other countries"	President
		"There is a country that has not report on HRs: the US"	Minister of Interior
US Department of State, March 2002	"Police abuse and jail poor conditions persist"	"Other country should not intervene in internal affairs" "There is over-population in jails but fighting delinquency has a cost"	President
Amnesty International, May 2002	"Police reportedly used excessive force in a number of incidents." "Police reportedly used excessive force during demonstrations and police operations."	"With few exceptions, AI allegations have not been documented in Court" "The use of force is proportionate to maintain order" "In the case of indigenous groups, the police have acted in self-defense"	Undersecretary of Interior
		"Police action is carried out in agreement with technical criteria established by legal norms and institutional rules" "The Chilean judicial system is the only competent institution to investigate and rule on alleged police abuse"	*Carabineros*

Sources: Press coverage in Chile, El Mercurio, La Epoca, La Tercera, El Mostrador.
HRs = human rights

Appendix Two

Testing Social Groups' Responsiveness

In order to test the level of Chilean actors' responsiveness toward the issue of police violence, I decided to run an experiment between August and December 2001. In this experiment, I provided an *input* (relevant information) to a sample of politicians, government officials, press, Chilean human rights organizations, international human rights organizations, embassies, and academic research centers. The input consisted in sending a short e-mail message titled "Police violence in Chile,"1 which stated that a new research made in Chile has demonstrated an increasing number of citizens' allegations of police violence since 1990. I sent this e-email in critical junctures, following actors' responses.

EXPECTED OUTCOMES

Following the results described above, I expected the following outcomes:

(a) Low levels of responsiveness to the input from: human rights organizations in Chile, Government officials, Congress representatives, and the media,
(b) High levels of responsiveness to the input from the Police and international actors.

INPUT

The experiment considered an input (an e-mail message) sent by the author of the work "Denuncias por Violencia Policial" ("*Police Violence Denounces*") published by FLACSO-Chile in August 2001. In this e-mail, I succinctly explain the main results of this work underlining as a main finding the important increase of citizens' allegations of police violence between

1990 and the year 2000. In this e-mail, I ask recipients *to visit a website* containing a summary of this work and free access to the whole document (Annex I). Additionally, I encouraged recipients to send me *feedback* and comments regarding my work.

In this sense, the experiment measures three types of responses:

1. *No response.* The recipient neither visits the webpage nor engages in a dialogue with the author.
2. *Passive responses:* In this case, the recipient just hit the website address and checked out the given webpage, without further consequences.[2]
3. *Active responses:* In this case, the recipient engages him/herself in a dialogue with the author of the work, asking for more information, providing feedback, etc. Another option is that the person visits the webpage and uses the information for his/her own interest. Even though it is difficult to control for such cases because we do not know what the person is doing with the information, we can trace whether the person uses the information publicly through the analysis of the press. As the experiment will demonstrate later, most of the people who actually hit the website did engage in a dialogue with the author.

TIMING

I run the experiment three consecutive times:

1. *First Juncture: restricted sample.* In August 31st and just after the printed document "*Denuncias por violencia policial*" was published by FLACSO, I sent a first e-mail to the Chilean media and the Embassy of the United States given the fact that the US publishes an annual report on human rights (27 recipients).
2. *Second Juncture: full sample.* In October 22nd, I sent a second e-mail to a sample of Chilean media, deputies and senators in Congress, human rights organizations, academic research centers, and the government (110 recipients). This e-mail was sent just after a scandal that affected the credibility of both the uniformed and civil police institutions. At that time, the media reported on the police's failure to capture a man who had raped and killed more than ten children during a period of two years. Several political and

social sectors were seriously questioning police institutions in their investigative capacity. Furthermore, the government and political parties questioned the police credibility given the fact that police officers hidden information from civilian authorities.

3. *Third Juncture: restricted sample.* In November 30th, I re-run the experiment. I sent the same e-mail to a selected sample of media, members of the Commission of Human Rights of the Chamber of Deputies and the Senate, and the government. (43 messages). Two days before, the uniformed police *Carabineros* was involved in a serious incident when they violently (desalojaron) the headquarters of the Communist Party. As a result, more than 20 people were injured, including the president of the Communist Party. Even though the police were complying with a judicial order, the way they acted caused a strong rejection by different political sectors and the government. After the incident, officers in charged of the procedure were dismissed.

ACTORS

The sample included the following actors:

Sector	E-mails sent	E-mails that achieved destination	Difference
Media	33	26	–7
Chilean HROs	13	10	–3
International HROs	11	11	0
Government	7	7	0
Police institutions	2	2	0
Congress	46	46	0
Academic Centers	8	8	0
US Dept of State	1	1	0
Total	—	111	—

I obtained e-mails addresses from several sources including databases listing governmental and non-governmental institutions, human rights organizations worldwide (*www.derechos.org*), and the Chilean Congress. The difference between e-mails sent and emails that achieved actual destination is due to the lack of specific organizations (mainly media agencies and human rights organizations) to update their electronic addresses in online directories.

RESULTS

First Juncture: Restricted Sample (27 recipients)

The objective of sending this first e-mail was to inform the media and the US Department of State regarding a new publication concerning police violence in Chile. As was stated before, the e-mail underlined the main finding of the research, that is, an increasing trend of citizens' allegations regarding police violence.

I chose to send it to the US Department of State because they publish an annual report on human rights which has some political impact in Chile given the fact that in the last 5 years this report has underlined the maintenance of police violence in Chile.

Because the main target was the media, I provided them a brief e-mail inviting them to check a summary of the findings (2 pages) and the whole document (65 pages). Given the timing constraints of the media, in general they prefer to receive summaries of documents rather than the complete document. To catch their attention, I titled the e-mail and the summary "Research proves Increasing Allegations of Police Violence." Finally, in order to increase the credibility of these findings, the e-mail mentioned that these findings are based on "official source," which is the case. It is important to notice that one month before, National TV-Channel (TVN) had made a special program focusing on the main findings for this research.

The document certainly did not call the attention of the media. A well-known radio station (*Radio Chilena*) had an active response, requesting the author to give an interview and a Santiago's newspaper (*La Hora*) published a note on the subject.3 On the other hand, the US Department of State showed an active response. 40 days after the message was sent, an official from the US Embassy in Chile contact the author asking for clarifications regarding the findings and for an authorization to quote this information in the US Annual Report on Human Rights.

First Juncture: Document publication

Actors	Total Recipients	No Response	Passive Response (Check website)	Active Response
Media	26	22	3	2
US Dept of State	1	—	—	1

Second juncture: Full Sample (110 recipients)

In October 22nd, a second e-mail containing the same information of the first e-mail was sent to 110 individuals and institutions. The political context made more likely for actors to show some interest in the information given the fact that both civil and uniformed police institutions were being seriously questioned by government officials and political parties after the failure to investigate a case of serial murders in the north of Chile.

What is interesting here is the behavior of local and international human rights organizations. Local human rights organizations such as *Comisión Chilena de Derechos Humanos*, derechoschile.org, Ombudsman-Chile, Comisión Funa, FASIC, and SERPAJ did not respond to the e-mail. The only response came from CODEPU (Santiago) requesting a copy of the printed document to include the report in its documentation center. International human rights organizations showed more interest, particularly Amnesty International and the Washington Office of Latin America (WOLA). In the case of Amnesty International (London), a representative contacted the author requesting additional information to be included in its annual report. Moreover and as result of the e-mail, a representative of WOLA invited the author to attend a seminar concerning police reforms in Latin America that was taking place few weeks later.[4]

In the case of public authorities, the government and Congress representatives did not show interest in the information. The only state institution that showed an active interest was the uniformed police *Carabineros*. 28 days after I sent the e-mail, a representative of the Department of Public Relations sent me a response apologizing for the late response, indicating

Second Juncture: Police's Efficiency Being Questioned

Actors	Total Recipients	No Response	Passive Response (Check website)	Active Response
Media	26	25	1	1
Chilean HROs	10	9	1	1
International HROs	11	8	2	2
Government	7	7	—	—
Police Institutions	2	1	2	1
Congress	46	46	—	—
Academic Centers	8	7	3	1
Total	110	—	—	—

that a further analysis of the document will take place, and thanking me for letting them know about this work.

In the case of the media, a radio-station identified with the left (*Radio Tierra*) sent an email back, asking for more information regarding the study.

Finally, in the case of academic centers, the only organization that showed an active interest was *policiaysociedad.org* dependent on the *Centro de Estudios del Desarrollo*. A representative of such organization got in touch with me, inviting me to publish a short article in their regular newsletter.

Third Juncture: Restricted Sample (43 recipients)

On mid-November an "ideal" juncture to release the information concerning police violence took place in Santiago. *Carabineros* violently (desalojo) the Communist party's headquarters, injuring 20 people, including the president of such party. The police's action took place after a court decision to (desalojar) the building for a property legal dispute. More than the legality of the action, what caused political impact was the aggressive way in which *Carabineros* conducted the procedure.

Two days after of this event, I sent the same e-mail to a target sample of media, government officials and the representative of the Commissions of human rights in Congress. In this case, it did not make sense to send the information to academic centers, human rights organizations and police institutions again.

In this case, we observe more interest to check the website out from people in Congress and the government but still we do not observe an active response neither from public authorities nor from the media.

Explaining the Results

The main objective of this experiment was to test actors' responsiveness toward the topic of police violence. Considering that my research shows an

Third Juncture: Police's procedures being questioned

Actors	Total Recipients	No Response	Passive Response (Check website)	Active Response
Media	26	26	2	—
Government	7	7	3	—
Congress	20	17	3	—
Total	42	—	—	—

Sector	Recipients	Active Response	%
US Dept of Stat	1	1	100.0%
Police institutions	2	1	50.0%
International HROs	11	2	18.1%
Academic Centers	8	1	12.5%
Media	26	3	11.5%
Chilean HROs	10	1	10.0%
Government	7	0	0.0%
Congress	46	0	0.0%
Total	111	—	—

important increase in levels of citizens' complaints in courts and given the fact that this information has not been made public, I decided to test whether political and social actors in Chile and abroad are receptive to the topic. I expected higher levels of responsiveness from international actors, the police, and the academia. Additionally, I expected lower levels of responsiveness from local human rights organizations, the government, the media, and representative in Congress.

Indeed, the experiment tends to confirm preliminary expectations. First, international actors tend to respond more than local human rights organizations. In two cases (Amnesty International and US Department of State), they do not only respond to my e-mail but also request clarifications. In both cases, it was clear that they took the time to read and criticize the document.

A second expected outcome is the low level of responses coming from human rights organizations in Chile, which supposedly are the most interested actors to use such information. The only response came from CODEPU, which did not ask about the content itself, but about a way to obtain a printed copy to save in the Documentation Center. While international actors saw this document as a source to make an statement, local actors tended not to respond, or respond passively.

The media, the government and representatives in Congress observe low levels of responsiveness. In the case of the media, the explanation may have to do with three factors: (a) *Personal relationship with journalists.* There are more chances to be published if you establish a personal relationship with journalists. In this case, e-mails were sent to the general e-mail address of a given media; (b) *Lack of interest in the topic.* Chile was living pre-electoral times and, therefore, the media may want to focus only on the

Congressional campaign; (c) *editorial decision.* Another option is the existence of an editorial decision not to get involved in this subject. In this respect, I have contradictory evidence. For instance, just after my research was known through the National TV-Channel "*Special Report,*"5 I offered the exclusive publication of my document "*Denuncias por Violencia Policial*" to an electronic newspaper (*El Mostrador*). After several weeks of delay, the newspaper's director told me that they decided not to publish the document (or a fragment of it) because "the uniformed police have not answered to our inquiry to respond to such information, and we do not want to publish something without having the other part of the story."[6] Few months later and after the Police's violent reaction against the communist party, I decided to send an article explaining the main findings of my research to a newspaper that have a relatively conservative editorial line (*La Tercera*). The article was published within three days and without censorship. Overall, it is not clear that Chilean mass media would censor information regarding police violence but it is very likely they may take steps to assure "neutrality" before the police by presenting alternative versions of the story.

The Congress' low responsiveness could be explained by (a) *Timing.* Given the fact that most representatives were running for re-election, it is very likely they did not pay attention to the information sent by e-mail; (b) *Method.* It is very likely that representatives do not read their e-mails and, therefore, the information was subject to some advisor or secretary who did not consider the information relevant. Additionally, we may think that e-mail is not a particularly important way by which representatives receive information.

In the case of the government, the low level of responsiveness may have similar causes than in the case of representatives; (a) *Timing.* The pre-electoral period may explain, in part, government's lack of interest; (b) *Method.* Another option is that governmental authorities do not use e-mail as a method to become informed. This option is more likely in this case because the e-mails were sent not to specific persons (as was the case of Congress representatives) but to institutional e-mail addresses (Ministry of Interior, Communications, Foreign Affairs, Defense, Presidency). One event that may support the previous statement is that just after I published an article in *La Tercera*, one of the main advisors of the Undersecretary of Interior asked me to write a memorandum considering specific policy recommendations regarding police violence in Chile.

What is interesting is that the only state authority that actually responded—even though only in formal terms—to my e-mail were Carabineros. This fact confirms preliminary findings regarding the efficiency of Carabineros' public relations system to respond to external criticisms by adopting a proactive position that consider the "promise" to study the subject in detail. However, we never know the result of these "studies."

Overall, this experiment tends to confirm the main expectations that raise the qualitative study of Chile; while international actors continue addressing the subject of police violence in Chile, few local actors respond to the subject in a pro-active way.

Appendix Three

Argentina: Selected Cases of Corruption

Table 1 Argentina: Police Corruption Indictments Reported by the Press. (Selected sample from Buenos Aires Province)

Involvement of Top and Lower-ranking officers*	Involvement of Lower-ranking officers
1992—Officers involved in kidnapping activities for profit reasons	1996—Officers involved in bombing attack against Jewish cultural center
1993—Officer involved in drug trafficking	1992—Officers involved in 22 robberies.
1993—Officers helped drug trafficking dealers	1992—Officers involved in drug traffic
1993—Officer involved in kidnapping	1995—Officers charging illegally to protect stores
1994—Eleven Police officers involved in massacre	1995—Officers involved in steeling banks
Involvement of Top and lower ranking officers*	Involvement of Lower-ranking officers
1994—Officers involved in helping inmates to escape from prison	1995—Officers involved in bribes
1995—Officers involved in a network of bribes to businessmen	1996—Officers helped delinquents to stole store

Involvement of Top and Lower-ranking officers*	Involvement of Lower-ranking officers
1995—Officers involved in network of drug trafficking	1996—Officers stole proves from Court
1995—Officers involved in network of Bribes	1996—Officers stole truck
1996—Officers involved in a network of trafficking of influence and documents involving lawyers and judges.	1996—Officer stole car parts after accident
1996—30 Officers involved in drug trafficking.	1996—Officer stole stores
1996—Officers involved in overcharging for services to municipality	1996—Officer used stolen car
1996—Officers involved in bribing a businessman to hide proves in court	1996—Officers help inmates to escape prison
1995—Officers involved in drug traffic	

* Top officers consider chiefs of police station or higher.
Sources: CELS (1993; 1994; 1995). Oliveira and Tiscornia (1996).

Table 2 Comparison Federal Police and BAPP abuse of power scandals reported by the Press Including Indictments, Sentences, and Allegations (Excluding Police Shootings), 1996 and July 1998–June 2001

Federal Police	BAPP
1996—Officer arrested after a friend used his weapon to kill a minor.	1996—Two police officers arrested on robbery of judicial files
	1996—Lawyers Professional Association denounce traffic of influence between some lawyers and police officers to obtain cases
	1996—Three officers arrested after a robbery
	1996—Two officers indicted because of false testimony

	1996—Officer arrested because of traffic of parts of stolen cars
	1996—Two officers arrested after robbery.
	1996—Officer suspended because he used a stolen car.
	1996—Thirteen police officers indicted in AMIA case
	1996—Seven officers arrested because their involvement in drug traffic and protection of drug dealers
	1996—Two officers arrested for extortion
	1996—One officer arrested because he helped prisoners to escape from prison
	1996—Judge investigate police organization that may overcharge police service to local government
	1996—One officer indicted for drug traffic
	1996—Thirteen officers indicted be cause of extortion of businessmen
1998—Officers sentenced for illegal detention. Fist time in history (*Página 12*, Oct 23)	1998—Officer detained for corruption and torture
1999—Three officers involved in whobank robbery **Federal police conduct investigation**	1998—Threats against officer who investigate police corruption
1999—Judiciary investigates police involvement in illegal gambling and prostitution business. **Government defend police**	1998—Threats against legislators who are reforming police services 1999—Ex-representative of the government recognize links between politicians and police
1999—Alleged threats against ex-officer who denounced police corruption	1999—4 police dismissed because of cover-up system of bribes in Buenos Aires public roads
	1999—Lawyer Union denounced police manipulate crime statistics
2000—Police investigate officers' repression	2000—Supreme Court requests internal investigation in BAPP for toture against children

Federal Police	BAPP
2000—**Police respond** to allegations of espionage of political parties	2000—Police officers indicted. They took bribed in exchange of security
	2000—Anonymous police office denounced he has been threatened by his boss
	2001—347 officers indicted for robbery and damages after a party
	2001—Documented torture in police stations against children. **Governor rejected them.**
2001—**Federal police** argue that 21 officers have been killed this year	2001—Increasing number of tortures in police stations. 280 this year according to the judiciary
2001—55 false police procedures are denounced.	2001—Judicial investigation for killing of a child in police station

Bold: institutional reactions defending police procedures or taking actions.
1996: Oliveira and Tiscornia (1997)
1998–2001: Online newspapers *Página 12* and *Clarín*.

Notes

NOTES TO THE INTRODUCTION

1. Governor Carlos Ruckauf, "Mano Dura en la Provincia," Clarín, August 5, 1999.
2. Penal Code procedures have been reformed in Ecuador (1991), Peru (1991) Guatemala (1992), Argentina (1992), Costa Rica (1996), El Salvador (1998), Chile (1998), Venezuela (1998), Paraguay (1998), Bolivia (1998). By 2002, other countries were debating reforms in Congress including Nicaragua, Honduras, Dominican Republic, and Panama (Domingo 1999; Struensee and Maier 2000)
3. This has been the case of El Salvador, Peru, Bolivia, Argentina, and Chile (Kincaid and Gamarra 1996; NACLA 1996; CELS 2001).
4. There are three other international agreements related to the subject: the U.N. optional protocol to file individual complaints (1966), the U.N. Convention against torture (1984), and the U.N. second optional protocol against death penalty (1989).
5. In an insightful article, Scharpf (2000) addresses the need to analyze not only the contextual (institutional) conditions under which actors operate but also the nature of the problem and characteristics of the actors involved in the policy process.
6. This situation is more complex in countries in which police officers are involved in networks of corruption and crime. In these cases, increasing police powers may lead to reinforcing patterns of crime and violence.
7. In making these assumptions, I rely on the advocacy coalition approach (Sabatier 1992; Sabatier and Jenkins-Smith 1999).
8. Chevigny argues that there is a correlation between the sociopolitical structure of the places (inequality, lack of accountability, low respect of rights) and the level of violence by the police (Chevigny 1995: 249).
9. Moreover, multi-ethnical countries face an additional dilemma regarding policing and race relations (Chevigny 1995; Bayley 1996).
10. According to recent studies, Latin America is the most unequal region in the world in terms of income distribution given its level of per capita GDP. Moreover, in the region levels of poverty and informal labor have increased in the last 10 years. By the year 2001, 44 percent of the population was living under the poverty line, a 4 percent increase since 1990. (ECLAC 1997; 2002).

11. As a comparison, between 1990 and 1999 the yearly average homicide rates are the following: Canada, 2.15; United States 8.2; Ecuador, 12.5; Mexico, 15.7; Brazil, 18.8; Venezuela, 19.1; Colombia, 64.5. Statistics based on the Pan-American Organization of Health and FBI. Cited by Ministerio de Justicia (Argentina) (2002). Homicides rates in some cities for the years 1997-99 are: London 2.3; Madrid 3.1; Copenhague 3.4; Buenos Aires Capital, 5.1; Amsterdam 5.4; New York 9.4; Moscu 18.2. Statistics based on the British Home Office. Cited by Ministerio de Justicia (Argentina) (2002).
12. As the Capital concentrates financial and commercial activities, higher rates on crimes against individuals and property are expected. For the period 1990-1999, in the Capital the average of crimes against property was 2,330 and the average of crimes against individuals was 460.3. In the Province the averages were 823.9 and 460.3 respectively. Unfortunately, Chile's indicators on crime consider other categories, making comparisons impossible. As a point of reference, in Chile, the yearly rate average of robbery with violence was 559 (for the period 1990-1998) and the yearly rate average of robbery without violence was 145 for the same period.
13. CELS is recognized as one of the most active NGOs promoting legal and procedural reforms in the Argentine police's behavior.

NOTES TO CHAPTER ONE

1. Interview with Daniel, Santiago, January, 2001.
2. My study departs from mainstream analyses on why police violence exists. Assuming the existence of police violence, I address the question of what factors inhibit or enable change. Regarding the former question, see a review of the literature in Ahnen (1999).
3. Policing is more than the sole use of force. Policing can be broadly defined as the exercise of authority of state over the civilian population (Waddington 1999). In this work, I just focus on one aspect of policing, which is related to the abuse of authority. For a critical view on the role of the police, see Neocleous (2000).
4. For discussion on norm internalization, see Axelrod (1986) and Schotter (1986).
5. For instance, Thomas (2002) argues that "states actors are more likely to respond positively to the demand of nonstate actors that identify with international norms. This is true because most states value the legitimacy they gain by appearing to comply with international norms, and because they value the material goods that others may link to certain behaviors."
6. A discussion of the socialization process and internalization of international human rights standards in Franck (1992) and Risse and Ropp (1999).
7. The cases of China and Cuba are examples of this trend. Even though in both countries violation of human rights have been documented, due to political and other strategic reasons international sanctions have had less impact than expected.
8. Latin America has not been the exception in this regard. See Friedman, Hochstetler, and Clark (2001).

9. Data extracted from Keck and Sikkink (1998: 11)
10. Meyer et al. (1997) put it in similar way: "If a nation-state neglects to adopt world-approved policies, domestic elements will try to carry out or enforce conformity. General world pressure favoring environmentalism, for example, have led many states to establish environmental protection agencies, which foster the growth of environmental engineering firms, activist groups, and planning agencies. Where the state has not adopted the appropriate policies, such local units and actors as cities, schools, scout troops, and religious groups are likely to practice environmentalism and call for national action." (p. 161).
11. A discussion on democratic consolidation in O'Donnell (2001b), Schedler (2001), and Mainwaring, Brinks and Pérez-Liñán (2001).
12. Analyzing the impact of global civil society, Clark, Friedman, and Hochstetler (1998) arrive to a similar conclusion, that is, "state sovereignty sets the limits of global civil society" (p.34).
13. Traditional pluralists make two critical assumptions: first, citizens respond to social conflicts by organizing themselves when their well-being is affected and, second, government policies are a reflection of interest group influence (Latham 1952; Truman 1951). See also critical analysis of pluralist approach in Gamson (1975). For a critical analysis on grievance and the emergence of social movements, see Mayer (1991).
14. Structures are defined by the arrangement or the ordering of the parts within a system. The distribution of capabilities (power), ordering principles within a society, and the specification of function (authority) will define a domestic political structure (Waltz 1979). In one view, structures are generative, that is, the arrangement of parts will shape and determine social interactions as well as political outcomes (Mahoney and Snyder 1999).
15. For a Marxian interpretation, see Schock (1996). For a critical analysis of a Marxian interpretation of police powers, see Walker (1977).
16. For a critical analysis of structuralism, see McKeown (1986).
17. Several Latin American countries have enacted laws restricting police powers after transitions to democracy (Chile, Argentina, El Salvador, Bolivia, Peru, and Brazil).
18. For an institutional criticism of the structuralist approach, see March and Olsen (1989).
19. Mitchell and McCormick conclude that "economic conditions can help us to understand and begin to account for variations in human rights violations. Yet even this assertion should not be pushed too far, for at least two reasons. First, the relationship is modest at best. Second, only in countries that never or rarely hold political prisoners do we approach a linear relationship with the level of economic development" (Mitchell and McCormick 1988: 488).
20. Other scholars have argued that economic openness (measured in terms of foreign investment) produces a short-term increase in human rights violations and a long-term improvement of citizens' rights (Mosley and Uno 2002).
21. For instance, Poe and Camp (2002) conclude that in situations of emergency, governments facing low-levels of threats (non-violent mobilizations)

are not likely to engage in repressive actions against the opposition. Repression is significant only when the state face high levels of threats (i.e. civil wars).

22. A discussion of modernization theory can be found in Klarén and Bossert (1986). A good discussion of the cultural arguments can be found in Waisman (1987).
23. Argentina (1976-1983), Uruguay (1973-1983), and Chile (1973-1989) are three examples of societies that had central components of a 'modern society' but they suffered reversals during the 1970s. Particularly striking is the case of Argentina where most of the population is comprised by immigrants (Waisman 1987).
24. Moreover, Weisman argues that the adoption of nationalist, anti-liberal orientations in Argentina after the depression was the result of the demonstration effect of the apparent success of fascist regimes in Europe rather than an actualization of latent contents or cultural legacies (Waisman 1987: 103). For a criticism of the cultural argument from a historical-institutional perspective, see Hartlyn (1998b).
25. North (1990) considers institutions as formal rules and standard operating procedures. According to North institutions are the rule of the game in a society or, are the humanly devised constraints that shape human interaction.
26. Historical institutionalism has defined institutions as formal organizations and rules and informal procedures that structure conducts. It includes formal rules, compliance procedures and standard operating practices (Thelen and Steinmo 1992).
27. The literature on democratization has extensively considered this argument. See, for instance, Agüero (1999) Hartlyn (1998b); Karl (1990; 1995); Karl and Schmitter (1994).
28. For instance, O'Donnell (1996; 1998) underlines the lack of mechanisms of vertical and horizontal mechanisms of accountability in new Latin American regimes. Horizontal accountability refers to legal mechanisms that allow state agencies to take actions in relation to possibly unlawful actions or omissions by other agents or agencies of the state. Congressional committees, the Judicial System, Ombudsmen, and Executive Commissions are examples of this type of accountability. Vertical accountability refers to legal mechanisms that allow citizens to control and to take actions over unlawful behaviors by agents or agencies of the state. The latter includes aspects such as regular elections, free press, right to public scrutiny, and right of association, among other aspects.
29. Policy shifts in early 1990s in Brazil are an example of this trend (Holston and Caldeira 1998). This is also the case of Chile in 1998 (see chapter three) and Argentina in the early 1990s (see chapter four).
30. Analyzing the case of Brazil, Chevigny (1995) makes a similar argument when he states that "an underground ideology, straight out of the Old Regime, was used to justify the use of torture [in democratic times]" (p.155). American political science, psychology, and sociology have produced extensive research on the issue of institutional isolation of the police (legal, administrative, and social) and likelihood of violent behavior. In this case,

police violence and corruption is considered as a dysfunctional product of the system. For a literature review, see Simpson (1977).

31. Some scholars have defined Latin American societies as "clientelistic," that is, marked by uneven patron-client relationships that imply a voluntary exchange between unequals of goods, favors, and influence for private and mutual benefits (Clapham 1982; Legg 1975). This may be embedded in patrimonial relationships which are also voluntary and for private and mutual benefits, always in search of just not the use but the abuse of state resources, and in which actors may assume different roles (patrons and clients) in the complex networks of patronage. I thank Jonathan Hartlyn for clarifying this point to me.
32. On Los Angeles Police Department, see the Warren Report (1991). On the New York Police Department see Silverman (1999).
33. The concept of structured contingency attempts to build a bridge between structural analyses that emphasize the set of arrangement and pre-conditions for change in a given political context and actors' ability to make contingent choices in a given time. It is assumed that actors' decisions respond to and are conditioned by their environment (socio-economic structures and political institutions already present). The environment provides a set of options from which actors may choose (Karl 1990)
34. The concept was first introduced by Eisinger (1973). Eisinger opens a research agenda to explain the link between political behavior and the environment, concluding that the intensity and frequency of protests in American cities is associated with the political configuration and specifically the degree to which groups are able to gain access to and manipulate the political system.
35. As Mahoney and Snyder suggest: "structures limit agency not by obstructing but by making available a finite repertoire of tools for action-a repertoire that actors can potentially modify and improve (Mahoney and Snyder 1999).
36. For instance, some structuralists suggest that domestic and international power structures will in fact determine outcomes no matter what individuals do or do not do (Moore 1966; Skocpol 1979; Meyer, Boli, Thomas and Ramirez 1997). In this case, structures are considered as generative forces that define and determine actors' behavior and even beliefs. Other authors suggest that structures provide 'constraining conditions' that may shape actors' behaviors but, at the same time, social actors have a certain level of freedom to influence the environment (Karl 1997; Bratton and van de Walle 1997; Berman 1998). I take a mid-range approach giving actors some room for maneuver. For an analysis of the structure-agent dilemma, see Wendt (1987) and Mahoney and Snyder (1999).
37. Scholars have considered factors such as state strength (Tarrow 1994), social and ethnical cleavages (Kriesi et al. 1995; Krain 1997), degree of openness of the political system (Kitschelt 1986), the institutional capacity to implement policies (Kitschelt 1986), state repressiveness (Schock 1996), the existence of international social networks (Della Porta and Kriesi 1999), the legacy from the previous structure of political opportunities (Kamenitsa 1998), major political changes (Tarrow 1994), and unforeseen events (Krain 1997).

38. For an economic approach, see Haggard and Kaufman (1995). For a political approach, see Mainwaring and Scully (1995) and Siavelis (2000).
39. Less work has been done to explore how such changes impact social actors outside the state. A good exception in the case of Latin America is Taylor (1998). For the case of Germany, see Kamenitsa (1998).
40. Scholars have argued that the number of veto points has an impact on policy outcomes (Immergurt 1992; Huber and Stephens 2001). In this case, veto points include institutional features such as presidential veto power, bicameral congressional system (as oppose to unicameral), and the Supreme Court veto powers. Given that in both Chile and Argentina these features are constant, I exclusively observe the presence/absence of veto points.
41. Here, I am using Janowitz's definition of professional institutions (Janowitz 1960). The notion of corporateness is from Huntington's work on the military institutions (Huntington 1959). For a discussion regarding state strength, see Huber (1995).
42. In this sense, political opportunity approach takes a similar theoretical stand to new institutionalism, regarding actors' agency and interests. First, there are several sources for actors' interests and they are not necessarily class based as a structuralist approach may suggest; second, the institutional context may affect actors' interests in a given time; and third, actors have some agency within a given context (See debate in Thelen and Theimo (1992) and Immergut (1998).
43. Della Porta (1996) mentions these two coalitions, studying policing protests in post-war Germany and Italy. I broaden her distinction suggesting that in issues related to control social protests and crime political authorities debate about the same trade off: liberty vs. security (individual rights vs. police powers).
44. Examples of this trade-off can be found in any democratic society regarding, for instance, increasing police powers to intervene personal communications, searching suspects in the street, allowing suspects to contact a relative once they are under custody, the right to have an attorney, etc.
45. For instance, it is argued that if police officers could detain individuals based on the suspicion they had or will commit a crime or that an officer could interrogate detainees just after a crime has been committed, this would increase the chances of abuses.
46. The advocacy coalition approach suggests that policy change is the result of large-scale social, economic, and political changes and strategic interaction of people that compete for power defending their beliefs. This approach attempts to explain policy change by assuming that actors who held similar beliefs will act collectively to advance such beliefs (Schlager 1999: 245). Beliefs are defined as a set of basic values causal assumptions, and problem perceptions (Sabatier 1988: 139). Beliefs systems determine individuals' choices and actions and according to these beliefs, citizens will form coalitions to advance their demands.
47. In some cases, the church assumes such a role, defending human rights. However, transition to democracy in Latin America was followed by a withdrawal of the Catholic Church from contention in human rights issues.

48. Most reforms imply introducing educational programs to re-capacitate officers, creating new standard operating procedures within the police, and creating external mechanisms of accountability that may have effective results after 2 or 3 years.
49. An interesting analysis on the difficulties of establishing mechanisms of accountability over police institutions in the United States is Chevigny (1995) and Human Rights Watch (1998b). For a comparative perspective, see Marenin (1996).

NOTES TO CHAPTER TWO

1. "Carabineros rechaza informe de Amnistía," El Mercurio, May 29, 2002.
2. "Gobierno resta validez a informe de Amnistía Internacional," La Tercera, May 29, 2002.
3. The last argument refers to the rejection by government authorities of the U.S. Department of State Annual Report on Human Rights.
4. Other distinctive features of the inquisitorial system is the written character of the procedures, the non existence of discretion, the extended use of pretrail detention, and the absence of hearings (Duce 1999; De la Barra 1998).
5. In Chile, a deep reform of the inquisitorial system is taking place. The reform considers public prosecutors and a jury, among other elements. This reform will be fully in place by the year 2003.
6. For a comparative study, see Frühling (1998b).
7. The Congress can recommend to the Executive an internal summary investigation when they consider there is evidence against a police officer. The Congress can even call police authorities to testify before Congress regarding a case. However, the Congress can only make recommendations and no independent investigation to collect information regarding a case is allowed.
8. Formally, appointed representatives are independent. However, the actual performance of the senators in the Senate clearly suggests that they defend their ex-institutions' interests (see the discussion on legal reforms later on in this chapter). An example that shows the close ties between the police and appointed senators is the fact that appointed senator and former director of the police Gen. Fernando Cordero has his office in one of the buildings of the Carabineros. He has publicly defended the police on several occasions (see "Con cintas de video, Cordero defiende a Carabineros" La Tercera, March 14, 1998)
9. This could be particularly observed the first four years of democratic government in the division of human rights at the Ministry of Foreign Affairs where former human rights advocacy leaders advanced the human rights agenda and kept in touch with NGOs. Interview with former advisor of the Ministry of Foreign Affairs Felipe Portales, September 14, 2000.
10. According to human rights organizations there were 435 incarcerated political and security related prisoners at the end of 1989. In January 1990, 47 escaped from Santiago's Prisoners detention center. By March 1990 a total of 335 remained in prison.
11. Upon the request of the police, however, once the detainee has been brought before the judge, he may extend this period for up to five days. In case of

terrorist offences, judges may order detainees to be held incommunicado for ten days. The original government's proposal suggested abolishing the power of judges to extend police detentions (Interview with former minister of Justice Francisco Cumplido, September 13, 2000).

12. This was clear in the Concertación's program of government (Concertación de partidos por la Democracia 1989). Interviews with Francisco Cumplido (September 13, 2000) and the representative of the National Commission of Human Rights Carlos López (August 29, 2000) confirm this government concern.
13. In hundreds of cases, people were held in jail without specific charges against them and several irregularities were detected in terms of the conditions of imprisonment and the legal procedures in court. Interview with former minister of Justice Francisco Cumplido, September 13, 2000.
14. Chamber of Deputies. Global framework agreed by the members of the Commission of Constitution, Law, and Justice to be considered by the government and political parties. June 5, 1990.
15. See for instance Amnesty International Report on 1990-1994, Amnesty International (1991), Human Rights Watch (1991a), and International Commission of Jurists (1992).
16. The Special Rapporteur received 17 complaints between 1990 and 1992, 47 new cases between 1991 and 1993, and 46 cases between 1992 and 1995. All these cases were reported by CODEPU (Interview with CODEPU personnel, September 2000).
17. The campaign involved three strategies: (a) the mobilization of activists in front of police buildings, (b) the formation of a "committee against the 'arrest on suspicion'" clause, supported by secondary and university student unions, by deputies sensitive to the issue, and by the National Institute of Youth (INJ)-a governmental office in charge of dealing with youth issues; and (c) the support of lawyers in other human rights organizations to initiate legal charges against police officers involved in such practices. Interview with former director of CODEJU, José Sabat, October 4, 2000.
18. The national press reported these manifestations extensively. One of the aspects the media always underlined was the high amount of arrested on suspicion. See La Epoca and El Mercurio February 8, 1993; La Nación, February 11, 1993; El Siglo, June 21, 1993; Las Ultimas Noticias, September 13, 1993; La Nación, May 16, 1994; La Epoca, May 20, 1994.
19. INJ several times called the police to adequate procedures to the democratic rule of law. See El Mercurio, October 21, 1992; La Cuarta, October 31, 1992;
20. In his speech, President Aylwin considered that "the amount of arrests on suspicion is excessive and we need to regulate this system in the short term" La Tercera, March 12, 1993.
21. La Nación, September 10, 1993 and Las Ultimas Noticias, September 21, 1993.
22. Private communication with a former advisor to the Ministry of Interior. October, 2000. By 1993, the government was clearly concerned about the high amount of arrest on suspicion. In March, the President mentioned the

need to reform the system (see footnote 20). In July, the government announced a bill to eliminate the arrest on suspicion (La Tercera, July 24, 1993).

23. Interview with former Director of the Police Fernando Cordero, September 29, 2000.
24. I thank Hugo Frühling for addressing this point to me.
25. Interview with José Sabat, October 4, 2000.
26. The Chamber of Deputies approved the bill unanimously (70 votes in favor and no votes against or abstentions). The mixed-commission unanimously approved the bill adding some changes. Finally, in the Senate the bill received the vote of the majority (Congress sessions May 13, 1998 and May 20, 1998).
27. Interview with appointed senator and former Director of the Police (1994-1998) Fernando Cordero, September 22, 2000.
28. Interview with lawyers at the Secretary of the Presidency, September, 2000.
29. The press registered only one politician criticizing these bills: "Leal rechaza reponer detención por sospecha." La Tercera, April 9, 2001.
30. The author collected this information during his field research in Chile. The author obtained unrestricted access to the military court books containing the number of cases filed between 1990 and 2000.
31. In another article, I discuss alternative explanations for this increase. One plausible explanation is that democracy creates incentives for citizens to take legal actions. While this is partly true, there has been no incentive for citizens to take these actions. For instance, the likelihood of winning a case against the police is close to zero, and neither the government nor advocacy groups have developed campaigns on the subject (Fuentes 2001).
32. These statistics were obtained by the author during his field research and consider Santiago and three other regions of the country, representing 65 percent of country's population.
33. A 1992 survey shows that 45 percent of the people who had a legal problem of all types decided not to file a complaint (Correa, 1993).
34. Interview with Nelson Caucoto, Corporation of Legal Assistance. September 29, 2000.
35. The author took a random sample of 165 cases-all those which the author had access to-, analyzing the socio-demographic characteristics of each complaint. These cases represent 4.2 percent of the universe. For specific methodological issues see Fuentes (2001).
36. Between 1990 and 1994, 104 civilians died in confrontations with the police while other 237 were seriously hurt. However, no comparative statistics on police deaths are available at this point. (See Ramos and Guzmán 2000:135).
37. Part of the study was released by a Chilean weekly magazine. See "Tortura en Democracia" Qué Pasa, August 2, 2002. See Universidad Diego Portales and CEJIL (2002).
38. For statistics on crime, see Carabineros and INE (1999).
39. A discussion of this point in Vanderschueren and Oviedo (1995), Correa and Jiménez (1995).

40. The comparative rate of judges per 100 thousand inhabitants is a good illustration of this point. In 1993, in Peru and Uruguay the rate were 18.8, in Costa Rica 10.9, in Colombia 9.7 and in Chile only 3.4 (Correa and Jiménez 1995).
41. In comparison, the sentencing rate for criminal cases in civil courts was 6 percent in the same period.
42. According to the Penal Code, the sentence for police violence (without the death of the victim) is between 2 and 5 years. As an average, military judges have sentenced officers to 532 days in prison (Fuentes 2001).
43. Concerning public opinion confidence in public institutions, see CERC-Chile. (www.cerc.cl).
44. Survey supervised by the Universidad Diego Portales, in four urban centers of Chile. Random sample with 1,642 interviews including exclusively lower classes sectors.
45. Survey conducted by CEP. Representative and random sample of 59% of the population in Chile. 1,885 interviews.
46. The author had free access to the military courts' registration book of complaints after sending a formal letter to the person in charge. It took me one week to be allowed to see this documentation and no special "connection" with any public authority. The analysis of this documentation allowed me to quantify the amount of cases in military courts since 1990, the status of each case (whether it was in a summary stage, close, or with sentence), the type of sentences applied by the judge, and the origin of the complaint (whether it was a case filed by an individual before a military court, a civil court, or a case originated in a police station). For details see Fuentes (2001).
47. In Chile, the coalition of government (Concertación) is formed by the Christian Democracy (PDC), Socialist Party (PS), and Party for Democracy (PPD). The opposition is constituted by two main parties, Renovación Nacional (RN), and Unión Demócrata Independiente (UDI). Major congress representatives that show consistent "pro-order" views are deputies Cristi (RN) Espina (RN), Guzmán (RN), Krauss (PDC) Senators Cordero (appointed), Stange (RN), Novoa (UDI).
48. For instance, the police have a legal division that has been very active in representing the police view before Congress (see the debate on the arrest on suspicion bill and Law 19,693). Additionally, the police have organized statistics on crime to sustain their claims before public authorities.
49. Former Director of the Police Gen. Fernando Cordero stated that "we are two former directors of the Police in Congress defending the interests of the institution." Interview with Fernando Cordero, September 22, 2000.
50. Within the government, particularly relevant is the relationship between the Police and key PDC close to the interest of the police. This was the case with former ministers of Interior Enrique Krauss (1990-1994) and Carlos Figueroa (1994-1998).
51. In Congress, particularly relevant are deputies Allende (PS), Elgueta (PDC), Letelier (PS), Naranjo (PS), Palma (PDC), and senator Gazmuri (PS).
52. Three types of organizations can be identified: the first type is Voluntary. The main objective of these organizations is to denounce specific acts and to

mobilize citizens around specific claims (disappearance of persons, torture, political prisoners). In general, these organizations emerge as initiatives of victims' relatives. (b) Professional. The main objective of these organizations is to conduct research on human rights and/or professional support (psychological, social) to the victims. (c) Political-Lobby. Although many organizations originally emerged with the clear objective of providing legal support for the victims and their relatives, some organizations adopted a more political role in trying to influence politicians and governments regarding the issue of human rights during and after Pinochet's regime.

53. For instance, between 1983 and 1988 the Vicariate of Solidarity coordinated a yearly average of two thousand organizations nationwide, which included the coordination of more than 70 thousand people every year (Lowden 1996).
54. To mention some of them, Alejandro González, Jorge Domínguez, Roberto Garretón, Carlos López, Felipe Portales, José Zalaquett, and several other professionals who used to work in the Vicariate of Solidarity and in the ChCHRs assumed new positions related to the subject in the government soon after the transition.
55. Interview with the secretary of the ChCHRs Carlos López. January 19, 2001.
56. Interview with CODEPU representative Hugo Gutiérrez, January 22, 2001.
57. The only options are through the Congress' requirement of an impeachment against the Director of the Police and through the President's request of the resignation of the Director of the Police to the National Security Council in which the armed forces and the police have half of the votes.
58. Interview with Alejandro Salinas, head of the Human Rights Division at the Ministry of Foreign Affairs, September 13, 2000.
59. See U.N. Commission on Human Rights (E/CN.4/2000/9/Add.1). After this commission requested information regarding the police investigative labor, the Carabineros responded that they could not provide information on internal administrative procedures. The government provided a list of seven cases that were under investigation by military courts.
60. I had access to the archives of the Corporation of Legal Assistance at the Ministry of Justice. I considered all letters sent to the police between November 1997 and October 2000.
61. When non-governmental organizations sent letters to the police (69 cases between 1997-2000), the police responded to 73 percent in the following way: 19 percent internal investigation will be initiated; 45 percent defense of police officers' behavior, 7.8 percent administrative sanction for clerical error. No specification of the type of sanction and no recognition of police violent behavior was registered. This data was obtained by the author during his field research. More recently, the police recognized having carried out 244 internal investigations in 1998, 274 in 1999, 303 in 2000, and 325 in 2001. The police said that in 27 percent of those cases some sanction was applied. However, no specification of the sanctions was mentioned. Qué Pasa, August 8, 2002.

62. This is a well-accepted view among lawyers on the police's culture of secrecy. Interview with Nelson Caucoto, September 29, 2000 and Julio Berrios, December 2000.
63. Comisión Verdad y Reconciliación (1991).
64. For instance, between 1990 and 1999, an average of six lawyers of CODEPU worked on cases related to past human rights violations and only one lawyer accepted cases regarding current violations of human rights. Interview with Miriam Reyes, October 11, 2000.
65. This becomes evident in several public declarations made by appointed senator Cordero, defending police interests (see La Tercera, March 14, 1998). The ex director of the police and currently elected senator, Rodolfo Stange assumed the same stand (see El Mercurio, January 12, 1998)
66. Two conservative groups dominate newspapers circulation in Chile: The Edwards group owns the newspapers El Mercurio, La Segunda, and Las Ultimas Noticias. The Copesa group owns La Tercera, La Cuarta, and the weekly magazine Qué Pasa. This represent 70 percent of national newspapers circulation.
67. Pro-government media includes the newspapers La Epoca (from 1990 to 1998) and La Nación, and the National TV station.
68. A reserved document produced by Carabineros suggests several irregularities in police procedures in the in dealing with Mapuches in the South of Chile-Mapuches are indigenous people who have rejected appropriation of land by hydroelectric private companies. The document suggests that officers have treated indigenous people in a hostile, aggressive, and offensive way. La Tercera, November 24, 2000. The document was given to the press by a government source. Personal communication with a journalist, September 2002.
69. An additional factor may refer to the internal acceptance of police violence as a mechanism to gain respect among officers: "being tough [with delinquents] is not a crime. If you are not tough, then, your boss thinks you are a 'chicken' and they punish you (. . .) If you do not allow low-ranking officers to be tough with detainees, you lose leadership among police officers." Police Officer. Anonymous interview, "Tortura en demoracia," Qué Pasa, August 9, 2002.
70. The original directory included senator Sergio Bitar (a moderate leftist from the Concertación), the Christian Democrat and former minister of Defense Edmundo Pérez-Yoma and the Christian Democrat Mónica Jiménez.
71. Interview with Javiera Blanco, December 21, 2000.
72. The debate of several bills regarding such subjects have included the participation of Paz Ciudadana in the period of public hearings in Congress.
73. In June 1998, the Ministry of Justice, Paz Ciudadana, and the Chilean Catholic University signed an agreement to support the modernization of police institutions. El Mercurio, June 23, 1998.
74. See "Suscrito convenio para modificación del Código Penal." El Mercurio, September 15, 2000.
75. Interview with Gen. Fernando Cordero, September 22, 2000.
76. The bill attempted to reduce police officers' administrative tasks in order to put more police officers on the streets.

77. Policymakers in charge of writing the bill in the Presidency expressed that the police was particularly concerned about the elimination of the 'arrest on suspicion' clause and that they lobbied policymakers in the Ministry of Interior to enact a clearer rule regarding detentions. Interview not for attribution at the Presidency, September, 2000. Gen. Cordero also expressed that the police was particularly concerned about not having powers to detain suspects. They lobbied the government and some Congressional representatives willing to reform the Penal Code. Interview with Fernando Cordero, September 22, 2000.
78. The name of the bill was "Reforms to make Police work more efficient," National Congress Library. History of the Law. Law 19,693.
79. The arguments were expressed by representatives Cordero (appointed Senator), Stange (RN), Espina (RN), Prat (RN), Parra (Radical Party), Sabag (PDC), Muñoz (Social Democrat), among other legislators. See Law 19,693 (2000).
80. Indeed, the bill and final law are very ambiguous in this regard. This clause (260bis) establishes that "the police could request identification to any individual who are suspected of committing a crime or simple crime, or who could provide information regarding a crime. (. . .). If individuals reject or cannot provide their identifications, the police will take individuals to a police station in order to facilitate means to establish a satisfactory identification." These opinions were expressed by senator Gazmuri (PS), and deputies Allende (PS), Cornejo (PDC), Elgueta (PDC), and Letelier (PS).
81. See "CODEJU denuncia detenciones por sospecha," La Tercera, January 24, 1999; "Eliminación de detención por sospechas causa sospechas" La Tercera, January 30, and "Carabineros pide más atribuciones" La Tercera, April 17, 1999; and "Carabineros critica discusión en Congreso," La Tercera, April 30, 2000.
82. The more active organization trying to address issues of individual rights is the Law School of the Universidad Diego Portales. However, they decided to support the government's initiative without engaging in further coordination with other civil rights groups.
83. The different congressional commissions invited the following institutions to discuss this bill: Ministry of Interior, under-secretary of Carabineros, the Carabineros, and Ministry of Justice.
84. Interview with José Sabat (CODEJU), October 4, 2000 and Loreto Hoecker, September 2000.
85. Interview with Felipe Portales, September 14, 2000.
86. Personal communication with a former advisor at the Ministry of Foreign Affairs. January 2001.
87. The only note regarding this visit appeared in the conservative newspaper "Visita Oficial a Chile de Relator sobre la Tortura," El Mercurio August 24, 1995.
88. Jorge Berguño, Chief of the Chilean Delegation in Geneve. "Controvertido Informe sobre la tortura en Chile entregó relator de la ONU," La Epoca, April 5, 1996.
89. Interview with lawyers of the Human Rights Division at the Corporation of Legal Assistance. October-December, 2000.

90. This program is the equivalent of the U.S. program 60 minutes.
91. Interview with National TV journalists, December, 2000. The documentary received, first, an editorial objection because of its title "torture in democracy," which was modified to "Police and Human Rights."
92. "Denuncian violencia innecesaria de Carabineros" La Tercera, December 7, 1999.
93. "Denuncian apremios ilegítimos contra mapuches" La Tercera, January 20, 2000.
94. "Cordero rejects Amnesty International report" El Mercurio, October 5, 2000.
95. See "Documento revela mea culpa de Carabineros en maltrato a mapuches." La Tercera, December 24, 2000. The journalist obtained the report from the government. Personal communication with the reporter, September, 2002.
96. Between July 1998 and March 2002, the printed press reported 24 cases of police violence. Eight cases were denounced by Congressional representatives, three by human rights groups, three by the victims, and ten by other sources (media, police release, Corporation of Legal Assistance).
97. Deputy Alberto Espina (RN) suggested using the anti-terrorist law because the indigenous protestors were threatening other sectors of the population, La Tercera, January 25, 2001.
98. Qué Pasa is an influential national magazine owned by COPESA-a corporation traditionally identified with conservative sectors.
99. "Tortura en Democracia," Qué Pasa, August 2, 2002.
100. "Por la razón o la fuerza," Qué Pasa, August 9, 2002.
101. I took a sample of 52 cases denounced in the press between 1993 and the year 2001. In all these cases, I analyzed press reactions during one week after the case was made public, unless cases were continued in press headlines, in which case I followed them longer.
102. See the gap between lawsuits channeled through CODEPU and the actual number of cases in courts, Graph 2.2.
103. See Table 2.4. Of the 52 incidents reported in the press, in 40 percent of these cases human rights groups did not react to the allegation.
104. Interview with Carlos López (CChHRs), August 29, 2000; Hugo Gutierrez (CODEPU) January 2001; José Sabat (CODEJU) October 4, 2000; Verónica Reina (FASIC), January 18, 2001.
105. An explicit division among human rights lawyers was evident in relation to the best strategies to deal with the Pinochet's case in the year 2000. See "El club de la pelea. Las querellas y contraquerellas de los DD.HH.," El Mercurio, October 22, 2000.
106. The Universidad Diego Portales, Centro de Estudios del Desarrollo, and FLACSO have developed academic programs to study reform of the military justice system and police autonomy but these efforts are rarely known by other non-governmental centers. Moreover, few academic institutions know about the work developed in the division of human rights of the Corporation of Legal Assistance.

107. A good example of this trend is the creation in March 2001 of an "Ethical Commission Against Torture," involving 13 Chilean human rights organizations. Most of this Commission's petitions are related to past human rights violations. (See, Comisión Etica contra la Tortura 2002).
108. Interview with Loreto Hoecker, September, 2000.
109. The author published a quantitative document called "Denuncias por Violencia Policial" [Accusations of Police Violence] in August 2001. The methodological aspects of the experiment are in Appendix 2.
110. In the case of the Department of State, a representative contacted the author requesting authorization to publish the findings their report. See U.S. Annual Report on Human Rights (2002). In the case of Amnesty International, they contacted the author to update their annual human rights report.
111. I distinguish between active responses (engaging in some contact with the author or using the material in public) and passive responses (visiting the webpage-which I monitored, and requesting the information for the library).

NOTES TO CHAPTER THREE

1. The Spanish translation is Corporación de Promoción Universitaria.
2. The first project funded by the USAID was U.S. $150,000 (1988-1990), the second project was U.S. $3,500.000 (Vargas 1998a; 1998b: 84).
3. See collection of Cuadernos de Análisis Jurídico, Universidad Diego Portales, 1992-1998.
4. The forum was integrated by 70 members, most of them lawyers linked to several left, center and right wing political parties or representatives of different Universities, professional associations, and policymakers (Vargas 1998b).
5. For instance, in 1994, newspapers published 91 articles and editorials regarding the reform. By 1996, this figure was 248 (Vargas 1998a: 107).
6. Representatives of CPU, Paz Ciudadana, and Universidad Diego Portales met with directors of mass media, Supreme Court Judges, presidents of several political parties, the head of the uniformed and civil police, the minister of Defense, congressional representatives, and representatives of the lawyers' professional association. Interview with Cristián Riego, September 28, 2000 and Vargas (1998b).
7. The reform is been implemented by stages, in different regions of the country. It is expected the reform will be fully implemented by 2003.
8. The study considered a random sample of 434 court files completed between 1992 and 1994 (González, Jiménez, and Riego 1998).
9. Interview with Cristián Riego, September 28, 2000.
10. The representatives included representatives of the center-left coalition Adriana Muñoz (PPD), Ramón Elizalde (PDC), Juan Pablo Letelier (PS), Carlos Montes (PS), Jaime Naranjo (PS), Andrés Palma (PDC), and Guillermo Yunge (PDC).
11. Interview with former Minister of Justice, Francisco Cumplido, September 13, 2000.

12. Minister of Justice, Soledad Alvear. Intervention in the Commission of Constitution and Legislation of the Chamber of Deputies, May 8, 1996.
13. Second Report of the Commission of Constitution and Legislation of the Chamber of Deputies, May 8, 1996 and Oficio number 1223, Ministry of Presidency, August 13, 1996.
14. See Report of the Commission of Constitution and Legislation of the Senate, March 31, 1996.
15. See discrepancies between the Senate and Chamber of deputies in Session 29, Chamber of Deputies, January 21, 1998, pp 14-24.
16. "Se dará suma urgencia a estatuto del detenido," El Mercurio, January 18, 1998
17. Report of the Mixed Commission. April 30, 1998.
18. Appointed senator Sergio Fernández expressed that "I support this bill because in this project there is an equilibrium between individual freedom and public safety." Senators Sergio Diez (RN) and Larraín (UDI) made similar statements. Senate, session 17, May 20, 1998.
19. "Sobre derechos del detenido: policías están entrenadas para aplicar la nueva ley" El Mercurio, July 2, 1998; "Nadie podrá ser detenido por sospecha." La Tercera, July 2, 1998.

NOTES TO CHAPTER FOUR

1. "Golpe en villa Ramallo, la polémica por la seguridad," Clarín, September 18, 1999.
2. "Hay que meterle bala a los ladrones," Clarín, August 4, 1999; and "Renunció Arslanián y comprometió a Duhalde," Clarín, August 6, 1999.
3. I thank Merike Blofield for her insights regarding this point.
4. This means there is 1 police officer every 270 inhabitants in Buenos Aires Province, 1 every 317 in the Capital and 1 every 416 in the case of Chile.
5. The government of the City of Buenos Aires has no direct control over the federal police. However, authorities at the City level have reformed legal procedures that affect the powers of the federal police.
6. This was the case of the federal police until 1992 and the provincial police until 1998. Penal Codes reforms created a judicial investigative police at both levels. However, budget problems have delayed the implementation of the reforms.
7. The penal code at the federal level specified that police officers could detain any individual in order to verify his/her police record (Blando 1995:140).
8 .Argentine lawyer Julio Maier developed the first Penal Code reform. Maier's ideas-along with other lawyers such as Binder and Zaffaroni-influenced Latin American current process of judicial reforms.
9 .The inefficiency of the system implied that, for instance, 84% of the adult population in jail was waiting for trial and from this figure only 16% was finally sentenced. 30.6% of trials took less than a year and 69.4% more than one year (Correa and Jiménez 1997).
10 .For a comparative analysis of these changes, see Correa and Jiménez (1997); Struensee and Maier (2000).

11. The new code abolished the spontaneous statement to the police and, therefore, police could not receive a testimony from a detainee. Additionally, the incommunicado period was restricted to 10 days and it was explicitly recognized the right of detainees to talk with a lawyer, even under incommunicado detention. The new 1994 Constitution introduced two other changes: it gave constitutional rank to international treaties regarding human rights and it provided constitutional status to the Ombudsman. Several of these legal changes did not enter into effect until the second wave of reforms.
12. Eduardo Duhalde, La Nación December 21, 1997.
13. See Página 12, January 14, 2000; and Clarín, February 24, February 27, and March 11, 2000.
14. Press reports suggest that the governor of the Buenos Aires province allowed criminal activities to continue in exchange of political and financial support to chiefs of police stations. The ex chief of the police Bronislao Rogosz claimed that he was dismissed by a governor in the early 1980s because he refused to protect an officer who was indicted by the court for corruption (See "plata sucia" Página 12, September 26, and "Plin Caja" December 19, 1999). Moreover, President Menem recognized the existence of stolen car trafficking within the provincial police ("El presidente y las bandas mafiosas," Clarín, August 13, 1996). Secretary of Justice and Security León Arslanián (1998-1999) said that "even though we faced pressures from Intendentes [heads of Buenos Aires provincial districts], we disarticulated some of the illegal finance network in the province" ("Plin Caja" Página 12, December 19, 1999).
15. In 1999, four former police officers, a police informer, and four civilians were detained in connection to the case. This case led the national government to push for several changes in the provincial police, including the dismissal of more than 400 officers connected to illegal activities, decentralization of the police's internal decision-making process, and the approval of several laws restricting police powers.
16. Police practice of shooting people without justified reasons (e.g. self-defense)
17. See, for instance, annual reports of Human Rights Watch (1991a), Amnesty International (1990-2001), and the U.S. Department of State Annual report on Human Rights (1995-2001).
18. Allegations of police violence in court have not been systematized. Additionally, the federal nature of the Argentine political system inhibits different state agencies from having a centralized account of such cases.
19. Interview with Gustavo Palmieri, CELS, April, 2001.
20. However, If we control the population, the proportion of yearly civilian deaths in the Capital (1 every 61,000 citizens) is actually greater than in the province (1 every 100,000). If we control of the number of police officers, the proportion of civilian deaths and police officers is higher in the Capital (1 every 193 officers) than in the province (1 every 358 officers).
21. For figures on crime, see Ministry of Justice, 2000. For figures on unemployment, see http://www.latin-focus.com
22. Between 1986 and 1990, police forces organized an average of 20 strikes a year. Between 1990 and 1999 the average fall to less than 3 strikes a year

(CEUNM, Centro de Documentación). The improvements for police officers focused on increasing the number of police cars (2,000 by 1993), increasing the number of police officers (the plan considered 6,000 more officers between 1993-1995), and improving communications (CELS and Facultad, 1994).

23. "Duhalde elogia la policía, pero también pide sanciones," Clarín, February 23, 1996.
24. Página 12, February 2, 1994. Cited in CELS (1995). Later on, Eduardo Pettiagini resigned from his position given increasing criticisms regarding police violence. Particularly important in this case was the publication of the U.S. State Department human rights annual report, increasing international attention to the subject.
25. Clarín, February 20, 1994. There are several government declarations supporting an "iron fist" approach. Minister of Interior Carlos Ruckauf suggested that "the police is requesting to increase the period in which police can hold citizens under custody and reduce legal concern during periods of interrogation" (Clarín March 25, 1994). After a police protest requesting higher salaries and "tough" rules, President Menem argued that "we need to speed up the approval of "iron fist" measures against delinquency" (Clarín, February 2, 1995). In June 1996 and facing new criticisms, Duhalde suggested that "the Buenos Aires provincial police is the best police in the world" (Clarín, June 17, 1996).
26. By the end of the 1990s, 66.2 percent of prisoners in federal prisons and 90 percent of prisoners in the Buenos Aires province were waiting for trial (CELS 2001).
27. See U.N. document UNCAT/C/SR/.307, December 10, 1997. Another source suggests that while 85,541 cases were filed in courts in 1996, only 3.1% ended in the oral stage of the process and only 1% ended with sentence (Comisión de Seguridad Interior, 1998).
28. Surveys conducted in the Buenos Aires Capital and Province. Representative and random sample. Samples are as follow: 1986-1994: 1,000 interviews; 1995: 993 interviews; 1996: 1,000 interviews; 1997-1999 1,140 interviews; 2000: 640 interviews.
29. Survey conducted by CEUNM in Buenos Aires Capital and Province. Random representative sample of adult population. 1,000 interviews. +/- 4 percent sample error.
30. Survey conducted by Catterberg and Assoc. in the Buenos Aires province. Random and representative sample of the adult population from the province. 1,000 interviews. +/- 3 percent sample error.
31. Surveys conducted by CEUNM in Buenos Aires Capital and Province. Random and representative sample of adult population. 900 interviews. +/- 4 percent sample error.
32. The methodological characteristics of the surveys are the following: 1998 survey, representative sample of citizens older than 15 years old with 2,001 interviews in Buenos Aires province (+/- 2.24% statistical error); 1999 survey, representative sample of citizens older than 15 years old with 5,611 interviews considering both Capital and Province (+/- 1.3 statistical error)

(Data shows only those of the province); and 2000 survey, representative sample of citizens older than 15 years old with 3,601 interviews in the Buenos Aires Province. (+/- 1.6 statistical error). Ministerio de Justicia (2002).

33. Two surveys confirm this trend. In 1998, w hen respondents were asked whether police forces should have more powers to fight crime, 44.7 percent supported this claim while 48 rejected it (survey conducted by CEUNM. Random and representative sample of the adult population in the Buenos Aires Capital and province. 1,140 interviews). In 2000, when respondents were asked the same question, 45.4 percent supported increasing police powers while 52 percent reject it (Survey conducted by Catterberg and Assoc. in the Buenos Aires province. Random and representative sample of the adult population from the province. 1,000 interviews. +/- 3 percent sample error).
34. Surveys conducted between 1998 and 2001 confirm that lower-class sectors have a comparatively better opinion of the police than upper-class sectors. See Centro de Documentación, CEUNM.
35. Voluntary. The main objective of these organizations is to denounce specific acts and to mobilize citizens around specific claims (disappearance of persons, torture, political prisoners). In general, these organizations emerge as initiatives of victims' relatives. (b) Professional. The main objective of these organizations is to conduct research on human rights and/or professional support (psychological, social) to the victims. (c) Political-Lobby. Although many organizations originally emerged with the clear objective of providing legal support for the victims and their relatives, some organizations adopted a more political role in trying to influence politicians and governments regarding the issue of human rights.
36. Activists in Argentina commonly refer to this distinction. Interview with Martín Abregú, January, 2001.
37. Several official documents and interviews with key policymakers and representatives of non-governmental organizations confirm this division within the government. Interviews with Martín Abregú, Andrea Pochack, and Gustavo Palmieri (CELS). April-June, 2001. See also Argentine reports on human rights presented before UN commission on human rights. For instance, Argentine representatives before the U.N. have shown critical views on the role of police forces in Argentine society (UN CAT/C/SR.307 December 10, 1997, 4). For a more moderate view, see Pierini (1999).
38. See for instance, Cecchi (2000), Dutil and Ragendorfer (1997), Salinas (1997), Sdrech and Colominas (1997), Sigal (1998).
39. Interview with Gustavo Palmieri, CELS, April and June 2001.
40. Comisión de Seguridad Interior (1998).
41. Interview with León Arslanián, former minister of Justice and Security, March 2001. Moreover, the police face serious problems regarding systematization and centralization of crime statistics even within a province, lack of databases with criminal records, and poor infrastructure (Comisión de Seguridad Interior, 1998). See particularly intervention of León Arslanián (pp. 125-133).

42. On December 1997, four anonymous chief of police stations publicly denounced illegal practices by police officers in Buenos Aires province. See Página 12, December 7, 1997. They mention illegal arrangements between active police officers, drug dealers and ex police officers, among others illegal activities.
43. I chose this period because of the availability of newspapers in Internet.
44. Interview with Gustavo Palmieri, CELS, April and June 2001.
45. Interview with María del Carmen Verdú, April 9, 2001.
46. Interview with Martín Abregú, January 26, 2001. See also CELS annual reports on human rights (1993-2001)
47. See, for instance, "Dicen que aumentan los casos de violencia policial en el país," Clarín, June 18, 1996; "Aumentan las víctimas incidentals, según el CELS," Página 12, July 1, 1998; "Para un solo año, demasiadas balas," Página 12, March 25, 1999; "Police violence on the rise" Buenos Aires Herald, April 18, 2000. In terms of politicians using this report, see 34 session, Buenos Aires Province Legislature, November 24, 1998; 27 session, December 11 1997; 22 session, 2000.
48. See "El CELS quiere saber," Clarín, November 18, 1996; and "la Justicia pregunta por qué la policía federal no da información" Página 12, October 25, 1996.
49. See, "Posible sucesor de Patti," Página 12, August 13, 1996; "Patti, Manual del buen torturador," Página 12, November 19, 1999.
50. "Queremos que el CELS nos ayude," Página 12, August 29, 2000.
51. Reforms were made in Ecuador (1991), Peru (1991) Guatemala (1992), Argentina (1992), Costa Rica (1996), El Salvador (1998), Chile (1998), Venezuela (1998), Paraguay (1998), Bolivia (1998). By 2002 other countries were debating reforms in Congress including Nicaragua, Honduras, Dominican Republic, and Panama (Domingo 1999; Struensee and Maier 2000).
52. As was said, Julio Maier wrote the original draft of the federal penal code reform in 1986. Alberto Binder and León Arslanián proposed and participated in the institutional reforms of the BAPP in 1997-1998. Binder is closely related to the FREPASO party and Arslanián is a member of the Permanent Assembly of Human Rights in Argentina. Raúl Zaffaroni wrote the original draft eliminating the detention on suspicion clause for the Buenos Aires City Council. All these authorities have participated in activities organized by CELS and have maintained contacts with CELS' researchers. Interview with Gustavo Palmieri (CELS), April 2001 and interview with Martin Abregú (CELS), January 2001.
53. Walter Bulacio was arrested outside of a stadium when he was trying to gain access to a rock concert in Buenos Aires. The police tortured him in the police station and transferred him to a hospital where he died as a result of serious contusions in his head. Until 2002, the police and the criminal system have failed to bring the responsible to justice. For example, the alleged officer responsible for this crime kept his job and was even promoted in the police, despite the fact he faced charges against him in court. Interview with María del Carmen Verdú, April 9, 2001. See also, "Sobreseyeron al comisario que detuvo al joven Walter Bulacio," Clarín, March 14, 1996; "Habrá condena en el caso Walter Bulacio" Diario Popular, March 24, 1996.

54. CORREPI's listserv address is correpi@fibertel.com.ar. CORREPI's online reports in: http://www.informativos.net.
55. The author interviewed six members of CELS between April and August 2001: Gustavo Palmieri, Sofía Tiscornia, Andrea Pochack, Laura Itchart, María Capurro, and Julieta Rossi.
56. Between 1989 and 2000, CORREPI's leaders have given 12 long interviews to the press, and newspapers register 53 reports on CORREPI's legal activities, and 38 reports on CORREPI's public demonstrations (Documentary Center, CORREPI).
57. Interview with Fernanda Doz Costa, representative of CEJIL, Washington DC, January 23, 2002.
58. Without considering news about the AMIA, more than 32 cases of police corruption were denounced by the press only in 1996 (Oliveira and Tiscornia 1997).
59. A prestigious lawyer, Alberto Binder, pro-civil rights was the main author of a proposal draft for the reform of the police.
60. Seminario sobre Control Democrático de los Organismos de Seguridad Interior. Buenos Aires, April 7 and 8, 1997. Marcelo Saín (who was in charge of writing the FREPASO proposal for the reform of the BAPP), and León Arslanián (who was the person in charge of implementing the BAPP reform) participated in this seminar.
61. In his study on the Peronist party, Steven Levitsky (2001) argues that local brokers or "problem-solvers" are informally linked to the Peronist party, accessing government resources. However, "there is a dark underside to this social embeddedness. Because urban slum zones are frequently centres of illicit activity such as drug trafficking, prostitution, and gambling, Peronist networks are inevitably linked to these forms of organization as well" (Levitsky 2001: 41).
62. Anonymous chief of a police station. "Los policías amenazan con huelga de brazos caídos," Página 12 December 21, 1997.
63. "Amenazan al comisario que investiga las agencies," Página 12, March 3, 1998.
64. "Amenazan a dos legisladores," Clarín, March 8, 1998. More cases were denounced during 1998. See "La policía está presa en su interna," Página 12, September 20, 1999.
65. "Plata sucia," Página 12, September 26, 1999. Moreover, former secretary of justice and security León Arslanián recognized pressures from several intendentes to maintain the illegal profit system in the police. "Plin Caja" Página 12, December 19, 1999.
66. "En Lomas de Zamora al defensor de seguridad lo eligen entre pocos," Página 12, March 18, 1998.
67. "Hay que meterle bala a los ladrones," Clarín, August 4, 1999.
68. "Renunció Arslanián y comprometió a Duhalde," Clarín, August 6, 1999.
69. "Renunció Arslanián y comprometió a Duhalde," Clarín, August 6, 1999. "La peor astilla," Página 12, August 8, 1999; "Una relación es ascenso," Clarín, October 28, 1999.
70. Interview with León Arslanián, March 2001.
71. "Reincorporarán a mil policías," Clarín, August 13, 1999.

72. "La Maldita policía, parte II," Página 12, August 13, 1999. A political reason may explain Duhalde's drastic change: he was interested on running for president in the next presidential election (1999) and he needed Ruckauf's support within the Peronist party.
73. Constant conflicts with the press and aggressive declarations made Ruckauf to request Rico's resignation few months after he was appointed.
74. The law implies that judges may take into account police's interrogatories but it was not allowed to use them during the trial.
75. "Las dos jugadas de Ruckauf," Clarín, February 27, 2000.
76. "Lo de meter bala ya era doctrina antes de Ruckauf," Página 12, August 13, 1999.
77. "Duhalde tuvo que despedir a su secretario de seguridad," Clarín, September 8, 1999.
78. "Joven y pobre es igual a delincuente," Página 12, May 17, 2001.

NOTES TO CHAPTER FIVE

1. Buenos Aires City government achieved full autonomy in 1994, after the approval of the new Constitution.
2. There are few studies regarding the amount of cases appealed. For instance, analyzing the year 1995, Oliveira and Tiscornia found that only 0.5% of individuals used their right to appeal a sentence (Oliveira and Tiscornia 1998:168). In 1996, the percentage of appeals dropped to 0.0029 percent (CELS and Human Rights Watch 1998).
3. This fact has recently been addressed by human rights organizations in Argentina (CELS 2000).
4. Interview of the advisors in charge of the platform of the Peronist party and Alianza coalition before the 1999 presidential campaign in Argentina. See "El futuro político de la policía federal. Qué hacer con ellos," Página 12, July 11, 1999.
5. Survey conducted by CEUNM in Buenos Aires Capital and Province. Random representative sample of adult population. 1,000 interviews. +/- 4 percent sample error.
6. Survey conducted by CEUNM (1998). Random and representative sample of the adult population in the Buenos Aires Capital and province. 1,140 interviews.
7. Presentation of the Federal Police before the Special Commission on National Public Safety, March 1998.
8. This was the case with Walter Bulacio, José Luis Ojeda, Juan Carlos Bayarri, and Gumercindo Ramoa (CELS and Human Rights Watch 1998; CELS 2000; 2001).
9. "Sistema para el cobro de coimas en la Federal," Clarín, March 4, 1999; "Investigan el patrimonio de un comisario implicado en coimas," Clarín, March 6, 1999.
10. "Cabo soportó tres atentados" La Nación, March 4, 1999; Martín Abregú, "Edictos viciosos," Noticias, March 6, 1999.
11. "Piden derogación de leyes que permiten espionaje. Los azules sin protección," Página 12, May 23, 2000.

12. For instance, after the approval of the restriction of police powers in 1998, the Federal Police began a campaign linking increasing levels of violence in the city with the reduction of such powers. See "No tenemos medios ideales" Página 12, August 29, 1998.
13. Interview with Gustavo Palmieri, CELS, April 2001.
14. Simón Lázara was particularly interested in this bill. He was a member of the Argentine NGO Permanent Assembly of Human Rights.
15. For a systematic account of this reform, see Blando (1995).
16. This memorandum Number 40 was date from April, 1965.
17. "Murió de un derrame cerebral el estudiante que estuvo detenido" Clarín, April 30, 1991; "Más de dos mil jóvenes pidieron que se aclare la muerte de estudiante" Clarín, May 3, 1991; "Otra Marcha por la Muerte de Walter Bulacio," Clarín May 10, 1991; "En silencio, los amigos de Walter reclaman justicia," Clarín, May 11, 1991; "Disturbios en la Plaza de Mayo," Clarín, May 24, 1991. "El Memorando Fantasma," Página 12, May 28, 1991; "En Diputados dicen que hay detenciones indiscriminadas" Clarín, May 29, 1991.
18. Several deputies pressured the Executive to clarify the Bulacio case, to create an investigate commission in Congress, and to speed up the debate regarding the "Verification of Records and Identity Detention" clause. See Chamber of Deputies, May 22, 1991. p. 302-309.
19. Walter Bulacio was arrested outside of a stadium when he was trying to enter to a rock concert in Buenos Aires. He later died under police custody. The case was widely publicized and even the rock group wrote a special song for him.
20. Between 1992 and 1996 a yearly average of 150,000 people was arrested under Federal Police edicts (Chillier 1998).
21. See "Presiones dan frutos" La Nación, September 8, 1996.
22. Deputy Jorge Zaffaroni, an influential pro-civil rights lawyer was the author of the proposal that was finally approved in the City Legislature.
23. "La policía lanzó el servicio metropolitano especial para prevenir delitos" Página 12, September 1, 1998.
24. "Más policía en la calle ayuda, pero no resuelve el problema," Minister of Justice Raúl Granillo Ocampo, Clarín, September 9, 1998.
25. See Clarín, July 4, 1998.
26. "Incidentes callejeros de vecinos con travestis y prostitutes," Clarín, March 20, 1998.
27. "Los unos y los Otros del barrio más caliente," Página 12, July 4, 1998.
28. "Investigan el patrimonio de un comisario implicado en coimas," Clarín, March 6, 1999.
29. "Corach vincula a los extranjeros con el aumento del delito. Criticó permisividad de la legislación en Capital," Clarín, January 25, 1999.
30. "Menem: vuelven los edictos," Clarín, February 25, 1999; "Menem insiste con los edictos," Clarín, February 27, 1999.
31. A good account of these reforms in Chillier (1998).
32. "La calle se puso dura," Página 12, March 5, 1999. The two most prominent leaders of the Alianza, Fernando de la Rúa and Chacho Alvarez, lobbied the legislature to "solve this controversial 'issue' fast."

NOTES TO CHAPTER SIX

1. "Conducir no es leer encuestas y correr," Página 12, August 6, 1999.
2. A recent WOLA report addresses that "in response to calls for a 'tough on crime' approach, governments have maintained or reintroduced a military role in policing, undermining the commitment to demilitarized internal security (. . .). Central America's police reform efforts have made important strides, but they face constant resistance and challenges from authoritarian sectors including the military, political parties, and elites who see their prerogatives threatened by democratic change" (Neild 2002: 1)
3. "Lawyers Protest Across France at Sweeping Anticrime Law," The New York Times, February 12, 2004, A11.
4. Several theoretical perspectives have addressed the importance of studying policy change and policy resistance. From a rational choice-institutional perspective see North (1990). From a historical-institutional perspective see debate in Thelen and Steinmo (1992). From a rational-choice perspective, see debate in Bates, Figueiredo and Weinsgast (1998).
5. Indeed, the 1994 Constitution allow Congress to examine presidential decrees within 10 days after being promulgated.
6. My study does not allow an exploration of such hypothesis in detail. However, comparative analyses of cases such as the New York Police Department and Los Angeles Police Department show that when top-ranking officers are committed and willing to enact internal controls, levels of police violence are likely to drop significantly (Kelling and Andrews 1999; Davis et al. 2002).
7. In this study, I have focused on CELS, but this has also been the case of other human rights organizations such as Madres de Plaza de Mayo, and Abuelas de Plaza de Mayo, among other organizations.
8. Here, I am referring to exclusively a change in internal mechanisms of accountability to control police misbehavior.
9. One of the most relevant projects to reform the police is a sub-regional academic initiative funded by Ford Foundation. However, the main issues addressed by this initiative in Chile are related to deployment, relationship with the community, improvement of resources, and training (see www.policiaysociedad.org). Moreover, in Chile here are some partial studies made by Universidad Diego Portales, FLACSO-Chile, and CED to reform the military judiciary system. However, these studies have not been extensively debated.
10. Keohane (1971) systematizes these conditions in his work on the influence of small powers over great powers.
11. As McAdam, Tarrow, and Tilly nicely put it, the main inquiry of the social movement literature has been explaining under what conditions apathetic, frightened, or disorganized people explode into the streets, put down their tools, or mount the barricades (McAdam, Tarrow, and Tilly 2002: 38).
12. Under certain circumstances issues like health care, education policy, and foreign policy affairs may not create polar views in society.

Bibliography

Abelson, Donald. 2002. *Do Think Tanks Matter? Assessing the Impact of Public Policy Institutes.* Montreal: McGill-Queen's University Press.

Abramovich, Víctor, and Christian Courtis. 2000. Estrategias de defensa de los derechos económicos, sociales y culturales. In *Rompiendo la Indiferencia. Acciones ciudadanas en defensa del interés público,* edited by Fundación Ford. Santiago: Fundación Ford.

Abregú, Martín, and Máximo Langer. 1992. Todo un ex ministro. Reportaje a León Arslanián. *No hay derecho* 3 (8):6–9.

Abregú, Martín, Gustavo Palmieri, and Sofía Tiscornia. 1998. Informe nacional: la situación y los mecanismos de control de los organismos de seguridad pública interior de la República Argentina. In *Control democrático en el mantenimiento de la seguridad interior,* edited by H. Frühling. Santiago: Centro de Estudios del Desarrollo (CED).

Agüero, Felipe. 1999. Legacies of Transition: Institutionalism, the Military, and Democracy in South America. *Mershon International Studies Review* 42 (2):189–240.

Agüero, Felipe, and Jeffrey Stark. 1998. *Fault Lines of Democracy in Post-Transition Latin America.* Miami: North-South Center Press.

Aguila Z., Ernesto, and Carlos Maldonado P. 1996. Orden público en el Chile del siglo XX: trayectoria de una policía militarizada. *Papeles de trabajo* 56:2–18.

Ahnen, Ronald. 1999. Defending Human Rights under Democracy: The Case of Minors in Brazil. Dissertation, Department of Political Science, The University of North Carolina, Chapel Hill.

Alger, Dean. 1996. *The Media and Politics.* Belmont: Wadsworth Publishing Company.

Almond, Gabriel, and Sidney Verba. 1963. *The Civic Culture: Political Attitudes and Democracy in Five Nations.* Princeton: Princeton University Press.

Alvarez, Sonia and Arturo Escobar eds. 1992. *The Making of Social Movements: Identity, Strategy, and Democracy.* Boulder, Co: Westview Press.

Americas Watch, and CELS (Centro de Estudios Legales y Sociales). 1991. *Police Violence in Argentina. Torture and Killing in Buenos Aires.* Buenos Aires: CELS, Americas Watch.

Amnesty International. 1991. Chile. Reports of Torture Since March 1990. London: Amnesty International.

Amnesty International. 2002. *Amnesty International Report 2002*. London: AI publications.

Andrian, Charles, and David Apter. 1996. *Political Protest and Social Change: Analyzing Politics*. New York: New York University Press.

Arias, Patricia. 1998. Las actuales propuestas en materia de seguridad y sus carencias metodológicas. *Papeles de trabajo* 61:5–16.

Arriagada, Irma. 2001. Latin America Violence and Citizen Security. Paper read at XXIII Latin American Studies Association Congress, September 6–8, 2001, at Washington DC.

Arslanián, León and Alberto Binder. 1998. *La reforma de la policía de la provincia de Buenos Aires*. Buenos Aires. (Mimeo).

Axelrod, Robert. 1986. An Evolutionary Approach to Norms. *American Political Science Review* 80 (4):1095–1111.

Baldez, Lisa. 2002. *Why Women Protest*. Cambridge: Cambridge University Press.

Barahona de Brito, Alexandra. 1997. *Human Rights and Democratization in Latin America. Uruguay and Chile:* Oxford University Press.

Barrientos Ramírez, Franklin. 2000. La gestión policial y sus métodos de evaluación. *Cuadernos del CED* 34:2–42.

Basombrío, Carlos. 2000. Looking Ahead. New Challenges for Human Rights Advocacy. *NACLA. Report on the Americas* XXXIV (1):7–11.

Bates, Robert, Rui Figuereido, and Barry Weingast. 1998. The Politics of Interpretation: Rationality, Culture, and Transition. *Politics and Society* 26 (4):603–642.

Baumgarther, Frank, and Beth Leech. 1998. *Basic Interests: The Importance of Groups in Politics and in Political Science*. Princeton: Princeton University Press.

Bayley, David, ed. 1977. *Police and Society*. Beverly Hills: SAGE Publications.

Bayley, David. 1993. What's in a Uniform? A Comparative View of Police-Military Relations in Latin America. Paper read at Conference on Police and Civil-Military Relations in Latin America, at Washington D.C.

Bayley, David. 1996. Police Brutality Abroad. In *Police Violence,* edited by W. Geller and H. Toch. New Haven: Yale University Press.

Berman, Sheri. 1998. Path Dependency and Political Actions: Reexamining Responses to the Depression. *Comparative Politics* 30 (4):379–400.

Binder, Alberto. 1997. *Política criminal: de la formulación a la praxis*. Buenos Aires: Ad-Hoc S. R. L.

Blando, Oscar. 1995. *Detención policial por averiguación de antecedentes*. Buenos Aires: Editorial Juris.

Boggian, Luis, and Antonio Tesolini. 1995. Argentina: Prevención de la tortura y de la violencia policial. Lucha contra la impunidad. In *Prevenir la tortura: un desafío realista,* edited by L. Valiña. Ginebra: Asociación para la prevención de la Tortura (APT).

Boli, John, and George Thomas. 1997. World Culture in the World Polity. *American Sociological Review* 62 (2):171–190.

Bolívar, Ligia. 1999. Comments on Rodley. In *The (Un)Rule of Law and the Underprivileged in Latin America,* edited by J. Méndez, G. O'Donnell and P. S. Pinheiro. Notre Dame: University of Notre Dame.

Booth, John, and Mitchell Seligson. 1994. Path to Democracy and the Political Culture of Costa Rica, Mexico, and Nicaragua. In *Political Culture & Democracy in Developing Countries,* edited by L. Diamond. Boulder, Co: Lynne Rienner Publishers.

Bovino, Alberto. 1992. ¡Hurra! por fin ninguno es inocente. *No hay derecho* 2 (6):1–3.

Bratton, Michael, and Williams Andrews. 1999. Combate a la delincuencia: lo que hemos aprendido. *Serie Informe Político* 56:1–16.

Bratton, Michael, and Nicolas Van de Walle. 1997. *Democratic Experiments in Africa.* Cambridge: Cambridge University Press.

Brett, Sebastian. 1998. *The Limits o Tolerance. Freedom of Expression and the Public Debate in Chile.* Washington D.C.: Human Rights Watch.

Brienes, W. 1982. *Community and Organization in the New Left: 1962–1968: The Great Refusal.* New York: Praeger.

Brisbin, Richard. 1993. Antonin Scalia, William Brennan and the Politics of Expression: A Study of Legal Violence and Repression. *American Political Science Review* 87 (4):912–927.

Bulcourf, Pablo. 2000. La problemática de la seguridad pública en los grandes conglomerados urbanos. *Revista de Ciencias Sociales* 11:157–196.

Cano, Ignacio. 1999. O controle da atividade policial: o uso da forca letal no Rio de Janeiro. *Cuadernos del CED* (31):3–23.

Carabineros de Chile and INE (Instituto Nacional de Estadísticas). 1999. *Anuario de estadísticas policiales de Carabineros de Chile.* Santiago: Carabineros de Chile, Instituto Nacional de Estadísticas (INE).

Caro, Isaac. 1999. Normas Informales de Comportamiento de la Policía en Chile. Santiago: Universidad Alberto Hurtado—ILADES.

Catterberg y asociados. 2000. Percepciones sobre el tema inseguridad en la provincia de Buenos Aires. Buenos Aires: Catterberg y asociados.

Cecchi, Horacio. 2000. *Mano dura. Crónica de la masacre de Villa Ramallo.* Buenos Aires: Colihue.

CELS (Centro de Estudios Legales y Sociales). 1996. *Informe anual sobre la situación de los derechos humanos en la Argentina. 1995.* Buenos Aires: CELS.

CELS (Centro de Estudios Legales y Sociales). 1997. *Informe anual sobre la situación de los derechos humanos en la Argentina-1996.* Buenos Aires: Centro de Estudios Legales y Sociales.

CELS (Centro de Estudios Legales y Sociales). 1998a. Control democrático de los organismos de seguridad interior en la república Argentina. *Pena y Estado* 3 (3):251–268.

CELS (Centro de Estudios Legales y Sociales). 1998b. *Informe sobre la situación de los derechos humanos en Argentina-1997.* Buenos Aires: Centro de Estudios Legales y Sociales/Eudeba.

CELS (Centro de Estudios Legales y Sociales). 1999. *Derechos humanos en la Argentina. Informe anual enero-diciembre 1998.* Buenos Aires: Centro de Estudios Legales y Sociales/ Eudeba.

CELS (Centro de Estudios Legales y Sociales). 2000. *Derechos humanos en Argentina. Informe anual 2000.* Buenos Aires: Centro de Estudios Legales y Sociales/ Eudeba.

CELS (Centro de Estudios Legales y Sociales). 2001. *Derechos humanos en Argentina. Informe anual 2001*. Buenos Aires: Centro de Estudios Legales y Sociales/ Eudeba.

CELS and Facultad (Centro de Estudios Legales y Sociales and Facultad de Filosofía y Letras UBA). 1994. *Informe sobre violencia institucional y urbana. Año 1993, Serie Extensión Universitaria Número 2*. Buenos Aires: Universidad de Buenos Aires.

CELS and Facultad (Centro de Estudios Legales y Sociales and Facultad de Filosofía y Letras UBA). 1995. *Informe sobre la situación de los derechos humanos en la Argentina. Año 1994, Serie Extensión Universitaria Número 5*. Buenos Aires: Universidad de Buenos Aires.

CELS (Centro de Estudios Legales y Sociales), and Human Rights Watch. 1998. *La inseguridad policial. Violencia de las fuerzas de seguridad en la Argentina.* Buenos Aires: Eudeba.

CEUNM (Centro de Estudios Unión para la Nueva Mayoría). 1998. *La seguridad pública, Colección Estudios 35*. Buenos Aires: Editorial Centro de Estudios Unión para la Nueva Mayoría.

CERC. 2002. Informe de prensa sobre temas económicos y políticos. Santiago: CERC.

Chevigny, Paul. 1969. *Police Power.* New York: Pantheon Books.

Chevigny, Paul. 1995. *Edge of the Knife. Police Violence in the Americas.* New York: The New Press.

Chillier, Gastón. 1998. La sanción de un código de convivencia urbana. Paper read at "Las reformas policiales en Argentina," 1–2 December, 1998, at Buenos Aires.

Chong, Dennis. 1991. *Collective Action and the Civil Rights Movement.* Chicago: University of Chicago Press.

Ciudad de Buenos Aires. 2000. *Código contravencional de la Ciudad de Buenos Aires*. Buenos Aires: Ediciones del país.

Clapham, Christopher ed. 1982. *Private Patronage and Public Power: Political Clientelism in the Modern State,* New York: St. Martin's Press.

Clark, Ann Marie, Elisabeth Friedman, and Kathryn Hochstetler. 1998. The Sovereign Limits of Global Society: A Comparison of NGO Participation in UN World Conferences on the Environment, Human Rights, and Women. *World Politics* 51 (1):1–35.

Comisión de Seguridad Interior. 1998. *Recopilación de las reuniones informativas y especiales. Informes y datos sobre seguridad pública y fuerzas nacionales de seguridad.* Buenos Aires: Cámara de Diputados de la Nación.

Comisión de Verdad y Reconciliación. 1991. *Informe de la Comisión Verdad y Reconciliación.* Santiago: Ministerio Secretaría General de Gobierno.

Comisión Etica contra la Tortura. 2002. Yo me pronuncio contra la tortura. Santiago.(Mimeo).

Concertación de Partidos por la Democracia. 1989. Programa de Gobierno. Santiago: Concertación de partidos por la Democracia.

Congreso de la Nación. 1997. *Informe de la Comisión Bicameral Especial de Seguimiento de las investigaciones de los atentados a la embajada de Israel y al edificio de la AMIA*. Buenos Aires: Congreso de la Nación.

Cooper Mayr, Doris. 1994. *Delincuencia común en Chile*. Santiago: LOM Ediciones.

CODEPU (Corporación de Promoción y Defensa de los derechos del Pueblo). 1994. *Informe derechos humanos 1990–1994*. Santiago: Comité de Defensa de los derechos del Pueblo.

CODEPU (Corporación de Promoción y Defensa de los derechos del Pueblo). 1999. Informe alternativo al cuarto informe períodico de Chile sobre la aplicación del Pacto Internacional de Derechos Civiles y Políticos. Santiago: CODEPU.

Correa Sutil, Jorge, ed. 1993. *Justicia y Marginalidad. Percepción de los pobres*. Santiago: Universidad Católica de Chile.

Correa Sutil, Jorge, and María Angélica Jiménez. 1995. Acceso de los pobres a la justicia en Chile. In *Acceso de los pobres a la justicia en países de América Latina*, edited by F. Vanderschueren and E. Oviedo. Santiago: Ediciones Sur.

Correa Sutil, Jorge, and María Angélica Jiménez. 1997. Acceso de los pobres a la justicia en Argentina, Chile, Perú y Venezuela. *Cuadernos de Análisis Jurídico* 35:21–216.

CORREPI. 1998. Listado de casos por violencia institucional. 1983–1998. Buenos Aires: CORREPI.

Cox, Sebastián. 2000. Acciones ciudadanas de interés público: protagonismo comunitario y de la sociedad civil en Chile. In *Rompiendo la indiferencia. Acciones ciudadanas en defensa del interés público*, edited by Fundación Ford. Santiago: Fundación Ford.

Cullen, Francisco. 2000. Programa de participación y fiscalización ciudadana en Argentina. In *Rompiendo la indiferencia. Acciones ciudadanas en defensa del interés público*, edited by Fundación Ford. Santiago: Fundación Ford.

Dahl, Robert. 1971. *Polyarchy: Participation and Opposition*. New Haven: Yale University Press.

Dallmayr, Fred. 1999. Globalization from Below. *International Politics* 36 (3):321–334.

Dammert, Lucía. 2000. *Violencia criminal y seguridad pública en América Latina: la situación en Argentina*. Santiago: Naciones Unidas.

Dassin, Joan. 1999. Building the Latin American Human Rights Field: Increasing Institutional and Financial Sustainability for Latin American Human Rights Organizations. New York.

Dávila Avendaño, Mireya. 2000. *Seguridad ciudadana: actores y discusión, Nueva Serie FLACSO*. Santiago: FLACSO-Chile.

Davis, Diane. 2002. From Democracy to Rule of Law? Police Impunity in Contemporary Latin America. *ReVista, Harvard Review of Latin America*. Fall, 2002.

Davis, Robert. 2000. *The Use of Citizen Surveys as a Tool for Police Reform*. New York: Vera, Institute for Justice.

Davis, Robert, Pedro Mateu-Gelabert, and Joel Miller. 2002. Can Effective Policing Also be Respectful? Two Examples in the South Bronx. New York: Vera Institute of Justice.

De la Barra Cousiño, Carlos. 1998. Adversarial vs. Inquisitorial Systems: The Rule of Law and Prospects for Criminal Procedure Reform in Chile. *Southwestern Journal of Law and Trade in the Americas* 5:323–364.

Della Porta, Donatella. 1996. Social Movements and the State: Thoughts on the Policing of Protest. In *Comparative Perspectives on Social Movements*, edited by D. McAdam, J. McCarthy and M. Zald. Cambridge: Cambridge University Press.

Della Porta, Donatella and Hanspeter Kriesi, ed. 1999. *Social Movements in a Globalizing World*. New York: St. Martin's Press.

Desimoni, Luis. 1996. *Garantías constitucionales, actividad prevencional y derechos humanos*. Buenos Aires: Editorial Policial.

Diamond, Larry, ed. 1994. *Political Culture and Democracy in Developing Countries*. Lynne Rienner Publishers.

Domingo, Pilar. 1999. Judicial Independence and Judicial Reform in Latin America. In *The Self-Restraining State*, edited by A. Schedler, L. Diamond and M. Plattner. Boulder, CO: Lynne Rienner Publishers.

Domínguez Vial, Andrés. 1996. *Policía y derechos humanos*. Santiago: Policía de Investigaciones de Chile. Instituto Interamericano de Derechos Humanos.

Domínguez Vial, Andrés. 1998. El estado democrático de derecho y el poder de la policía. *Pena y Estado* 3 (3):27–50.

Duce, Mauricio. 1999. Criminal Procedural Reforms and the Ministerio Público: Toward the Construction of a New Criminal Justice System in Latin America. Master, Stanford Law School, Stanford University, Stanford.

Duce, Mauricio. 2000. Problemas en torno a la reconfiguración del ministerio público en América Latina. *Informes de Investigación* 2 (6):3–24.

Duce, Mauricio, and Felipe González. 1998. Policía y estado de derecho: problemas en torno a su función y organización. *Pena y Estado* 3 (3):51–62.

Dutil, Carlos, and Ricardo Ragendorfer. 1997. *La Bonaerense. Historia criminal de la policía de la Provincia de Buenos Aires*. Buenos Aires: Planeta.

ECLAC (Economic Commission for Latin America) 1997. Estudio Económico de América Latina y el Caribe. Santiago: ECLAC.

ECLAC (Economic Commission for Latin America) 2002. *Panorama social de América Latina 2001–2002*. Santiago: ECLAC.

Eisinger, Peter. 1973. The Conditions of Protest Behavior in American Cities. *American Political Science Review* 67 (1):11–28.

Ensalaco, Mark. 2000. *Chile Under Pinochet*. Philadelphia: University of Pennsylvania Press.

Estévez, Eduardo. 2000a. Estructuras y su aplicación en policías en proceso de reforma. *Cuadernos de IEPADES* 1:37–91.

Estévez, Eduardo. 2000b. Reforma de sistemas de seguridad pública e investigaciones judiciales: tres experiencias en la Argentina. *Colección* VI (10):139–182.

Estévez, Francisco. 1993. Discurso del director del Instituto Nacional de la Juventud el 11 de marzo de 1993 al cumplirse 3 años de gobierno democrático. Santiago.

Estévez, Francisco. 1994. El legado de una búsqueda de identidad generacional. i.ene.jota 9:12–20.

Evans, Peter. 1995. *Embedded Autonomy: States and Industrial Transformation*. Princeton: Princeton University Press.

Evans, Tony. 1997. Trading Human Rights. In *Global Trade and Global Social Issues*, edited by A. Taylor and C. Thomas. London: Routledge.

Evans, Tony. 2001. *The Politics of Human Rights*. London: Pluto Press.

Finnemore, Martha, and Kathryn Sikkink. 1998. International Norms Dynamics and Political Change. *International Organization* 52 (4):887–917.

FLACSO-Chile. 1997. *Informe de Encuesta: Representaciones de la sociedad chilena* (Three volumens). Santiago: FLACSO-Chile

Forsythe, David. 2000. *Human Rights in International Relations.* Cambridge: Cambridge University Press.

Foweraker, Joe. 2001. Grassroots Movements and Political Activism in Latin America: A Critical Comparison of Chile and Brazil. *Journal of Latin American Studies* 33 (3):839–861.

Fraizer, Heather. 2002. Searching for Success in Post-Transition Chile: An Examination of Tactics Employed by the Chilean Environment Movement. Paper read at American Political Science Association, August 28—September 1, at Boston.

Franck, Thomas. 1992. The Emerging Right to Democratic Governance. *The American Journal of International Law* 86 (1):46–91.

Friedman, Elisabeth, Kathryn Hochstetler, and Ann Marie Clark. 2001. Sovereign Limits and Regional Opportunities for Global Civil Society in Latin America. *Latin American Research Review* 36 (3):7–35.

Frühling, Hugo. 1989. Organismos no gubernamentales de derechos humanos en el paso del autoritarismo a la democracia en Chile. In *Una puerta que se abre,* edited by J. A. e. a. Abalos. Santiago: Taller de Cooperación al Desarrollo.

Frühling, Hugo. 1998a. Carabineros y consolidación democrática en Chile. *Pena y Estado* 3 (3):81–116.

Frühling, Hugo, ed. 1998b. *Control democrático en el mantenimiento de la seguridad interior.* Santiago: Centro de Estudios del Desarrollo (CED).

Frühling, Hugo. 2001. Las estrategias policiales frente a la inseguridad ciudadana en Chile. In *Policía, sociedad y Estado: Modernización y reforma policial en América del Sur,* edited by H. Frühling and A. Candina. Santiago: CED.

Frühling, Hugo, and Azun Candina. 2001. *Policía, sociedad y Estado: modernización y reforma policial en América del Sur.* Santiago.

Fuentes, Claudio. 2001. *Denuncias por Violencia Policial.* Santiago: FLACSO-Chile.

Fundación Ford. 2000. *Rompiendo la indiferencia. Acciones ciudadanas en defensa del interés público.* Santiago: Fundación Ford.

Fundación Paz Ciudadana. 1998. *Propuestas para la prevención del delito.* Santiago: Fundación Paz Ciudadana.

Fundación Paz Ciudadana. 1999. *Anuario de Estadísticas Criminales.* Santiago: Fundación Paz Ciudadana.

Gajardo Contreras, Francisco, and Ricardo Rivera Vallejo. 1999. Estudio sistemático del delito de tortura, Facultad de Ciencias Jurídicas y Sociales, Universidad Central de Chile, Santiago.

Galiano, José. 1996a. *Derechos humanos. Tomo I: teoría e historia.* 2 vols. Vol. 1, *Colección sin norte.* Santiago: LOM ediciones. Universidad Arcis.

Galiano, José. 1996b. *Derechos humanos. Tomo II: Vigencia y legislación.* 2 vols. Vol. II, *Colección sin norte.* Santiago: LOM ediciones. Universidad Arcis.

Gamson, William. 1975. *The Strategy of Social Protest.* Homewood: The Dorsey Press.

Gamson, William, and David Meyer. 1996. Framing Political Opportunity. In *Comparative Perspectives on Social Movements,* edited by D. McAdam, J. McCarthy and M. Zald. Cambridge: Cambridge University Press.

Garretón, Manuel Antonio. 1996. Human Rights in Democratization Processes. In *Constructing Democracy. Human Rights, Citizenship, and Society in Latin America,* edited by E. Jelin and E. Hershberg. Boulder, CO: Westview Press.

Garrido, Manuel, Fabricio Guariglia, and Gustavo Palmieri. 1997. Control judicial de las actividades preventivas y de investigación policiales en el ámbito de la justicia nacional y federal. Paper read at Control democrático de los organismos de seguridad interior en la república Argentina, at Buenos Aires.

Garrido, Manuel, Fabricio Guariglia, and Gustavo Palmieri. 1998. Control judicial de las actividades preventivas y de investigación policiales en el ámbito de la justicia nacional y federal. In *Control democrático en el mantenimiento de la seguridad interior,* edited by H. Frühling. Santiago: Centro de Estudios del Desarrollo (CED).

Gingold, Laura. 1997. *Memoria, moral y derecho. El caso de Ingeniero Budge (1987–1994)*. Mexico City: FLACSO-Mexico/Juan Pablos Editor.

Gitlitz, John and Paul Chevigny. 2002. Crisis and Reform: The Police in the Dominican Republic. *WOLA Citizen Security Monitor.* November.

Gobierno de la provincia (Buenos Aires). 1998. *La transformación del sistema de seguridad.* Buenos Aires: Secretaría de la Gobernación.

Gobierno de la Provincia (Buenos Aires). 2001. *Legislación policial de la Provincia de Buenos Aires.* Buenos Aires: Editorial Universidad.

González, Felipe, María Angélica Jiménez, and Cristián Riego Ramírez. 1998. La policía y el proceso penal: antecedentes empíricos. *Cuadernos de Análisis Jurídico* 38:265–393.

González, Felipe, and Cristián Riego Ramírez. 1994. Las garantías de la detención en Chile. In *Proceso penal y derechos fundamentales,* edited by Corporación Nacional de Reparación y Reconciliación. Santiago: Corporación Nacional de Repación y Reconciliación.

Goretti, Mateo, and Delia Ferreira. 1998. When the President Governs Alone: The Decretazo in Argentina, 1989–1993. In *Executive Decree Authority,* edited by J. Carey and M. Shugart. Cambridge: Cambridge University Press.

Guidry, John, Michael Kennedy, and Zald Mayer, eds. 2000. *Globalizations and social Movements: Culture, Power, and the Transnational Public Sphere.* Ann Arbor: University of Michigan Press.

Gunther, Richard, and Anthony Mughan, eds. 2000. *Democracy and the Media.* Cambridge: Cambridge University Press.

Hafner-Burton, Emilie. 2002. External Pressures and Human Rights: The State of the Globalization Debate. Paper read at American Political Science Association, August 30—September 1, at Boston.

Haggard, Stephan and Robert Kaufman. 1995. *The Political Economy of Democratic Transitions.* Princeton: Princeton University Press.

Hardin, Russell. 1993. *Collective Action.* Baltimore: The John Hopkins University Press.

Hartlyn, Jonathan. 1998a. Political Opportunities, missed Opportunities and Institutional Rigidities: Another Look at Democratic Transitions in Latin

America. In *Politics, Society and Democracy: Latin America,* edited by S. Mainwaring and A. Valenzuela. Boulder, CO: Westview.

Hartlyn, Jonathan. 1998b. *The Struggle for Democratic Politics in the Dominican Republic.* Chapel Hill: University of North Carolina Press.

Hawkins, Darren. 2002. Human Rights Norms and Networks in Authoritarian Chile. In *Restructuring Wolrd Politics,* edited by S. Khagram, J. Riker and K. Sikkink. Minneapolis: University of Minnesota Press.

Hipsher, Patricia. 1997. Democratization and the Decline of Urban Social Movements. *Comparative Politics* 28 (3):273–298.

Hojman, David. 1993. Non-governmental Organisations (NGOs) and the Chilean Transition to Democracy. *European Review of Latin American and Caribbean Studies* 54:7–24.

Holston, James, and Teresa Caldeira. 1998. Democracy, Law, and Violence: Disjunctions of Brazilian Citizenship. In *Fault Lines of Democracy in Post-Transition Latin America,* edited by F. Agüero and J. Stark. Miami: North-South Center Press.

Horvitz, María Inés. 1998. La justicia militar: justificación, competencia, y organización en el derecho comparado. Los principios de independencia e imparcialidad en la organización de los tribunales militares chilenos. *Cuadernos de Análisis Jurídico* 40:79–160.

Huber, Evelyne. 1995. Assessments of State Strength. In *Latin America in Comparative Perspective: New Approaches to Method Analysis,* edited by P. Smith. Boulder, CO: Westview Press.

Huber, Evelyne, and John Stephens. 2001. *Development and Crisis of Walfare State. Parties and Policies in Global Markets.* Chicago: The University of Chicago Press.

Human Rights Watch. 1991a. *Human Rights and the "Politics of Agreements."* Washington DC: Human Rights Watch.

Human Rights Watch. 1991b. Police Brutality in the United States. New York: Human Rights Watch.

Human Rights Watch. 1998a. *Los límites de la tolerancia. Libertad de expresión y debate público en Chile, Colección Nuevo Periodismo.* Santiago: LOM Ediciones.

Human Rights Watch. 1998b. *Shielded From Justice. Police Brutality and Accountability in the United States.* New York: Human Rights Watch.

Human Rights Watch. 2002. World Report 2001 (Americas section). http://www.hrw.org/2k2/americas.html.

Huntington, Samuel. 1959. *The Soldier and the State.* Cambridge, MA: The Belknap Press of Harvard University.

Hutchison, Elizabeth. 1989. El movimiento de derechos humanos en Chile bajo el régimen autoritario, 1973–1988. In *El movimiento de derechos humanos en Chile, 1973–1988,* edited by P. Orellana and E. Hutchison. Santiago: CEPLA.

Immergut, Ellen. 1992. *The Political Construction of Interests: National Health Insurance Politics in Switzerland, France and Sweden, 1930–1970.* New York: Cambridge University Press.

Immergut, Ellen. 1998. The Theoretical Core of the New Institutionalism. *Politics and Society* 26 (1):5–34.

Instituto Nacional de Estadísticas (INE). 2001. *Compendio Estadístico 2001.* Santiago: Instituto Nacional de Estadísticas.

International Commission of Jurists, and Centre for the Independence of Judges and Lawyers. 1992. *Chile: A time of Reckoning.* Geneva: International Commission of Jurists.

Janowitz, Morris. 1960. *The Professional Soldier:* The Free Press of Glencoe.

Jelin, Elizabeth. 1996. Citizenship Revisited: Solidarity, Responsibility, and Rights. In *Constructing Democracy. Human Rights, Citizenship, and Society in Latin America,* edited by E. Jelin and E. Hershberg. Boulder, CO: Westview Press.

Jiménez, María Angélica. 1994. El proceso penal chileno y los derechos humanos. *Cuadernos de Análisis Jurídico* 4:1–275.

Jiménez, María Angélica. 2000. *Adolescentes privados de libertad y justicia de menores, Informe de Investigación.* Santiago: Universidad Diego Portales.

Johnson, Lyman, ed. 1990. *The Problem or Order in Changing Societies: Essays on Crime and Policing in Argentina and Uruguay.* Albuquerque: University of New Mexico Press.

Kamenitsa, Lynn 1998. The Process of Political Marginalization: East German Social Movements After the Wall. *Comparative Politics* 30 (3):313–334.

Karl, Terry. 1990. Dilemmas of Democratization in Latin America. *Comparative Politics* 23:1–21.

Karl, Terry. 1995. The Hybrid Regimes of Central America. *Journal of Democracy* 6 (3).

Karl, Terry. 1997. *The Paradox of Plenty: Oil Booms and Petrostates.* Barckeley: Barckeley University Press.

Karl, Terry, and Philippe Schmitter. 1991. What Democracy is . . . and is not. *Journal of Politics* (2):75–88.

Karl, Terry, and Philippe Schmitter. 1994. The Conceptual Travels of Transitologists and Consolidologists: How Far the East Should they Attempt to Go? *Slavic Review* 53:173–185.

Keck, Margaret E., and Kathryn Sikkink. 1998. *Activists Beyond Borders: Advocacy Networks in International Politics.* Ithaca: Cornell University Press.

Keith, Linda. 1999. Do Constitutional Provisions For States of Emergency Discourage or Enable Human Rights Abuse? Paper read at Annual Meeting of the American Political Science Association, September 1–4 1999, at Atlanta.

Kelling, George, and Williams Andrews. 1999. Experiencias exitosas contra la delincuencia en una sociedad moderna. *Serie Informe Político* (60):1–14.

Keohane, Robert. 1971. The Big Influence of Small Allies. *Foreign Policy* 2 (3):161–182.

Keohane, Robert. 1984. *After Hegemony.* Princeton, NJ: Princeton University Press.

Keohane, Robert and Gary King, and Sidney Verba. 1994. *Designing Social Inquiry. Scientific Inference in Qualitative Research.* Princeton: Princeton University Press.

Khagram, Sanjeev, James Riker, and Kathryn Sikkink, eds. 2002. *Restructuring World Politics.* Minneapolis: University of Minnesota Press.

Kielbowicz, Richard, and Clifford Scherer. 1986. The Role of the Press in the Dynamic of Social Movements. In *Research in Social Movements, Conflicts and Change,* edited by L. Kriesberg. Greenwich: Jai Press Inc.

Kincaid, Douglas, and Eduardo Gamarra. 1996. Disorderly Democracy: Redefining Public Security in Latin America. In *Latin America in the World-Economy,* edited by R. Korzeniewicz and W. Smith. Wesport: Conn.: Praeger.

Kitschelt, Herbert. 1986. Political Opportunity Structures and Political Protest: Anti-Nuclear Movements in Four Democracies. *British Journal of Political Science* 16 (1):57–85.

Klarén, Peter, and Thomas Bossert. 1986. *Promise of Development. Theories of Change in Latin America.* Boulder, CO: Wesview Press.

Kollman, Ken. 1998. *Outside Lobbying: Public Opinion and Interest Group Strategies.* Princeton: Princeton University Press.

Krain, Matthew. 1997. State-Sponsored Mass Murder. *Journal of Conflict Resolution* 41 (3):331–360.

Kriesi, Hanspeter, Ruud Koopmans, Jan Willem Duyvendak, and Marco Giugni. 1995. *New Social Movements in Western Europe. A comparative Analysis.* Edited by B. Klandermans. 5 vols. Vol. 5, *Social Movements, Protests, and Contention.* Minneapolis: University of Minnesota Press.

Latham, Earl. 1952. *The Group Bias of Politics: A Study in Busing Point Legislation.* Ithaca: Cornell University Press.

Lauzán, Silvana. 2000. Cambio de régimen político y burocracia estatal. Una mirada sobre la policía Federal Argentina. Tesis de Licenciatura, Departamento de Ciencia Política y Gobierno, Universidad Torcuato di Tella, Buenos Aires.

Legg, Keith. 1975. *Patrons, Clients, and Politicians: New Perspectives on Political Clientelism.* Berkeley: University of California.

Levitsky, Steven. 1998. Institutionalization and Peronism. *Party Politics* 4 (1):71–92.

Levitsky, Steven. 2001. An "Organized Disorganization": Informal Organization and the Persistence of Local Party Structures in Argentine Peronism. *Journal of Latin American Studies* 33 (1):29–61.

Linz, Juan, and Alfred Stepan. 1996. *Problems of Democratic Transitions and Consolidation: Southern Europe, South American and Post-Communist Europe.* Baltimore: John Hopkins University Press.

Lipschutz, Ronnie. 1996. *Global Civil Society and Global Environmental Governance: The Politics of Nature from Place to Planet.* Albany: State University of New York Press.

Lipsky, Michael. 1980. *Street-Level Bureaucracy: Dilemmas of the Individual in Public Services:* Russell Sage Foundation.

Lohmann, Susanne. 1998a. Federalism and Central Bank Independence: The Politics of German Monetary Policy, 1957–92. *World Politics* 50 (3):401–446.

Lohmann, Susanne. 1998b. An Information Rationale for the Power of Special Interests. *American Political Science Review* 92 (4):809–827.

Londregan, John. 2000. *Legislative Institutions and Ideology in Chile.* Cambridge: Cambridge University Press.

Loveman, Brian. 1995. Chilean NGOs: Forging a Role in the Transition to Democracy. In *New Paths to Democratic Development in Latin America,* edited by C. Reilly. Boulder, CO.: Lynne Rienner Publishers.

Lowden, Pamela. 1996. *Moral Opposition to Authoritarian Rule in Chile, 1973–1990.* London: MacMillan Press Ltd. and St. Martin's Press Inc.

Lowery, David, Virginia Gray, and Matthew Fellowes. 2002. Sisyphus Meets the Borg: Understanding the Diversity of Interest Communities. Paper read at American Political Science Association, August 28-September 1, at Boston.

Mahmud, Jacinto. 2000. *Régimen disciplinario para la policía federal Argentina. Manual práctico.* Buenos Aires: Editorial Policial.

Mahoney, James, and Richard Snyder. 1999. Rethinking Agency and Structure in the Study of Regime Change. *Studies in Comparative International Development* 34 (2):3–33.

Maier, Julio Bernardo. 1996. Breve historia institucional de la policía argentina. In *Justicia en la calle,* edited by P. Waldmann. Bogota: Bibliteca Jurídica Diké, Fundación Konrad Adenauer.

Maier, Julio Bernardo, Martín Abregú, and Sofía Tiscornia. 1996. El papel de la policía en la Argentina y su situación actual. In *Justicia en la calle,* edited by P. Waldmann. Bogota: Biblioteca Jurídica Diké, Fundación Konrad Adenauer.

Mainwaring, Scott. 1999. The Surprising Resilience of Elected Governments. *Journal of Democracy* 10 (3):101–114.

Mainwaring, Scott, Daniel Brinks, and Aníbal Pérez-Liñán. 2001. Classifying Political Regimes in Latin America, 1945–1999. *Studies in Comparative International Development* 36 (1):37–65.

Mainwaring, Scott, and Timothy Scully. 1995. *Building Democratic Institutions: Party Systems in Latin America.* Stanford: Stanford University Press.

Manzetti, Luigi, and Charles Blake. 1996. Market Reforms and Corruption in Latin America. *Review of International Political Economy* 3 (4):662–697.

March, James, and John Olsen. 1984. The New Institutionalism: Organizational Factors in Political Life. *American Political Science Review* 78 (3):734–749.

March, James, and John Olsen. 1989. *Rediscovering Institutions: The Organizational Basis of Politics.* New York: The Free Press.

Marenin, Otwin, ed. 1996. Policing Change, Changing Police: International Perspectives. New York: Garland Publications.

Martínez, María Josefina, Gustavo Palmieri, and María Victoria Pita. 1998. Detenciones por averiguación de identidad: policía y prácticas rutinizadas. In *Violencia social y derechos humanos,* edited by I. Izaguirre. Buenos Aires: Eudeba.

Mayer, Margit. 1991. Social Movement Research and Social Movement Practice: the U.S. Pattern. In *Research on Social Movements,* edited by D. Rucht. Boulder: CO: Westview.

McAdam, Doug. 1996. The Framing Function of Movement Tactics: Strategic Dramaturgy in the American Civil Movement. In *Comparative Perspectives on Social Movements,* edited by D. McAdam, J. McCarthy and M. Zald. Cambridge: Cambridge University Press.

McAdam, Doug, John McCarthy, and Mayer Zald, eds. 1996. *Comparative Perspectives on Social Movements.* Cambridge: Cambridge University Press.

McAdam, Doug, Sidney Tarrow, and Charles Tilly. 2001. *Dynamic of Contention.* Cambridge: Cambridge University Press.

McCarthy, J., and M. Zald. 1973. *The Trends of Social Movements in America: Professionalization and Resource Mobilization.* Morristown, NJ: General Learning Press.

McCarthy, John. 1987. *Social Movements in an Organizational Society.* New Burnswick, NJ: Transaction Books.

McCarthy, John, Jackie Smith, and Mayer Zald. 1996. Accessing public, Media, Electoral, and Governmental Agendas. In *Comparative Perspectives on Social Movements,* edited by D. McAdam, J. McCarthy and M. Zald. Cambridge: Cambridge University Press.

McGuire, James. 1995. Political Parties and Democracy in Argentina. In *Building Democratic Institutions. Party Systems in Latin America,* edited by S. Mainwaring and T. Scully. Stanford, CA: Stanford University Press.

McKeown, Timothy. 1986. 'Structural' Theories of Commercial Policy. *International Organization* 40 (1):43–64.

Medina, Cecilia. 1993. Chile: obstáculos y desafíos para los derechos humanos. *Cuadernos de Análisis Jurídico* (26):11–31.

Méndez, Juan. 1999. Problems of Lawless Violence: Introduction. In *The (Un)Rule of Law and the Underprivileged in Latin America,* edited by J. Méndez, G. O'Donnell and P. S. Pinheiro. Notre Dame: University of Notre Dame.

Méndez, Juan, and Guillermo O'Donnell and Paulo Pinheiro, ed. 1999. *The (Un)Rule of Law and the Underprivileged in Latin America.* Notre Dame: University of Notre Dame.

Mera Figueroa, Jorge. 1992. Seguridad ciudadana, violencia y delincuencia. *Cuadernos de Análisis Jurídico* 21:11–23.

Merenin, Otwin, ed. 1996. *Policing Change, Changing Police: International Perspectives.* New York: Garland Publishers.

Meron, Theodor. 1995. International Criminalization of Internal Atrocities. *The American Journal of International Law* 89 (3):554–577.

Meyer, David, and Suzanne Staggenborg. 1996. Movements, Countermovements, and the Structure of Political Opportunity. *American Journal of Sociology* 101 (6):1628–1660.

Meyer, John, John Boli, George Thomas, and Francisco Ramírez. 1997. World Society and the Nation-State. *American Journal of Sociology* 103 (1):144–181.

Ministerio de Justicia (Argentina). 2002. *Comparación de homicidios dolosos en países americanos* http://www.jus.gov.ar/polcrim/Internacionales/Estadisticas2.htm, 2002 [cited 2002].

Ministerio del Interior. 1997. Plan nacional de seguridad ciudadana. Santiago: Ministerio del Interior.

Ministerio del Interior. 1998. Programa de seguridad ciudadana. Memoria 1998. Santiago: Ministerio del Interior.

Ministerio del Interior. 1999. Plan integral de seguridad ciudadana. Informe primer semestre 1999. Santiago: Ministerior del Interior.

Ministerio Secretaría General de Gobierno. 2000. Informe Consejo Ciudadano para el desarrollo de la sociedad civil. Santiago: División de Organizaciones Sociales.

Mitchell, Neil, and James McCormick. 1988. Economic and Political Explanations of Human Rights Violations. *World Politics* 40 (4):476–498.

Moore, Barrington. 1966. *Social Origins of Dictatorships and Democracy: Lord and Peasant in the Making of the Modern World.* Boston: Beacon Press.

Mosley, Layna, and Saika Uno. 2002. Racing to the Bottom or Climbing to the Top? Foreign Direct Investment and Human Rights. Paper read at Annual Meeting of the Midwest Political Science Association, at Chicago.

Moulián, Tomás. 1997. *Chile: Anatomía de un Mito.* Santiago: LOM Ediciones.

NACLA. 1996. Report on Crime and Impunity. *NACLA. Report on the Americas,* 30:17–43.

Neild, Rachel. 1995. *Policing Haiti. Preliminary Assessment of the New Civilian Security Force.* Washington DC: WOLA.

Neild, Rachel. 1998a. *Capacitación Policial, Temas y debates en la reforma de la seguridad pública. Una guía para la sociedad civil.* Washington DC: WOLA.

Neild, Rachel. 1998b. *Controles internos y órganos disciplinarios policiales, Temas y debates en la reforma de la seguridad pública. Una guía para la sociedad civil.* Washington D.C.: Washington Office on Latin America, WOLA.

Neild, Rachel. 1998c. *Convocatoria y selección policial, Temas y debates en la reforma de la seguridad pública. Una guía para la sociedad civil.* Washington DC: WOLA.

Neild, Rachel. 1998d. Derechos humanos y seguridad ciudadana: el marco de un orden policial democrático. In *Control democrático en el mantenimiento de la seguridad interior,* edited by H. Frühling. Santiago: Centro de Estudios del Desarrollo (CED).

Neild, Rachel. 1998e. *Policía comunitaria, Temas y debates en la reforma de la seguridad pública. Una guía para la sociedad civil.* Washington D.C.: Washington Office of Latin America, WOLA.

Neild, Rachel. 2000a. Confronting a Culture of Impunity: The Promise and Pitfalls of Civilian Review of Police in Latin America. In *Civilian Oversight of Policing. Governance, Democracy, and Human Rights,* edited by A. Goldsmith and C. Lewis. Oxford: Hart Publishing.

Neild, Rachel. 2000b. *External Controls, Themes and Debates in Public Security Reforms.* Washington DC: WOLA (Washington Office on Latin America).

Neild, Rachel. 2001. Democratic Police Reforms in War-torn societies. *CSD. Conflict, Security, Development* 1 (1):21–43.

Neild, Rachel. 2002. Sustaining Reform: Democratic Policing in Central America. *Citizen Security Monitor* 1 (1):1–36.

Neocleous, Mark. 2000. *The Fabrication of Social Order. A Critical Theory of Police Power.* Sterling, VA: Pluto Press.

North, Douglass. 1990. *Institutions, Institutional Change, and Economic Performance.* Cambridge: Cambridge University Press.

O'Brien, Robert, Anne Marie Goetz, Jan Aart Scholte, and Marc Williams. 2000. *Contesting Global Governance.* Cambridge: Cambridge University Press.

O'Donnell, Guillermo. 1996. Illusions about Consolidation. *Journal of Democracy* 7 (2):34–51.

O'Donnell, Guillermo. 1998. Horizontal Accountability in New Democracies. *Journal of Democracy* 9 (3):112–126.

O'Donnell, Guillermo. 2000. The Judiciary and the Rule of Law. *Journal of Democracy* 11 (1):25–31.

O'Donnell, Guillermo. 2001a. Democracy, Law, and Comparative Politics. *Studies in Comparative International Development* 36 (1):7–36.

O'Donnell, Guillermo. 2001b. Reflections on Contemporary South American Democracies. *Journal of Latin American Studies* 33 (3):599–609.

O'Donnell, Guillermo, and Philippe Schmitter. 1986. *Transitions from Authoritarian Rule: Tentative Conclusions About Uncertain Democracies.* Baltimore: John Hopkins University Press.

Oliveira, Alicia, and Sofía Tiscornia. 1997. Estructura y prácticas de las policías en la Argentina. Las redes de ilegalidad. In *Control democrático de los organismos de seguridad interior en la república Argentina,* edited by CELS (Centro de Estudios Legales y Sociales). Buenos Aires: CELS.

Oliveira, Alicia, and Sofía Tiscornia. 1998. Estructura y prácticas de las policías en la Argentina. Las redes de ilegalidad. In *Control democrático en el mantenimiento de la seguridad interior,* edited by H. Frühling. Santiago: Centro de Estudios del Desarrollo (CED).

Olson, Mancur. 1971. *The Logic of Collective Action.* 2nd ed. Camdridge: Harvard University Press.

Oxhorn, Philip. 1998. The Social Foundations of Latin America's Recurrent Populism: Problems of Class Formation and Collective Action. *Journal of Historical Sociology* 11 (2):212–246.

Oxhorn, Philip. 1999. The Ambiguous Link: Social Movements and Democracy in Latin America. *Journal of Interamerican Studies and World Affairs* 41 (2):126–146.

Oxhorn, Philip. 2001. When Democracy Isn't All That Democratic: Social Exclusion and the Limits of the Public Sphere in Latin America. *The North-South Agenda* Paper 44:1–23.

Palma, Andrés, Juan Pablo Letelier, Adriana Muñoz, Mario Devaud, and Carlos Montes. 1994. Boletín número 914–07. Modifica el código de procedimiento penal y el código penal en lo relativo a la detención, y dicta normas de protección a los derechos del ciudadano. *Cuadernos de Análisis Jurídico* 30:59–64.

Palmieri, Gustavo. 1997. Normativa y estructura de los organismos de seguridad pública interior. In *Control democrático de los organismos de seguridad interior en la República Argentina,* edited by CELS (Centro de Estudios Legales y Sociales). Buenos Aires: CELS.

Palmieri, Gustavo. 1998. *Investigación criminal, Temas y debates en la reforma de la seguridad pública. Una guía para la sociedad civil.* Washington DC: WOLA.

Palmieri, Gustavo, María Josefina Martínez, Máximo Sozzo, and Hernán Thomas. 2001. Mecanismos de control interno e iniciativas de reforma en las instituciones policiales argentinas. Los casos de la policía federal argentina, la policía de la Provincia de Santa Fe y la policía de la provincia de Buenos Aires. In *Policía, sociedad y Estado: Modernización y reforma policial en América Latina,* edited by H. Frühling and A. Candina. Santiago: CED.

Pelacchi, Adrián. 2000. *Tratado sobre la seguridad pública*. Buenos Aires: Editorial Policial.

Peña González, Carlos. 1998. La policía y el sistema democrático. In *Control democrático en el mantenimiento de la seguridad interior,* edited by H. Frühling. Santiago: Centro de Estudios del Desarrollo (CED).

Perry, Michael. 1998. *The Idea of Human Rights: Four Inquiries*. New York: Oxford University Press.

Peruzzotti, Enrique. 1999. Constitucionalismo, populismo y sociedad civil. Lecciones del caso argentino. *Revista Mexicana de Sociología* 61 (4):149–172.

Pierini, Alicia. 1995. Argentina: Subsecretaría de derechos humanos del Ministerio del Interior. In *Prevenir la tortura: un desafío realista,* edited by L. Valiña. Ginebra: Asociación para la Prevención de la Tortura (APT).

Pierini, Alicia. 1999. *1989–1999. Diez años de derechos humanos*. Buenos Aires: Ministerio del Interior.

Pierson, Paul. 2000. Increasing Returns, Path Dependence, and the Study of Politics. *American Political Science Review* 94 (2):251–268.

Pinheiro, Paulo Sérgio. 1996. Democracies without Citizenship. *NACLA. Report on the Americas,* 30:17–23.

Pinheiro, Paulo Sérgio. 2000. Navigating in Uncharted Waters. Human Rights Advocacy in Brazil's "New Democracy.." *NACLA. Report on the Americas* XXXIV (1):47–51.

Poe, Steven, and Linda Camp. 2002. Personal Integrity Abuse during Domestic Crises. Paper read at American Political Science Association, at Boston, MA.

Poe, Steven, and Neal Tate. 1994. Repression of Human Rights to Personal Integrity in the 1980s: A Global Analysis. *American Political Science Review* 88 (4):853–872.

Policía Federal. 1995. Policía Federal Argentina: Misión, funciones, Jurisdicción y competencia. *Revista de policía y criminalística* 1 (1):55–66.

Posner, Paul. 1999. Popular Representation and Political Dissatisfaction in Chile's New Democracy. *Journal of Interamerican Studies and World Affairs* 41 (1):59–85.

Provincia de Buenos Aires. 2001. *Código Procesal Penal de la Provincia de Buenos Aires. Leyes complementarias*. Buenos Aires: Ediciones del País.

Przeworski, Adam. 1992. The Games of Transitions. In *Issues in Democratic Consolidation: The New South American Democracies,* edited by S. Mainwaring, G. O'Donnell and S. Valenzuela. Notre Dame: University of Notre Dame.

Quintana, Augusto. 1998. Informe nacional: control democrático de los organismos de seguridad interior en Chile. In *Control democrático en el mantenimiento de la seguridad interior,* edited by H. Frühling. Santiago: Centro de Estudios del Desarrollo (CED).

Ragin, Charles. 1987. *The Comparative Method*. Berkeley: University of California Press.

Ramos, Marcela, and Juan Guzmán. 2000. *La Guerra y la Paz Ciudadana*. Santiago: LOM Ediciones.

Reiss, Albert. 1971. *The Police and the Public*. New Haven: Yale University Press.

República de Chile. 1996. *Código de procedimiento penal.* Santiago: Editorial Jurídica de Chile.

República de Chile. 1999a. *Código de Justicia Militar.* Santiago: Ediciones Publiley.

República de Chile. 1999b. *Código Penal.* Santiago: Ediciones Publiley.

República de Chile. 1999c. *Leyes de control de armas y de seguridad interior del Estado.* Santiago: Ediciones publiley.

Reyes, Myriam, Federico Aguirre, and Oliver Bauer. 1999. Tortura durante la transición a la democracia. El trabajo de CODEPU en el período. *Serie Retrospectiva y Reflexión* 4:1–62.

Richards, David, Ronald Gelleny, and David Sacko. 2001. Money with a Mean Streak? Foreign Economic Penetration and Government Respect for Human Rights in Developing Countries. *International Studies Quaterly* 45 (2):219–239.

Riego Ramírez, Cristián. 1992. Juventud y represión penal. *Cuadernos de Análisis Jurídico* 21:65–86.

Riego Ramírez, Cristián. 1994. Una visión de la realidad del proceso penal chileno. *Cuadernos de Análisis Jurídico* 4:245–254.

Riego Ramírez, Cristián. 1998. La reforma procesal penal chilena. *Cuadernos de Análisis Jurídico* 38:15–54.

Riego Ramírez, Cristián. 1999. Las reformas judiciales y la seguridad ciudadana. *Perspectivas en Política, economía y Gestión* 3 (1):43–61.

Riego Ramírez, Cristián, and Mauricio Duce. 1994. Informe acerca del proyecto de ley que modifica los artículos 110, 272 y 363 del código de procedimiento penal. *Cuadernos de Análisis Jurídico* 30:65–72.

Riego Ramírez, Cristián, and Mauricio Duce. 2000. Evolución histórica del proceso penal en Chile. *Cuadernos de Trabajo* 2:11–26.

Risse, Thomas, and Stephen Ropp. 1999. International Human Rights Norms and Domestic Change: Conclusions. In *The Power of Human Rights,* edited by T. Risse, S. Ropp and K. Sikkink. Cambridge: Cambridge University Press.

Risse, Thomas, Stephen Ropp, and Kathryn Sikkink, eds. 1999. *The Power of Human Rights.* Cambridge: Cambrindge University Press.

Risse-Kappen, Thomas. 1994. Ideas Do Not Float Freely: Transnational Coalitions, Domestic Structures, and the End of the Cold War. *International Organization* 48 (2):185–214.

Risse-Kappen, Thomas, ed. 1995. *Bringing Transnational Relations Back In: Non-State Actors, Domestic Structures, and International Relations.* Cambridge: Cambridge University Press.

Roberts, Kenneth. 1997. Beyond Romanticism: Social Movements and the Study of Political Change in Latin America. *Latin American Research Review* 32 (2):137–151.

Roniger, Luis, and Mario Sznajder. 1999. *The Legacy of Human Rights Violations in the Southern Cone:* Oxford University Press.

Ropp, Stephen, and Kathryn Sikkink. 1999. International Norms and Domestic Politics in Chile and Guatemala. In *The Power of Human Rights. International Norms and Domestic Change,* edited by T. Risse, S. Ropp and K. Sikkink. Cambridge: Cambridge University Press.

Ross Fowler, Michael, and Julie Bunck. 1992. Legal Imperialism or Disinterested Assistance? American Legal Aid in the Caribbean Basin. *Albany Law Review* (815):1–26.

Rucht, Dieter, ed. 1991. *Research on Social Movements*. Boulder, CO: Westview.

Rueschemeyer, Dietrich, Evelyne Huber, and John Stephens. 1992. *Capitalist Development and Democracy*. Chicago: University of Chicago Press.

Rusconi, Maximiliano Adolfo. 1998. Reformulación de los sistemas de justicia penal en América Latina y policía: algunas reflexiones. *Pena y Estado* 3 (3):189–198.

Russo, Eduardo Angel. 1999. *Derechos humanos y garantías. El derecho al mañana*. Buenos Aires: Eudeba.

Saba, Roberto, and Martín Bohmer. 2000. Participación ciudadana en Argentina. Estrategias para el efectivo ejercicio de los derechos. In *Rompiendo la Indiferencia: Acciones ciudadanas en la defensa del interés público*, edited by Fundación Ford. Santiago: Fundación Ford.

Sabatier, Paul. 1988. An Advocacy Coalition Framework of Policy Change and the Role of Policy-Oriented Learning Therein. *Policy Sciences* 21 (2):129–168.

Sabatier, Paul. 1992. Interest Groups Membership and Organization: Multiple Theories. In *The Politics of Interests: Interests Groups Transformed*, edited by M. Petracca. Boulder, CO: Westview Press.

Sabatier, Paul, ed. 1999. *Theories of Policy Process*. Boulder, CO: Westview Press.

Sabatier, Paul, and Hank Jenkins-Smith. 1999. The Advocacy Coalition Framework: An Assessment. In *Theories of the Policy Process*, edited by P. Sabatier. Boulder, CO: Wesview Press.

Saín, Marcelo. 1998a. Control parlamentario de las actividades de inteligencia en la Argentina. In *Control democrático en el mantenimiento de la seguridad interior*, edited by H. Frühling. Santiago: Centro de Estudios del Desarrollo (CED).

Saín, Marcelo. 1998b. Democracia, seguridad pública y policía. Paper read at Las reformas policiales en Argentina, 1–2 December 1998, at Buenos Aires.

Saín, Marcelo. 2000. Crisis y colapso del "modelo tradicional" de seguridad pública. *Revista de Ciencias Sociales* 11:113–156.

Saín, Marcelo. 2001. La ¿reforma? del sistema de seguridad y policial bonaerense. Buenos Aires. (Mimeo).

Salinas, Juan. 1997. *AMIA. El atentado*. Buenos Aires: Planeta.

Salisbury, Robert. 1969. An Exchange Theory of Interest Groups. *Midwest Journal of Political Science* 13 (1):1–32.

Saltzstein, Grace. 1989. Black Majors and Police Policies. *The Journal of Politics* 51 (3):525–544.

Samhat, Nayef. 1999. Human Rights Regimes and the Emergence of International Political Community. *International Politics* 36 (4):503–527.

Sandoval, Luis. 2001. Prevención local de la delincuencia en Santiago de Chile. In *Policía, sociedad y estado: Modernización y reforma policial en América del Sur*, edited by H. Frühling and A. Candina. Santiago: CED.

Scharpf, Fritz. 2000. Institutions in Comparative Policy Research. *Comparative Political Studies* 33 (6–7):762–790.

Schedler, Andreas. 2001. Measuring Democratic Consolidation. *Studies in Comparative International Development* 36 (1):66–92.

Schlager, Edella. 1999. A Comparison of Frameworks, Theories, and Models of Policy Processes. In *Theories of the Policy Processes,* edited by P. Sabatier. Boulder, CO: Westview Press.

Schock, Kurt. 1996. A Conjunctural Model of Political Conflict. *Journal of Conflict Resolution* 40 (1):98–133.

Schotter, Andrew. 1986. The Evolution of Rules. In *Economics as a Process,* edited by R. Langlois. Cambridge: Cambridge University Press.

Schumaker, Paul. 1975. Policy Responsiveness to Protest-Group Demands. *The Journal of Politics* 37 (2):488–521.

Scully, Timothy. 1995. Reconstituting Party Politics in Chile. In *Building Democratic Institutions. Party Systems in Latin America,* edited by S. Mainwaring and T. Scully. Stanford, CA: Stanford University Press.

Sdrech, Enrique, and Norberto Colominas. 1997. *Cabezas. Crimen, mafia y poder, Colección pistas.* Buenos Aires: Atuel.

Shaw, Greg, Robert Shapiro, Shmuel Lock, and Lawrence Jacobs. 1998. The Polls-Trends. Crime, The Police, and Civil Liberties. *Public Opinion Quarterly* 62 (3):405–426.

Shaw, Timothy. 2000. Overview. Global/Local: States, Companies and Civil Societies at the End of the Twentieth Century. In *Global Institutions and Local Empowerment: Competing Theoretical Perspectives.,* edited by K. Stiles. New York: St. Martin's Press.

Shelton, Dinah. 1994. The Participation of Nongovernmental Organizations in International Judicial Proceedings. *The American Journal of International Law* 88 (4):611–642.

Shifter, Michael. 1997. Tensions and Trade-Offs in Latin America. *Journal of Democracy* 8 (2):114–128.

Siavelis, Peter. 2000. *The President and Congress in Postauthoritarian Chile. Institutional Constraints to Democratic Consolidation.* University Park, PA: The Pennsylvania State University Press.

Sigal, Eduardo, Alberto Binder, and Ciro Annichiarico. 1998. *El final de la maldita Policía?* Buenos Aires: Ediciones FAC.

Sikkink, Kathryn. 1993. Human Rights, Principled Issue-Networks, and Sovereignty in Latin America. *International Organization* 47 (3):411–441.

Silverman, Eli. 1999. *NYPD. Battles Crime.* Boston: Northeastern University Press.

Simpson, Antony. 1977. *The Literature of Police Corruption.* New York: The John Jay Press.

Skaar, Elin. 1994. *Human Rights Violations and the Paradox of Democratic Transitions.* Norway: Chr. Michelsen Institute.

Skocpol, Theda. 1979. *States and Social Revolutions: A Comparative Analysis of France, Russia, and China.* Cambridge: Cambridge University Press.

Smulovitz, Catalina. 2001. Jucialización y accountability social en Argentina. Buenos Aires. (Mimeo).

Smulovitz, Catalina, and Enrique Peruzzotti. 2000. Societal Accountability in Latin America. *Journal of Democracy* 11 (4):147–158.

Snow, David, and Robert Benford. 1992. Master Frames and Cycles of Protest. In *Frontiers in Social Movement Theory,* edited by A. Morris and C. McClurg Mueller. New Heaven: Yale University Press.

Sozzo, Máximo. 2000. Hacia la superación de la táctica de la sospecha? Notas sobre prevención del delito e institución policial. In *Detenciones, facultades y prácticas policiales,* edited by CELS (Centro de Estudios Legales y Sociales) and CED. Santiago: CELS, CED.

Stanley, William. 1996. *Protectors or Perpetrators? The Institutional Crisis of the Salvadoran Civilian Police.* Washington DC: WOLA.

Street, John. 2001. *Mass Media, Politics, and Democracy.* New York: Palgrave.

Struensee, Eberhard, and Julio Bernardo Maier. 2000. Introducción. In *Las reformas procesales penales en América Latina,* edited by J. B. Maier, K. Ambos and J. Woischnick. Buenos Aires: Ad-Hoc S.R.L.

Tarrow, Sidney. 1994. *Power in Movement. Social Movement, Collective Action and Politics.* Cambridge: Cambridge University Press.

Tarrow, Sidney. 1996a. Social Movements in Contentious Politics: A Review Article. *American Political Science Review* 90 (4):874–883.

Tarrow, Sidney. 1996b. State and Opportunities: The Political Structuring of Social Movements. In *Comparative Perspectives on Social Movements,* edited by D. McAdam, J. McCarthy and M. Zald. Cambridge: Cambridge University Press.

Taylor, Lucy. 1998. *Citizenship, Participation, and Democracy. Changing Dynamics in Chile and Argentina.* New York: St. Martin's.

Thelen, Kathleen, and Sven Steinmo. 1992. Historical Institutionalism in Comparative Politics. In *Structuring Politics. Historical Institutionalism in Comparative Analysis,* edited by S. Steinmo, K. Thelen and F. Longstreth. Cambridge: Cambridge University Press.

Thomas, Daniel. 2002. Human Rights in U.S. Foreign Policy. In *Restructuring World Politics,* edited by S. Khagram, J. Riker and K. Sikkink. Minneapolis: University of Minnesota Press.

Thome, Joseph. 2000. Heading South But Looking North: Globalization and Law Reform in Latin America. Paper read at Latin American Studies Association XXII International Congress, March 16–19, at Miami.

Tilly, Charles. 1978. *From Mobilization to Revolution.* Mass: Addison Wesley Publications.

Tilly, Charles. 1999. Conclusion. From Interactions to Outcomes in Social Movements. In *How Social Movements Matter,* edited by M. Giugni, D. McAdam and C. Tilly. Minneapolis: University of Minnesota Press.

Tiscornia, Sofía. 1998. Violencia policial. De las prácticas rutinarias a los hechos extraordinarios. In *Violencia social y derechos humanos,* edited by I. Izaguirre. Buenos Aires: Eudeba.

Tiscornia, Sofía. 2000. El teatro de la furia. *Encrucijadas* 1 (1):49–59.

Tiscornia, Sofía, Lucía Eilbaum, and Vanina Lekerman. 2001. Detenciones por averiguación de identidad. Argumentos para la discusión sobre sus usos y abusos. In *Policía, sociedad y Estado: Modernización y reforma policial en América del Sur,* edited by H. Frühling and A. Candina. Santiago: CED.

Toch, Hans, and William Geller, eds. 1996. *Police Violence.* New Haven: Yale University Press.

Tolley, Howard. 1990–91. Interest Group Litigation to Enforce Human Rights. *Political Science Quarterly* 105 (4):617–638.

True, James, Bryan Jones, and Frank Baumgartner. 1999. Punctuated Equilibrium Theory: Explaining Stability and Change in American Policymaking. In *Theories of the Policy Process,* edited by P. Sabatier. Boulder, CO: Westview Press.

Truman, David. 1951. *The Governmental Process: Political Interests and Public Opinion.* New York: Alfred A. Knopf Inc.

Ungar, Mark. 2001. Prisions and Politics in Contemporary Latin America. Paper read at XXIII Latin American Studies Association Congress, September 5–8, 2001, at Washington DC.

United Nations. 1966. *International Convenant on Civil and Political Rights.* New York: United Nations.

United Nations. 1980. Sixth U.N. Congress on the Prevention of Crime and the Treatment of Offenders, 25 August- 5 September, at Caracas.

United Nations. 1984. *Convention against Torture and Other Cruel, Inhuman or Degrading Treatment or Punishment.* New York: United Nations.

United Nations. 1996. Report of the Special Rapporteur, Mr. Nigel S. Rodley, submitted pursuant to the Commission on Human Rights. Resolution 1995/37. E/CN.4/1996/35/Add.2. Geneve: United Nations.

United Nations. 2000. *Human Development Indicators.* New York: United Nations.

Universidad Diego Portales, and CEJIL. 2002. *Tortura, derechos humanos y justicia criminal en Chile. Resultados de una investigación exploratoria.* Santiago: Universidad Diego Portales and CEJIL.

Urzúa Troncoso, Paula. 2000. El uso del conocimiento en el caso de la reforma procesal penal. *Estudios Sociales* trimestre 1 (103):111–172.

Valdivieso, Carlos. 1998. La gravedad a que ha llegado la delincuencia exige acciones inmediatas. *Revista Libertad y Desarrollo* 74:14–16.

Valdivieso, Carlos. 1999. Violencia y delincuencia en Chile. *Perspectivas en Política, economía y Gestión* 3 (1):5–41.

Valenzuela, Arturo. 1999. Chile: Origins and Consolidation of a Latin American Democracy. In *Democracy in Developing Countries. Latin America,* edited by L. Diamond, J. Linz, J. Hartlyn and S. M. Lipset. Boulder: CO: Lynne Rienner.

Vanderschueren, Franz, and Enrique Oviedo, eds. 1995. *Acceso de los pobres a la justicia en países de América Latina.* Santiago: Ediciones Sur.

Vargas, Juan Enrique. 1998a. La modernización de la justicia criminal chilena. *Perspectivas en Política, economía y Gestión* 2 (1):1–22.

Vargas, Juan Enrique. 1998b. La reforma a la justicia criminal en Chile: el cambio del rol estatal. *Cuadernos de Análisis Jurídico* 38:55–169.

Waddington, A.P.J. 1999. *Policing Citizens: Authority and Rights.* London: UCL Press.

Waisman, Carlos. 1987. *Reversal of Development in Argentina: Postwar Counterrevolutionary Policies and Their Structural Consequences*. Princeton: Princeton University Press.

Waisman, Carlos. 1999. Argentina: Capitalism and Democracy. In *Democracy in Developing Countries. Latin America*, edited by L. Diamond, J. Hartlyn, J. Linz and S. M. Lipset. Boulder, CO: Lynne Rienner Publishers.

Waldmann, Peter, ed. 1996. *Justicia en la calle*. Bogota: Biblioteca Jurídica Diké, Fundación Konrad Adenauer.

Walker, Samuel. 1977. *A Critical History of Police Reform*. Lexington, Ma: Lexington Books.

Waltz, Kenneth. 1979. *Theory of International Politics*. Mass: Addison Wesley Publications.

Warren, Christopher. 1991. *Report of the Independent Commission on the Los Angeles Police Department*. Los Angeles, CA: LAPD.

Washington Office on Latin America (WOLA). 1993. *The Colombian National Police, Human Rights and US Drug Policy*. Washington DC: WOLA.

Washington Office on Latin America (WOLA). 1995. *Demilitarizing Public Order. The International Community, Police Reform and Human Rights in Central America and Haiti*. Washington DC: WOLA.

Weingast, Barry. 1997. The Political Foundations of Democracy and the Rule of Law. *American Political Science Review* 91 (2):245–263.

Weissbrodt, David. 1984. The contribution of International Nongovernmental Organizations to the Protection of Human Rights. In *Human Rights in International Law: Legal and Policy Issues*, edited by T. Meron. Oxford: Clarendon Press.

Wendt, Alex. 1987. The Agent-Structure Problem in International Relations Theory. *International Organization* 41 (3):335–370.

Weyland, Kurt. 1998. The Politics of Corruption in Latin America. *Journal of Democracy* 9 (2):108–121.

Wiarda, Howard. 2001. *The Soul of Latin America. The Cultural and Political Tradition*. New Haven: Yale University Press.

Wilson, James. 1995. *Political Organizations*. Princeton: Princeton University Press.

Winston, Morton. 1999. Human Rights and International Political Economy in Third World Nations: Multinational Corporations, Foreign Aid, and Repression. *Human Rights Quaterly* 21 (3):824–830.

Wiseberg, Laurie, Guadalupe López, and Sarah Meselson. 1990. *Human Rights Internet Reporter*. Vol. 13. Cambridge, MA: Human Rights Internet.

WOLA. 2000. Facing the 21st Century: Challenges and Strategies for the Latin American Human Rights Community. *Cross Currents* 2 (1):1–8.

Wolfsfeld, Gadi. 1997. *Media and Political Conflict*. Cambridge: Cambridge University Press.

Woods, Gerald. 1993. *The Police in Los Angeles. Reform and Professionalism*. New York: Garland Publishing, Inc.

Yamin, Alicia. 1999. *Facing the 21st Century: Challenges and Strategies for the Latin American Human Rights Community*. Washington DC: WOLA-Instituto de Defensa Legal.

Zakaria, Fareed. 1997. The Rise of Illiberal Democracy. *Foreign Affairs* 76 (6):22–43.

Ziegler, Melissa, and Rachel Neild. 2002. *From Peace to Governance. Police Reform and the International Community.* Washington DC: WOLA.

PERIODICAL SOURCES

Clarín (Argentina)	http://www.clarin.com.ar
El Mercurio (Chile)	http://www.emol.com
El Mostrador (Chile)	http://www.elmostrador.cl
La Nación (Argentina)	http://www.lanacion.ar
Página 12 (Argentina)	http://www.pagina12.com.ar
Qué Pasa (Chile)	http://www.quepasa.cl
La Tercera (Chile)	http://www.latercera.cl

ONLINE SOURCES

CELS (Argentina)	http://www.cels.org.ar
CERC Chile	http://www.cerc.cl
CIMA, Iberoamerican Barometer	http://www.cimaiberoamericana.com
CODEPU (Chile)	http://www.codepu.cl
Department of State (United States).	http://www.state.gov
Derechos Chile	http://www.derechoschile.cl
ECLAC (Economic Commission for Latin America)	http://www.eclac.cl
Freedom House	http://www.freedomhouse.org/
Latin Focus	http://www.latin-focus.com
Ministry of Justice—Argentina (2002)	http://www.jus.gov.ar/polcrim/
Policía y Sociedad	http://www.policiaysociedad.org
United Nations	http://www.un.org

CENTERS OF DOCUMENTATION

Archivo—Justicia Militar—Chile
(Archive of legal complaints on police violence)
Centro de Estudios Para una Nueva Mayoría (CEUNM)
(Surveys, Chronologies, and Monthly reports on Argentine's Social Conflicts).
Centro de Estudios Públicos—(CEP Chile)
(Surveys 1990–2000)
Centro de Documentación—CORREPI—Argentina
(Newspapers' clips on public activities organized by CORREPI).
Centro de Documentación—CELS—Argentina
(Newspapers' clips on public activities organized by CELS).
Centro de Documentación—CODEPU—Chile
Centro de Documentación—Corporación de Asistencia Judicial—Chile
(Files on cases of police violence- 1995–2001)

INTERVIEWS

Chile

Non governmental Organizations

Carlos López, Chilean Commission of Human Rights (ChCHRs), August 29, 2000
Harim Villagra, CODEPU. September 2000
Juan Domingo Milos, President Chilean Chapter Ombudsman, September 12, 2000
Sebastián Cox, Secretary Chilean Chapter Ombudsman, September 22, 2000
Mauricio Duce, lawyer, University Diego Portales, September 20, 2000
Cristián Riego, laywer, University Diego Portales, Advisor Ministry of Justice, September 28, 2000
María Angélica Jiménez, University Diego Portales, September 28, 2000
Gabriel Pozo, director CODEJU (Corporación Derechos Juveniles), October 3, 2000
José Sabat, ex director CODEJU, October 4, 2000
Francisco Cox, Lawyer, International Association of lawyers, October 5, 2000
Jorge Mera, lawyer, Universidad Diego Portales, October 10, 2000
Miriam Reyes, lawyer, CODEPU, October 11, 2000
Hugo Fruhling, lawyer, Centro de Estudios del Desarrollo, October 18, 2000
Daniel, victim of police violence, December, 2000
María Inés Horvitz, lawyer, Universidad de Chile, December 5, 2000
Roberto Garretón, Lawyer, ChCHRs, December 20, 2000
Javiera Blanco, Corporación Paz Ciudadana, December 21, 2000
Hugo Gutierrez, Corporación Asistencia Judicial. CODEPU, January 2001
Elena Deltone, Agrupación de trabajadoras sexuales, January 2001
Alejandro González, UN expert on human rights, ChCHRs, January 2001
Mirna Schindler, journalist, January 12, 2001
Verónica Reina, FASIC, January 18, 2001
Luis Cárdenas, SERPAJ, January 24, 2001

State Organizations

Tita Aranguiz, Regional Director Corporación Asistentia Judicial, January, 2000
Patricio Morales, Undersecretary Carabineros, September 9, 2000
Francisco Cumplido, former Minister of Justice, September 13, 2000
Rodrigo González, advisor ministry of Presidency, September 12, 2000
Alejandro Salinas, Director Human Rights Division, Ministry of Foreign Affairs, September 13, 2000
Felipe Portales, ex advisor Human Rights section, Ministry of Foreign Affairs, September 14, 2000
Jorge Vives, Lawyer, advisor Ministry of Interior. September 21, 2000
Nelson Caucoto, Lawyer, Corporación de Asistencia Judicial, September 29, 2000
Fernando Cordero, Appointed Senator, former director of Carabineros, September 22, 2000
José Antonio Viera Gallo, Deputy (1990–1998) Senator (1998–2000), September 20, 2000

Carlos Pecci, lawyer, former general auditor Carabineros de Chile, September 22, 2000
Gonzalo Miranda, undersecretary Investigaciones, September 27, 2000
General Smith, Director of Order and Security, Carabineros, October 2000
Kenneth Mcfarland, lawyer, advisor National Institute for Youth, INJ, October 2000
Alfredo Garrido, Prefecto, Director Legal Affairs Division, Investigaciones Police, October 3, 2000
Harry Gruwenbalt, general Director of Legal Affairs Division, Carabineros, October 5, 2000
Mario Meza Director Civil Police Academy, October 10, 2000
Andres Dominguez, lawyer, advisor Civil Police, October 10, 2000
Francisco Estévez, Former Director National Institute for Youth, INJ October 24, 2000
Eugenio Baeza, lawyer, advisor ministry of Interior, November, 2000
Julio Berrios, Lawyer, Corporación Asistencia Judicial. December 2000
Andres Palma, Deputy, December 2000
Jorge Burgos, Undersecretary of Interior. January 2001
Raúl Troncoso, Former Minister of Interior, January 10, 2001
Carlos Figueroa, Former Minister of Interior, January 29, 2001
Jose Miguel Insulza, Minister of Interior, Former Ministry of Foreign Affairs, January 30, 2001

Argentina

Non-governmental organizations

Martin Abregú, CELS, January, 2001
Ana Chávez, Servicio Paz y Justicia, March, 2001
Gustavo Palmieri, Centro de Estudios Legales y Sociales (CELS), April and June 2001
Sofía Tiscornia, CELS, Defensor del Pueblo, April 2001
Horacio Ravena, Lawyer, April 2001
Maria Teresa de Schiavini, COFAVI, April 2001
María del Carmen Verdú, CORREPI, April 2001
Catalina Smulovitz, Universidad Torcuato Di Tella, April 2001
Andrea Pochak, CELS April 9, 2001
Maria Capurro, CELS, May, 2001
Julieta Rossi, CELS, May, 2001
Memoria Activa, Collective inverview, May, 2001
Laura Gingold, May 2001
Diana Maffia, Lawyer, May, 2001
Sergio Delgado, Defensoria del Pueblo, May 15, 2001
Sergio Digiogia Asamble Permanente de DDHH, June 2001
Mariana Ponce de León, Amnistia Internacional, June 2001
Laura Itchart, CELS, June, 2001

State Agencies

Leon Arslanian, Ex ministro justicia y seguridad provincia, March 2001
Alberto D'Aloto, Ministerio de RREE. Derechos Humanos, May 2001
Eduardo Jozami, Diputado legislatura, Gobierno de Buenos Aires, May, 2001
Eduardo Estévez, ex Instituto Criminal Provincia, May 2001
Nora Chardianasqui, Instituto Criminal Provincia, May 2001
Edgardo Abramovich, Ministry of Interior, Gobierno Buenos Aires, May 2001
Mario Baizán, May 2001
Marcelo Sain, advisor FREPASO, National Congress, March and May 2001
Colombo, former advisor ministry of Interior, June 2001
Alicia Pierini, Legislatura de Buenos Aires, June, 2001

United States

New York
Larry Cox, Ford Foundation, Human Rights Division, January 16, 2002
Christopher Stone, Vera Institute for Justice, January 18, 2002
Robert Davis, Vera Institute for Justice, January 18, 2002
Emma Phillips, Vera Institute for Justice, January 18, 2002
Washington D.C.
Rachel Neild, Washington Office on Latin America, January 22, 2002
Fernanda Doz Costa, CEJIL, January 23 2002
Loreto Biehl, Interamerican Development Bank, January 23, 2002

Index

R

S

T

U

V

For Product Safety Concerns and Information please contact our EU representative GPSR@taylorandfrancis.com
Taylor & Francis Verlag GmbH, Kaufingerstraße 24, 80331 München, Germany

www.ingramcontent.com/pod-product-compliance
Ingram Content Group UK Ltd.
Pitfield, Milton Keynes, MK11 3LW, UK
UKHW021430080625
459435UK00011B/223

* 9 7 8 0 4 1 5 6 4 6 9 7 0 *